Amazon FBA, Dropshipping Shopify, Social Media & Affiliate Marketing

Make a Passive Income Fortune by Taking Advantage of Foolproof Step-by-step Techniques & Strategies

By

Steven Sparrow

Table of Content

Dropshipping E-commerce Business Model #2020 5

Introduction 6

Chapter 1: Understanding How Dropshipping Works...7

Chapter 2: The Benefits of Working in Dropshipping 9

Chapter 3: The Drawbacks of Dropshipping..12

Chapter 4: How to Get Started with Your Dropshipping Business 15

Chapter 5: How to Pick a Supplier and How to Pick Out a Product..................................20

Chapter 6: How to Handle Your Customers and Provide Exemplary Customer Service.............23

Chapter 7: How to Handle Security Issues With Your Business...27

Chapter 8: How to Scale Your Business 29

Chapter 9: How to Dropship with Shopify 31

Chapter 10: How to Dropship On Amazon and eBay...33

Chapter 11: Creating a Personal Website for Your Dropshipping Business 36

Chapter 12: Do I Need to Use Social Media for My Business?..39

Chapter 13: What About Using Affiliate Marketing? 41

Chapter 14: How Amazon FBA Can Help You Grow Your Business..................................43

Chapter 15: Tips to Make Your Dropshipping Business As Successful As Possible 46

Conclusion..50

Affiliate Marketing 2020 51

Introduction 52

Chapter 1: What Is Affiliate Marketing?..53

Chapter 2: Steps to Getting Started with Affiliate Marketing...58

Chapter 3: Picking Out a Strategy to Use with Affiliate Marketing 62

Chapter 4: How to Pick Out a Profitable Niche in Affiliate Marketing.............................67

Chapter 5: Where Can I Place My Affiliate Marketing Links...70

Chapter 6: How to Do Affiliate Marketing Through My Blog...72

Chapter 7: How to Do Affiliate Marketing Through Facebook...75

Chapter 8: How to Do Affiliate Marketing with Instagram 78

Chapter 9: How to Do Affiliate Marketing Through YouTube..81

Chapter 10: How to Do Affiliate Marketing Through Google 84

Chapter 11: Other Unique Ways to Do Affiliate Marketing..87

Chapter 12: Things to Avoid with Affiliate Marketing to Get the Most Success...........................92

Chapter 13: How Can I Turn Affiliate Marketing into a Passive Income?....................97

Chapter 14: Email Marketing to Make Your Affiliate Links Beat Out the Competition............102

Chapter 15: Tips and Tricks to Get the Most Out of Affiliate Marketing....................106

Conclusion...110

Amazon FBA E-commerce Business Model $10,000/mo Ultimate Guide 111

Chapter 1: What is Amazon FBA?...112

Chapter 2: Steps to creating an FBA Account 123

Chapter 3: Most Profitable Products 141

Chapter 4: Product Listing..146

Chapter 5: Four Elements of a Product Listing..152

Chapter 6: Product Launch..158

Chapter 7: AMS ADS (Advertising) 172

Bonus Chapter: How to Setup AMS ADS UK...175

Social Media Marketing for Business #2020 178

Introduction 179

Chapter 1: Why Social Media is Getting a Primary Pole in Building Businesses Online 180

Chapter 2: Becoming an Influencer...187

Chapter 3: Starting a Business on Social Media..194

Chapter 4: Monetize Your Audience..200

Chapter 5: Facebook Marketing 202

Chapter 6: Facebook Ads 208

Chapter 7: Instagram Marketing 213

Chapter 8: Twitter Marketing..219

Chapter 9: YouTube Marketing 223

Chapter 10: SnapChat 228

Chapter 11: Pinterest Marketing 231

Chapter 12: Things to Remember 235

Conclusion..237

Dropshipping E-commerce Business Model #2020

$10,000/month Ultimate Guide - Make a Passive Income Fortune with Shopify, Amazon FBA, Affiliate marketing, Retail Arbitrage, Ebay and Social Media

By

Steven Sparrow

Introduction

Congratulations on downloading *Dropshipping E-commerce Business Model 2019* and thank you for doing so.

The following chapters will discuss everything that you need to know in order to get started with your own dropshipping business. There are a lot of different types of businesses that you can choose to work with. Many of them claim to be part-time and can offer you a lot of money on the side but most of them end up failing, taking up too much time, and not providing you with the money that was promised.

Dropshipping is a process that is different from these other options. With this method, you get the benefit of working the hours that are best for you. If you want to just work a few hours a week, you simply have to just sell a few products at a time to keep the time management easy. If you want to turn this into a full-time income, you simply scale the business up and start selling more products and advertising more. There really isn't any other business model that works as successfully as working with dropshipping.

This guidebook is going to take some time to look at all the information that you need to know in order to get started with dropshipping. We will take a look at what dropshipping is, some of the advantages of working with dropshipping, how to choose a good supplier and a good product to work with, and more just to get things started.

Inside, we will also have a discussion about which platforms are the best for helping you to see results with your selling. You can choose to create your personal website and sell the products through that method, or you can work through some other popular websites such as Shopify, Amazon, or eBay to sell your products.

In addition, we will spend time looking at all the other parts of dropshipping that you need to know to get the most out of this business and get it to work for you. We will look at how to keep your website safe so customers trust you with their payments, how to work with social media to grow your website, how to provide the best customer service each time and even some methods on how you can beat out the competition and get ahead.

While there are many other business opportunities out there that you can choose to work with, none are going to be as successful and as easy to start as dropshipping. While you will need to put in a little bit of work to get this started, you will find that compared to some of the other methods of making money from home, this is one of the best. When you are ready to get started with your own dropshipping business, make sure to read through this guidebook to learn how! There are plenty of books on this subject on the market, so thanks again for choosing this one! Every effort was made to ensure it is full of as much useful information as possible. Please enjoy!

Chapter 1: Understanding How Dropshipping Works

Before we can get into some of the steps on how to start your own dropshipping business, it is important to have a good understanding of what this process is all about. Dropshipping is basically a business model where a company or an individual is able to do all of their operations without having to own a warehouse to store the products, without having to maintain inventory, and they don't even need to ship out the products to the customers.

The way that this process works is that the retailer is going to partner up with a supplier. This supplier will either warehouse or manufacture various products for the retailer to choose from. The supplier will then pack the product and ship directly to the customer once they received an order from the retailer (which is you in this supply chain). The supplier is doing this on your behalf during this process.

To break this down a bit further, here are some of the steps that explain better how dropshipping works:

1. The customer is going to go to an online store for a retailer and then places an order for a product that is there.
2. The retailer, either manually or automatically, forwards the order, as well as the details about the customer over to the supplier.
3. The supplier will then pack the order and ship it out to the customer. The package will have the name of the retailer to help maintain the business image of the dropshipper.

This kind of business model has gotten a lot of popularity in recent years because it has helped to eliminate the need for a store owner to be in a physical location such as in their own office space or warehouse. Anyone can join this business model as long as they have an internet connection and a laptop.

Typically, the profit margin for a dropshipping business will be somewhere between 15 and 45 percent. However, depending on the product, it is possible that the amount could be higher, sometimes up to 100 percent. How do you determine how viable this option is and how much you are going to make?

This is often going to do more with finding the right niche and a good supplier so that you can enter into a market that has good demand but isn't overly saturated already. The more saturated the market is, the harder it is going to be for you to find your voice there. As an effect, your margins and your sales are going to be much lower.

A good way to help you to get higher margins is to try and source right from the manufacturer directly rather than going through a supplier or a vendor. This is a bit harder to do, but if you can accomplish it, this effectively cuts out the middleman in the scenario and can save you some money in the process.

Once you have been able to get your dropshipping business off the ground and gain a bit of traction in the market, you will find that this kind of business can quickly start being a money-making machine, one that only needs a little bit of input. It does take some time and some work, and you won't be able to get it done within a few weeks. You have to be willing to put in a lot of work. But if you are good at finding reputable suppliers, good at finding products that will sell well and earn you a higher margin, you can become successful in this kind of business as well.

Who Can Dropshipping Be Good For?

There are a lot of people who can benefit from starting their own dropshipping business. Anyone who wants to earn a side income to help pay the bills and who can devote at least a little bit of time each day to this endeavor would do well at dropshipping. Anyone who wants to get started with growing their business but who doesn't have a lot of capital to spend from the beginning can benefit from his business model. Anyone who wants to be able to stay at home and pursue things other than their traditional job will benefit from this type of business model, too.

There are a few different types of entrepreneurs who will really benefit from the idea of dropshipping. Some of these include:

- Validating Entrepreneur: This business model can be a good way for the individual to test out a new product or a new startup before they invest a lot of money into inventory they are worried may not sell.
- Budget Entrepreneur: Dropshipping is a very inexpensive method of selling online because you are not responsible for purchasing any inventory upfront. This can work out as a great business model for those individuals who want to start a business but want to keep their startup costs low or who are on a limited budget.
- The First Time Entrepreneur: This model of business is a great option for someone who is just starting out with the idea of selling online. Selling online isn't something that everyone finds easy. Driving traffic to your website and then converting that traffic can take a lot of time for a new marketer. Because dropshipping is low in cost, it can allow a new entrepreneur some time to learn how to set up a store, drive traffic, and optimize conversions before they invest more money into their own business.
- Walmart Entrepreneur: This type of business can also be good for someone who would like a chance to sell a ton of models and products. Depending on how much each item costs and how big you want to grow, acquiring all of this inventory for a traditional business can be really expensive. But with dropshipping, this is possible without spending a lot of money.

As you can see, there are many benefits that come with working in dropshipping. Many different individuals will find this as a great option to starting their own business, whether they are doing it as a method to help them to see if this is right for them before starting their own business, if they are using it as a part-time income, or if they are using it to make a full-time income on their time. Dropshipping can be a great business model for anyone who is willing to put in the time and the work.

Chapter 2: The Benefits of Working in Dropshipping

There are a lot of different business opportunities out there that you can choose to go with. However, none of them provide the same benefits that you can get from starting your own dropshipping business. This kind of business doesn't require a lot of money to start, can take just a few steps to get it up and running, introduces you to a global market right from the start, and so much more. Let's take a look at some of the benefits of working with your own dropshipping business and why you should consider starting yours today.

Little Investment to Start

Starting your own dropshipping business requires very little investment to get going. You don't have to pay to make the products, you don't have to keep an inventory for the products, and you do not have to hire a team to help you run the business or even to pay for shipping. In fact, it is possible to get started with drop shipping without paying for anything upfront.

If you choose to sell the products from your own website (and there are some benefits to that), you will have to pay a bit to get the website up and running. If you decide to go with Amazon or eBay, you can get the item listed and then you will pay once the item actually sells. If you plan to use a bit of advertising to draw more interest to your items, then you will need to pay for that as well.

As a dropshipper, it is really in your control how much you would like to spend to get started. Some people are able to start this kind of business for nothing, and others like to spend a bit to help set themselves apart from other sellers. The great thing about this business is that you get to be the one who decides all of it and you can keep the costs as low as you need.

Easy to Get Started

While we will discuss this in a bit more detail later, it is pretty easy to get started with your own dropshipping business. Unlike some other business models, you will find that this business can be started relatively quickly. Keep in mind that you do need to do a bit of research on suppliers and products. It is important that you don't rush in and pick the first product you see. But comparatively, you can't find an easier type of business.

With dropshipping, you simply need to find a niche to work in, find a product and the right supplier of that product to fill that niche, list it in some manner online (such as on Amazon or your own website), and then wait for a customer order. Once the customer orders, you will take what they pay you and place an order directly with the suppliers. The supplier will then send the item out to the customer, and you will end up with a happy customer.

Of course, there are times when things won't work out exactly as you had planned, but there are steps you can take to limit issues and keep things going smoothly. Those basic steps above are really all you need to get started with this kind of business model.

Little to No Overhead Costs

As a dropshipper, you will have limited to no overhead costs. You are not required to keep any of the products on hand or to have an inventory of any kind at all. With this business model, you simply list the products that you want to sell somewhere online such as on Amazon or eBay. Then, when a customer orders, you will use that money to place an order directly with the supplier. The supplier sends the item directly to the customer, not to you. You don't have to worry about keeping all of the products on hand for each customer, which means there is very little cost for you.

There are a few costs that come with dropshipping but you do have some control over them. For example, if you use your own website, you may have to put a bit of money into that. There are usually a few fees associated with listing on eBay and Amazon as well. If you wish to advertise on social media, you will also need to pay a little bit. But as a business owner, you can choose how much you would like to spend on the products. And despite the other expenses, there will never be an overhead cost for running your business.

Lots of Products to Choose From

When it comes to dropshipping, you will find that there are a ton of products that you can sell for your business. There are hundreds of suppliers and each of them can offer you something unique to work with. This means that it is easier for you to reach your own niche because there is sure to be a product out there that will work for you.

Make sure that you take the time to really look through a bunch of suppliers and the products that they offer. You want to make sure that you find a good supplier, a unique product, and something that is in high demand but is still not getting reached well by other sellers. If you can combine all of these together, you will find that it is easier to get more sales on your site.

A Global Market

Since dropshipping and all of the business you do with it will occur online, you get the opportunity to work with a global market, even as a beginner. With a traditional business, you will have to start out by working in your local community. After some time has passed and you see a good amount of profits and interest, you may decide to expand out into your area, then the state, and then the country. Eventually, you may decide to reach out to a global market, but that is only if your business gets that far. Many businesses are happy to just expand a little bit in their region.

But with dropshipping, you can make your products available to a large market right from the beginning. If you list on sites like eBay, Amazon, and Shopify, or even if you do your own website, you are already reaching a potential global market. This is huge. That means more people who may potentially be interested in your product, and more potential to grow your own dropshipping business in no time.

Easy to Scale Later on If You Want

When you first get started with this kind of business, you want to keep it simple. You may only want to start out with a few products to keep it simple and learn the ropes, and that is just fine. But over time, as you start to get the hang of dropshipping and everything that goes along with it. You can then decide to scale your business and make it bigger later on.

That is part of the beauty of working with this kind of business. You can make it as small or as big as you would like. Some people keep it smaller with just a few products for sale. Others decide to grow this into a large business with hundreds of products that they want to sell. And scaling it in this manner is so easy. You simply do a bit of research and decide what other products you would like to sell on your chosen sites and then you list them. That is all there is to it! It's no wonder that so many people want to figure out how to work with dropshipping; it can easily go from a side business to a full-time income with very little work.

Easy to Automate

In the beginning, you will have to put a lot of time and effort into your business. This is necessary to get any business up and running properly. You have to find good suppliers, pick out the right products to sell, get things listed and so on. This takes up some time and can be a big reason why a lot of people give up with dropshipping early on.

But if you are able to get through the beginning work with dropshipping and you are able to be successful with growing your business, you will find that you can then change-up your business and make it more automated. This can really help to save you a lot of time and hassle. You can get your social media posts to be automated, you can handle the orders and any emails within a few hours at any time of the day that you choose, and most of the business will run itself.

Think of how it will feel to make unlimited money with a side business where most of the work is automated! This is what most people dream about when they get started with dropshipping in the first place. You have to go through and put in the hard work from the beginning, but if you can do that, you will soon be able to automate the whole business, and this can really help things to grow.

There are so many benefits that come with starting your own drosphipping business. You can reach a global market, it doesn't cost a lot to get started, you don't have to keep inventory or worry about the overhead costs, and so much more. For those who are willing to put in the hard work to make a good income, dropshipping is the way to go!

Chapter 3: The Drawbacks of Dropshipping

Dropshipping business has a lot of things that you can enjoy. It is a great way to start earning an income on the side along with your regular line of work. You can enjoy a wide range of products to sell, you can choose how much or how little you would like to sell, and you get the freedom of choosing times to work that go around your busy schedule. With that said, there are a few drawbacks that when you decide to get into the dropshipping business, which is why only a few people have seen success with this business model. Some of the main drawbacks that you may notice with dropshipping include:

Sudden Shortages in Stock

As a dropshipper, it is your responsibility to keep up with the amount of stock that is available from your supplier. You can then keep this information updated on your shop so customers know when an item is out of stock or not. Sometimes, this is easy to do. But around the holidays, or with a really popular item, it is hard to keep up with the numbers.

If there is a sudden shortage in the stock of an item, this can pose a problem for you. Your customers may get frustrated that they can't get ahold of that item right away. And if the customer already placed an order for that item, and then you found out that item was out of stock, this can really make it difficult on you and the customer.

The best way to handle this is to have multiple suppliers for the same item, or at least two or three suppliers with similar items. This way, if your main supplier ends up running out of a particular item, and you have customers interested, you still have some options. If the items are the same, you just switch suppliers for a time and send the item out. If the items are a bit different, you can contact the customer and give them the alternative. You can also add a little extra incentive to it as well.

Customer Service is All on You

When the customer gets upset about something, they are not going to call up or email the supplier. You are the front of the business. And for all they know, you are completely in control over that product. When things go wrong, you have to handle all of the customer service yourself.

This can get tedious and hard on some occasions. You have to handle any questions that the customer has. You have to answer emails when you get comments or questions or complaints from a customer. If there need to be any returns or exchanges, you are the one who will have to handle all of this. As one person, this can seem like a lot and can really add to the workload in some situations.

Less Control Over Your Own Business

Dropshipping is a great business to get into. You can start to earn money on products that other companies make, and you don't have to keep any inventory on hand or actually make the product yourself. But, the tradeoff here is that you have very little control over your own business. The suppliers you pick will be the ones in most control over this kind of business. And if you pick the wrong supplier, it could mean the end of your business.

As a dropshipper, you are basically listing items for sale online for other companies. You list them for higher than the supplier has them, and then you take the profits. You will have a customer place the order through you, and then you take that money and place the order through the supplier. From there, the supplier takes over.

If you have picked out good suppliers to work with, this process should be easy to handle. After placing your order, they will make the product, ship it out, and your customer will be happy. But you have very little control over this. It is possible that the supplier could send the product to the wrong place, orders can get mixed up, and more. And when these happen, you have to handle the downfall, even though you didn't have control over any of it.

Potential Issues with Quality Control

Since you are not the one making the product and you never actually touch the product, there could be problems with the quality of the product. The supplier will often try to do the best they can because that is how they make money as well. But if there are quality control issues, you are the one who is going to get harmed the most. Your customers will leave bad reviews, and there isn't really much you can do since you don't make the product.

There are a few things that you can do to make sure that you provide high-quality products to your customers. First, when you are looking for a supplier, do some research on them. Look around and see what other dropshippers have thought about the products. Look and see if there are any major problems with that company that you should be worried about. If there are a lot of bad reviews, or other issues, choose to go with someone else.

Before you decide whether you are going to sell a particular product or not, consider ordering one for yourself. This way, you can get a good feel for the experience the customer will have if they order through you. You can check how the shipping is, check in with the customer service, and see how the product actually works when you have it in your hand. Do this any time you decide to work with a new supplier for your business.

Hard to Find Products That Will Make Enough Money

One challenge that a lot of dropshippers will run into is finding a product they can make a good profit margin on. There are tons of companies and suppliers who will work with this kind of business model, but you have to make sure that you pick out a product that is worth your time to sell. If you look at the price from the supplier and the product is listed as $10, but everyone online is charging $10.50, then this is probably not a good product for you to sell because you will have to sell quite a few to make anything for your time.

Many companies are like this, which is why dropshipping sometimes gets a bad name. It is important to take your time and not rush into the product that you want to work with. The bigger the margin, the easier it is for you to make a good deal of profit on it, and the more worth your time it is.

Don't waste your time making just $0.50 on each item that you sell. By the time you put in the work, do your social media, and pay the fees for the listing site, you will end up losing money. Find products that make as much as possible. For example, if you are able to find a product that costs $50 from the supplier, but other similar sellers have it listed online at $200, then this is definitely a product you should look into.

Supplier Errors

There are times when the supplier may make an error in one of the orders that you place. They may get an address mixed up and send the product to the wrong place. They may send the wrong product to one of your customers. Or they could make some other mistake that makes the customer upset.

When you are a dropshipper, it is hard to get the supplier to take on the hassle with this one. Some of the good ones will help out with this, but the customer is still going to be mad at you if something goes wrong with one of the orders. If this happens too often, you could run into the issue of too many mistakes and bad reviews, and then no customer will want to purchase from you in the future.

It is best to find a supplier you can trust. One that is known for getting orders right and for great customer satisfaction. Remember that you are the face of the business. If you sell the product, then the customer is going to blame you for things going wrong. Even though you are only listing the product and placing the order, the customer will assume you are the one in charge of everything and will take their disappointment and frustration out on you. Picking out a good supplier who takes care of their customers can make a world of difference when it comes to how successful you will be.

While there are many benefits to choosing dropshipping as your new business, there are also a few things that you need to be aware of before starting. There is some work that comes with this kind of business. And even though the income potential can be high, you do have to put in the time and effort to find a good supplier, someone who has great customer satisfaction, creates a high-quality product, and who will get the orders to the right people each time. If you are able to do that, you can easily avoid some of the negatives that come with dropshipping.

Chapter 4: How to Get Started with Your Dropshipping Business

Now that we know a bit more about dropshipping and why it is such a great business to get started with, it's time to look at the different steps that you can follow to get your business up and running. We will look at how to choose a niche, how to pick out products, and so much more to make this business successful for you.

How to Choose Your Dropshipping Niche

Before you get started, it's important to pick out the niche you would like to sell with. You want to find a niche that has higher demand but doesn't necessarily have numerous people selling to it yet. This can be the tricky part when it comes to starting your business. Dropshipping has become very popular and there many other sellers out there as well. Making sure that you can reach your customers in a new way can be a great way to actually make money.

The more specific you can make your niche, and the bigger the audience that comes with it, the better you will do. One misconception that comes with this business is that it's possible to be profitable and successful in any niche that you choose. But if the niche you want to work in has thousands of other sellers, how are you going to stand out from the crowd and make money? Some of the things that you can consider when picking out your own niche include:

1. Start with your own passion and interest: Tap into your interests and hobbies and see if you can come up with some good idea from there. There may be a nice market just waiting for you.

2. Scratch your own itch: The theory behind this one is that if you have a certain problem in your own life, then it is likely that someone else is dealing with the same issue. If you can find a product that will solve that problem, then this could be the new niche that you work on.

3. Research more about the competition: Is the niche you are taking a look at oversaturated? Are you able to beat out the competition in some manner, or is it even worth beating them? The less competition you can find in a niche, the easier it will be to win and make money.

4. Make sure you pick out a profitable niche: The more profitable the niche is that you choose, the more money you can make from this business. You should always look into the profitability of any niche or product you want to work with. Remember, you want to come up with a profit margin that is at least 40 percent after shipping costs, taxes, and fees. If it doesn't meet up to that, then pick a different niche.

When you are picking out a niche, it is also important to take some time to really get to know the customer that you want to work with. Each niche is going to have a different type of customer and a different demographic that you will need to concentrate your energy on. The more you know about that customer, the easier it will be to market and sell to them later on.

As you are going through things and picking out your niche, think about the type of person you want to sell your product to. If you have the time, sit down and write out to your perfect customer. If you could sell the product to any person out there, what would they be like? What gender is there, what age range, what is their job, what do they like to do in their free time, where do they live, what problems do they need to be solved, do they have a family and more. When you have this done, you will be able to plan out your social media strategy, better pick out your platform a bit better and even have a better idea of how you want to market and use the products that you plan to sell. Having this demographic information and the perfect customer all set up and ready to go can make a big difference in providing you with a path to follow for your new business plan.

Find a Supplier

We will get into this a bit more in the next chapter, but it is important to find a good supplier to work with on your business. While you are the face of your own business and have the responsibility of taking care of your customers, the supplier will be the one who actually creates and ships out the product. Finding a good supplier can either make or break your business.

If you pick out a good supplier, things are going to work out so much better for your business. You will have someone who takes care of your customers. Someone who always has a high-quality product that is readily available and shipped out right away when the customer needs it. You will have someone who is easy to work with if there are any complaints or other issues that come up. And you will always be able to rely on them.

On the other hand, if you pick out a bad supplier or one who isn't reliable, things will become a mess. You will have unhappy customers, lots of returned products, and even issues with getting good reviews. If you really want your business to thrive and do well, then you must make sure that you pick out a supplier who is ready to properly take care of your customers.

Take your time to look through all the different suppliers who are out there. You want to find someone who is going to take care of your customers, someone who has good reviews for providing excellent service, and ones who will provide high-quality products at affordable prices so that you can still make some profits for your work. This is definitely a place where you should take your time to search around to find the right company for you.

Get Your Sales Tax ID

If you are setting up this business in the United States or in Canada, then you will probably need a sales tax ID, or a retail license, resale number, vendor's license, or a tax ID. The sales tax is a tax that is levied on all the sales of physical goods sold to consumers, and depending on where you live, it will fall somewhere between six to nine percent of the price. Most states will require that you have this kind of ID but there are some exceptions such as in Oregon, New Hampshire, Montana, Delaware, and Alaska.

It is standard for a business to pass the sales tax on to the consumer by adding it into the price that they charge. Applying for this kind of ID is easy and won't cost significant amounts. You can do it online or you can visit your local county clerk's office to get it done. To do this, you need to either be a sole proprietor (which is what a lot of people will be with this since they are a home online business), a company, or a business entity.

There are some sites, such as eBay, that don't require this kind of ID. But most suppliers and wholesalers will want you to have this before they even consider doing business with you. It is best to have this number in place to make things easier when they are doing taxes at the end of the year.

Pick Out Your Products

Part of the process of picking out a supplier should include a look through the products that you want to sell. If you look at a supplier and find that they don't offer the type of products that you would like to sell, then that is not the right supplier for you. Always go in with an idea of the kind of products that you would like to sell.

When you first get started with this journey, you are going to be amazed at how many different products are for sale and what you can choose from. Try not to get overwhelmed or entranced by a product that seems cool but which has no market and won't make you any profits. Before you even go and look at any products, at least have some guidelines in place that you need to follow to ensure that you are going to find a profitable and valuable product to sell to your customers.

Make sure that you pick out at least a few products to sell. You don't want to take on too much at the beginning. Having a few products, especially ones that are related to each other, can help you to get the dropshipping business off the ground and do well.

Choose Your Selling Platform

Now that you have picked out the product that you want to use and you have set up the right supplier, it is time to find the platform you will use to start selling the product and making money. It is important to pick out the right selling platform if you want to have a business that is successful. But how do you make sure that you pick the right platform that works for you?

We will take some time to talk about each one in more detail in a bit, but there are a few options that seem to be the most popular when it comes to running a dropshipping business. Many people like to work with either Amazon, Shopify, eBay, or their own personal website. There are advantages and disadvantages to each one and the choice is often going to depend on your own goals and the types of products you want to sell.

Setting Up a Strategy to Bring Customers in

At this point, you already have a selling platform set up for the business, but you need to find a way to get people to come and look at the items that you are selling. This is why you need to come up with a strategy for gaining new customers. This is going to include amassed persuasion on your part and it is a combination of marketing and advertising. You can choose between doing either the fast path and paying for the customers, or the slower path that can be free. Often doing a combination of the two can be the right option. Let's take a look at both of these strategies to see how they can work.

Fast results with paid advertising

The first place you may consider advertising is on Facebook ads. Facebook is the biggest social media platform throughout the world, which means it's a great place to advertise your products and reach a bunch of people. Facebook makes its money by promoting your business, so every customer that you get with this method is going to come with a cost. There are many reasons to choose to advertise with Facebook, including:

- It is really easy to get the process started.
- You get all the control over how much you decide to spend each day.
- You can be very specific on your demographics, such as picking out people of certain ages, locations, interests, and even relationship statuses.
- If it is used properly, you can also get results fast.
- It helps when you want to create more awareness for your brand.
- A good ad or a good boosted post has the potential to go viral.

Another option that you can go with is Google Ads. Google is known as one of the most popular of search engines out there. If you have your own online store, you want to make sure that it gets as high up on the list of Google search as possible. You can take your time and do this organically, or you can purchase ads for the store that appear near the top of the page for any of the keywords you are ranking for. Below are several reasons for using Google ads to help grow your business:

- You can achieve better exposure when it comes to search results.
- As mentioned, it is known as the largest platform for advertising throughout the world.
- You can also target demographics in a highly specific manner.
- You will find that the exposure you get with your ads with some of your high volume keywords can be amazing.

You can also choose to do marketing with a social media influencer. Influencer marketing has started to become a big part of gaining new customers, and it is definitely something that you should consider in your strategy for 2019. It can be really effective if you choose a niche that is really trendy. For example, if you are selling a handbag that has a new style, you could reach out to someone famous on Instagram and ask if they are willing to share a post with one of the bags while tagging your business.

There will have to be some agreement between you and the influencer. Potentially, just one post can bring in a lot of new followers and customers to your business. The amount you pay is going to depend on how famous the influencer is, how many people follow them, and other factors of your choices.

Slow results that are free

Now, as a dropshipper, it is important to keep your costs down a bit so that you can keep those margins up as high as possible. While it is fine to do the paid advertising listed above, it is also wise to save some of your budget and work on a more organic reach that doesn't cost you anything. This will take a bit more of your time but can really help with your budget overall.

The first option here is forum or blog marketing. With this one, you are going to find blogs or other types of forums that are related to the niche you are selling in. You want to then actively participate in any discussions that occur on that page. By working to position yourself as an authority in that niche and having a link to your website attached, you are going to find that, over time, you will increase the amount of traffic that heads to your site.

Content marketing is next on the list. In most cases, this is going to take in form as a blog on your store website, some trendy posts on Instagram, a YouTube channel, or something posted on Twitter. Content marketing is meant to involve some creative content that is valuable to your customers and it can really work to build up an audience that will hopefully become your customers. It is more about serving the audience rather than the brand, so make sure it isn't as explicit as advertising.

Social media is another option, but because so many other businesses are using it as well, it is harder to get an organic reach. Note, however, that while it is challenging, it is possible. You just need to consistently share and create great content on these channels. Over time, you will be able to build up a great following that can later be converted into the customers you need.

And finally, you should consider working with email marketing as well. This is still considered one of the most effective ways to acquire new customers. You must first set up a channel that will help you capture the email addresses that you want, such as a request at checkout for them to sign up. Once you have had a chance to build up your email list, you will have a great way to reach a large group of people when you need, for free.

As you can see, dropshipping is a simple idea that anyone can get started with. It isn't meant to be complicated or hard to work with. And it isn't meant to be exclusive to anyone who wants to give it a try. If you just follow the steps above, you will be able to see some great results with your own dropshipping business as well.

Picking the Right Price

Another important aspect of your dropshipping business that we need to discuss here is how to price your items the right way. Many beginners have trouble with this because they want to price it at a point where they can be attractive to the buyers and beat the competition but they also want to make sure that their price margin is high enough that the work is worth their time. Here, we will take a look at how to pick out the right pricing to make sure you get the most out of your business.

First, you do not want to price the item too high. Sure, this may make your price margin seem higher. But if your pricing is much higher than the competition, then customers will notice. They will wonder why your pricing is so high, and most of them are going to choose the cheaper option if the products are the same. The profit margins may look higher, but you aren't going to end up with any sales so you don't really want to do this at all.

Another trap that you need to avoid with this is pricing too low. Pricing a bit lower than the competition isn't bad but it still isn't the best practice to go with. The first issue with this is that you are cutting your price margin when you price it too low. The lower you price the item, the less you are able to make a profit for it. If you would like to earn a good income from this, then you need to try and make as much as possible on the items you sell.

Another issue with pricing too low is that it can make the customer wary of purchasing from you. Yes, customers like to get a good deal when it comes to purchasing any item. But when they see your price is way below the competition, they may worry that the product is something different or that it is lower quality than the others. When you price too low, it's likely that the customer will choose to go with the competition.

It is best to take a look at what the competition is pricing their items at, and then try to stay somewhere near there. This helps you earn as much as possible on the items that you want to sell but still make your items attractive to the customer so they will purchase them from you.

Chapter 5: How to Pick a Supplier and How to Pick Out a Product

Two of the most important things that you will need to do with your business is to pick out a good supplier to work with and a high-quality product to offer to your customers. These two are the basis of a good dropshipping business, and if you don't take the time to get them in place, your new business isn't going to get anywhere very fast.

There are a number of things that you will want to look into when it comes to picking out a good supplier and a good product to help you get your business up and running. Some of the things that you should consider when picking out both of these include:

How to Pick Out a Good Supplier

The entire model of this business is going to be based on the idea that the supplier will be able to do their job well and that they will work to fulfill all their orders punctually and efficiently. This is why picking out the right supplier is so important when it comes to growing your own business. If your supplier ever makes a mistake and messes up one of the orders, you, as well as your business, are the ones who are going to be responsible for this. The key here is to make sure that you find a seller that not only sells a good product but one that will also take care of your customers.

There are a few factors that you should consider when it comes to choosing a supplier for your business. The first thing to look into is finding a company that is experienced, one who has some sales representatives who know what they are doing. This can help any time you get stuck with something, when you have a question, and with other concerns. A company who knows what they are doing and has a reputation for doing it well can be a big asset to your business.

The next thing that you can look for in your supplier is to find one who can provide you with excellent products. The better the product, the higher the level of customer satisfaction. This is great news for you. It not only means some great reviews on your page and more sales, but it also means a much lower rate of returned items and unhappy customers.

If you can, it is also a good idea to find a supplier who has some technical abilities. You want to work with a supplier who has the right technological capabilities to keep up with the times. At some point, you will want to scale your business. You don't want to end up breaking off with a business partnership with the supplier simply because they wouldn't be able to keep up with the growth that you are working for.

And finally, you want to work with a supplier who is punctual and who can be efficient with their shipping process. You should pick out a supplier who is regular with shipping, someone who can ship out the products within 24 to 48 hours after placing the order. This can help ensure that you get happy customers. Since there is so much competition in the market, longer shipping times are generally bad for your customers.

If you are worried about how long the shipping time will be, consider placing a test order ahead of time. This gives you the experience of your customer through the whole process. You can see how long the shipping takes, how the product looks when it gets there, and more. This can go a long way in helping you choose which supplier you would like to work with.

How to Pick Out the Right Products to Sell

To have a successful dropshipping business, you need to make sure that you are picking out the right products to sell. There is no guaranteed way to find the perfect products for your business. However, you need to make sure that you aren't picking out items that are already being sold by a bunch of people, and also items that have a high demand so you can make some money in the process.

Each business is going to be different, so finding the right products for your needs can sometimes prove to be a big challenge. But there are a few criteria you can consider following to help you decide whether a product is going to work well for your business.

The first thing to consider is the retail price of that item. The wholesale and retail price of the product are going to be crucial. You want to hit a sweet spot in the way you price the products. Having a product at a lower price may encourage more sales, but you aren't going to make a big profit margin on those products. On the other hand, items that are priced higher may sell fewer items, but you will earn a bigger profit from each one.

As a business owner, it is important that you find a good balance that works the best for you and for the expectations of your customers. You want to make sure that you get a profit margin that is somewhere between 15 to 45 percent (or higher if you can) to ensure that the work you put into the sale is actually worth it all.

The next thing that you should consider is the size and weight of the item. The packaging and the shipping costs are going to vary based on each product, the effort it takes to ship the product, and how much packaging material will be needed. In this sense, the smaller and the lighter items are often the best to dropship because they will give you a bigger profit margin. You can find larger products that fit in with this as well, but often starting out with smaller items is the best.

Cross-selling is going to become very important to your business. Selling a set of products that are related can be a great way to provide some value to your customers, and it can encourage them to purchase more each time they place an order. If you only have one item available in each category, it is going to be hard to do any cross-selling at all.

When picking out a product, consider what other products you could sell with it to serve your niche. For example, if you sell easels, you may want to also sell paint brushes, canvases, and other art supplies because it is more likely that your customers will want to purchase these kinds of items as well. When you choose to go with this option, consider the ways that you can price the products in a strategic way to make the sale worth as much value for your business as it will for the customer.

You also need to make sure that you pick out products and goods that are going to meet customer expectations. If the products or the goods you sell are renewable or disposable, there is a better chance that the customer will come back and place a repeat order, which can increase your sales. This is why so many retailers will set up a subscription option for their customers to ensure that they keep getting a repeat purchase. If you want to really impress your customers, offer a good discount to customers who are going to subscribe to the product or service you offer.

In addition to this, you need to make sure that your product is as durable as possible. You do not want to send your customers products that don't work in the manner that they should, or products that fall apart and don't work at all. This is the worst way to retain your customers and will end up with you getting bad reviews in the process. Always make sure that you are getting products that are going to impress your customers, not ones that will turn the customer away from you.

And finally, you need to take a look at the turnover rate of the products. As a retailer working through an online store, you will find that the majority of the business you get will come from the copy/content and the photography of the product that you publish on the website. These can be time-consuming and will cost you some money as well.

This means that if you decide to go with products that are going to change soon, then you will have to spend more time switching up the content to keep up. This will result in more time and money wasted. And since you have to do it all physically, it can be stressful. It is best if you find a product that has a low turnover in order to ensure that you can get the most out of the products you sell and the work that you do.

Picking out the right supplier and the right products to start your business is critical. This is going to really determine how well your business is able to do overall and how much money you are able to make in the process as well. Take your time to pick out a good supplier who will take care of you and find products that are in demand, aren't found in a saturated market, and that will earn you a good margin on your profit. If you can do this, you have most of the work accomplished for starting your dropshipping business.

Chapter 6: How to Handle Your Customers and Provide Exemplary Customer Service

The biggest thing to remember when you want to create a long-lasting and sustainable dropshipping business is to maintain a good reputation with your customers. This is all going to come down to the experience that your customer has with you and your product. Sometimes you will find that it is hard to build up that trust with your customers since the whole business is online and there is no face-to-face interaction with your customers.

But when you are starting your dropshipping business, you need to take the reigns and all of the responsibility for how well the customer service of your business is handled. Your suppliers are the ones who will take care of fulfilling all the orders. And if you picked a good supplier, you should find that part of the process good. However, the supplier is never going to have any contact with the customer. This means that you need to be the one who provides good customer service in order to keep your business growing strong.

You are the One Responsible

The first thing that you have to keep in mind with this business is that no matter how well it is all running, there will be times when things will go wrong. This can happen even for the best companies out there. Even the most trusted suppliers will run into trouble on occasion. But in the dropshipping business, when this does happen, you are the one who needs to go through and fix that situation.

In some cases, this may mean that you will lose some money to fix an order. But this loss of money is going to pay off in the long run. Fixing the mistake, even at a cost, means that you will have a customer who is more likely to come back. And they may even leave a more favorable review, rather than a bad review, to help your business grow a bit more in the future.

Understand Your Customers

If you are able to understand the wants and the needs of your customers, then this will be a big factor when it comes to how well you are able to provide customer satisfaction in your business. Your customers want to feel secure when they shop with you. Making sure that your customers have a safe and secure checkout and that they will have their personal information safe when they shop with you can be very valuable to your customers.

How do you do this? If you aren't using sites like eBay and Amazon, and you choose to sell on your own website, make sure that you build one that looks professional. Customers will run the other way if the website doesn't look professional and looks like it has been thrown together (this is a big sign of someone who is out to steal their information). In addition, on your personal website, you should consider adding in some extra security features to show customers that you value their personal information.

Know About Your Products

Customers are never happy when they purchase a product and it comes in completely different from what they expected. They are going to be mad at you and possibly even leave a bad review if they end up getting something that wasn't what they expected at all. Make sure that you provide very detailed and good product descriptions to your customers and take pictures that actually showcase the product well.

Moreover, you can add in a few other parts to help answer any questions that the customer may have. Starting an informative blog, making sure there is a good FAQ page on the website, and even sending out a newsletter on a regular basis to explain products and other information can be helpful to your customers. Remember, the less that a customer has to come to you to ask a question, the more comfortable they are going to feel when they make the purchase and the less work you have to do. If you offer the knowledge for free, they are going to appreciate that, and they will see you as more of an expert on those products and that niche.

Happiness is the Top Priority

And finally, remember that a happy customer is the best when it comes to growing your own business. Transactions that are successful and have very little friction are going to lead to happy customers. Happy customers are most likely to come back, leave positive reviews, and tell their friends about the product. All of these things will lead to your business growing and you make more money.

As you are working with your customers and creating a good experience for them, remember that a happy customer can be one of the best tools for marketing your brand out there. Treating your customers well and making them happy can help you to get your business out of there. It will also help your business grow much better than it would with any of the other tactics that we have discussed in this guidebook.

An unhappy customer can do the opposite. They will still leave reviews and share information about you with their friends and family. But often this information will be in a negative light that you do not want. Negative word of mouth spreads faster than positive word of mouth. So take the customer service of your business seriously and try to avoid any problems before they happen. And if these problems do happen, and they will at some point, do your best to handle them in a way that can satisfy your customer.

Customer service is completely your responsibility when it comes to your dropshipping business. Making sure that you always take care of the customer and that you are willing to handle any of their questions, complaints, and concerns can make a big difference in how the customers feel when purchasing you, whether they will share information with others about the business, and also if they will become repeat customers.

How to Set Yourself Apart from the Competition

When it comes to dropshipping, you will see there is plenty of competition out there. Not only are there other companies selling the exact same product that you are, but there are also other individuals selling those products and other similar ones that can fit the same kind of demographic as you. It is important that you find some methods that help you to stick out from the crowd to get customers to find you and to ensure that you will get them to come back.

There are different methods that you can use to make this happen. And often, it will depend on the products that you are selling and the type of business plan you follow. One thing to note is that lowering the price too much is usually not a good method to use. Yes, it may mean that you can offer a price that is much lower than what the competitors can do, but this often backfires. Many customers will be worried about why you price so low, thinking that you are selling a substandard product. This can harm your sales. Plus, when you price things lower, you can end up with lower price margins, and it is harder to make the profits that you want.

It is better to find other methods that can help you to stand out from the competition, methods that show that you are ready to provide exceptional products and customer service to all of your customers, without having to hurt your bottom line too much.

One option that you can consider is starting a subscription service. If your product lends itself well to this, you could offer a discount to customers who agree to sign up for a few months of your service or product. This is a great way to get repeat customers and can make things easier for the customer since they can continue to get the product sent to them automatically when they need it each month.

Depending on the type of supplier you choose to use, you may want to add something special to the packaging that you send out to the customer. Adding in a personalized note to it or finding a way to showcase your business entity can go a long way for you to showcase your work and feel like there is that personal touch. If you can't do this with your supplier, another option would be to get the email address of the customer and send them a personalized message in this manner. This helps the customer to feel valued and provides you with the start of your own email list that you can use later.

As a business owner, you will soon find that positive word of mouth can go a long way in growing your business. If a customer takes the time to share your products with their friends and is willing to talk up the product, then you are more likely to make sales in the future. You can choose to use this to your advantage to make more sales.

When a customer finishes their order, ask them to share the word. You can ask them to refer a friend or place a little advertisement on Facebook or another social media site talking about their experience. Many businesses choose to offer discounts, such as 10 percent off the next purchase if their customers are willing to do this. It may cost a bit out of your pocket, but it can result in a high number of sales if you can get a few customers to agree to help you. it is well worth the investment as well.

With some types of products, you may find that it is helpful to put add-ons with it to sell more. You can offer it as a special gift that goes with the product or make some bundle deals to help make things easier for your customers when they are shopping. Customers love to be able to save money on their purchases and they love one-stop shopping. If you can provide them with a place where they can get several items that they need in one place, and you can offer your customers a discount on buying the items altogether, you can earn a big profit in the process as well.

Any time that you are able to add some freebies in with your sales, you should consider doing it. Maybe if you are selling a technology item, sending off a pamphlet with tips on how to use it, or your own personalized manual to help them use the item can make a difference. Or, if you are selling a product for making life easier in the kitchen, you can also send out a recipe book with the product to your customer.

The point here is that you want to find some ways that you can differentiate yourself from the competition. There are always going to be other people out there selling products, and sometimes they will even sell the same product that you are. You have to find a way to provide more value to the customers than that which they are getting from the competition or they have no reason to choose you over someone else.

If you are unsure of ideas on how to set yourself apart, go and look at what the competition is doing. See what the best sellers are doing in your industry and decide what you like and don't like then implement these ideas into your own strategy. You will be amazed at the different things that other competitors are doing in your industry, and taking the time to learn from them a bit can really help you to see the best results in your own dropshipping business when you first get started.

Providing good customer service can be so important when it comes to your new business. And this customer service is going to come in a bunch of different shapes and sizes. If you are able to provide an exceptional product at a good price and find other ways to beat the competition on the same or similar items, then you are well on your way to seeing success when you get started with this business model.

Chapter 7: How to Handle Security Issues With Your Business

If you choose to create your own website and sell your products through there, there's another step that you have to handle when it comes to your customers. Any customer who chooses to purchase through your website expects that website to be as safe as possible. They don't want to provide you with payment and personal information, just to find out that someone can come and steal that information right after. As a business owner, it is your responsibility to set up the site so it is secure and so your customers can shop with peace of mind.

Select a Platform that is Secure

The first thing you can do to help protect your customers is to select a platform for your site that already has some security built in. There are different platforms out there that you can choose from, but pick out one that offers PCI-compliant payment gateways and SSL security throughout the site.

Another thing that you should look for on your platform is a checkout page that is secure. You also need to make sure that there is a session timeout function so that when the user isn't active for a certain amount of time, the session will log them out to keep them safe. The more security features that you can find on your chosen platform, the better it is for your customers.

Set Higher Standards for Passwords

One of the best ways that you can make sure that your customers are shopping as safe as possible online is to insist that they use strong passwords. It is common for users to use the same kind of password on more than one account, or going through and picking something that is simple just so they won't forget it later. However, these kinds of passwords make it easy for cyber crooks to get information and it can make things even more difficult from a security standpoint.

While you can't do much about your customers using the same password that they have on another site, you can set some requirements that ensure the passwords they pick for this website are complex. For example, enforce a minimum number of lowercase and uppercase letters and add in symbols to help keep the website and the user account as safe as possible.

Protect Against Any DoS Attacks

As you will quickly see with your own e-commerce site, you will see that the DoS attacks can be a very big threat against your website. And if they are done effectively, they can keep genuine customers from getting onto your website when they need access.

DoS stands for denial of service. This kind of attack is when a hacker is going to get on a system and deliberately inundate a site, sending over more requests than that site is able to handle. The website is going to be overwhelmed and it won't be able to respond to anything at all. The hacker is then able to use some backdoor techniques in order to cause issues, steal information, and do what they want while the system is down and real customers are not able to get onto the site.

To help avoid his issue, you can use a mitigation service. This service is able to filter out the traffic that comes into your website and it will check to see that the requests that are coming in actually are done by real people rather than from bots. This is a simple way to help prevent against a large-scale attack that could really put your business and the personal information of your customers at risk when they visit your site.

Use an SSL Protection Layer

And finally, adding in a layer of protection with SSL can be a great way to keep your website site. Since you are an e-commerce business, you will have to collect sensitive customer information to complete the transactions and receive payment. This means that you will have access to the customer name, their address, and their credit card or other payment information. This is all just part of the e-commerce business.

As a business owner in this industry, it is important for you to protect all of this information as much as you can. This is where the SSL protection is going to come into play. The SSL, or Secure Socket Layer, is able to encrypt any information that is sensitive as it travels from the customer (point A) to you (point B). This encryption is going to make it harder for any outsider to come in and intercept the information.

SSL is actually the standard when it comes to using websites online, especially when sensitive information is shared between two parties, so you need to make sure that you have it in place on your website. In fact, most customers are going to look for the padlock sign on their browser before they make a purchase to make sure that their information won't be stolen. If you don't have this in place, you will lose out on a lot of customers.

In addition to providing your customers with some extra peace of mind when it comes to shopping online with you, the SSL protection may even be able to give your site a boost in SEO. This helps you to get seen by more customers and makes it easier for your business to grow.

Protecting the information of your customers can be very important when you sell any item online and when you are growing your business. You want to make sure that your customers will feel safe and secure when they come to your website, and that they will come back again and again. Make sure to put as much security on your business website as possible to ensure that customers can shop and make payments without worry.

Chapter 8: How to Scale Your Business

When you first get started with your dropshipping business, you will probably work with just a couple of products. This helps you to learn the ropes, try a few things out, and get used to everything. But over time, you will want to scale your dropshipping business and make it grow. After you have gained some experience, you will be able to add in more products, and really see the business, and your income, grow.

The nice thing about dropshipping is that you can scale it to be however big you would like and you can choose how quickly you would like to scale the business as well. This chapter is going to show you a few of the strategies that you can use in order to scale your business and make as much money as you would like with this revenue stream.

Add More Products to Your Inventory

The best way to scale your business is to just add more products to your list. You can go through the supplier you like to use and pick out a few different items that you want to add to your site. You can choose to go with something that is completely new or find other items that can complement the items that you are already selling.

As a business owner, it is best to just add in a few products at a time. You don't want to overwhelm yourself with some of the work that can come, and each product can add in a lot more work for you. If you have ten products, it's not a good idea to instantly jump to selling forty products overnight. Adding in five or six new products, seeing how that goes, and then adding in more can be a great way to ensure you are prepared for the extra work.

The nice thing about your dropshipping business is that you are able to scale this business as large as you would like. If you only start out with a few products but want to grow it to have 100 products over time, this is possible with dropshipping. Just make sure to only take on as much as you can handle and still provide good customer service at the same time.

Consider Seasonal Items

If you are working on a few products that seem to be doing well and you now want to see about scaling the business to make it bigger, seasonal items can be a great option. These are items that sell well during a certain time of the year but won't be available all the time. Things like beach items, Christmas items, or Halloween items can do well with this.

When you want to scale your business, these products can be nice to work with. They allow you to sell items that are really popular and unique and there can be a good margin on them if you pick the right ones. You can get some experience with selling more items, but then you still have times when you get a break during the process as well.

If you are going with seasonal items, make sure that you start selling them early. If you start selling them just a week before the holiday or before that season, you are too late to the party and you have missed out. Starting earlier than other sellers is a great way to get more customers and get your name at the top of search engines for these items. Also, try to find items that are unique rather than selling the same items that other competitors to put yourself ahead of the competition.

Hire Others to Help You Manage the Business

Over time, as you sell more products and gain more inventory, you may find that you are making enough in profits that you are able to hire on some help to do some of the work. This is when your business has really started to do well. In the beginning, you will be in charge of everything. You have to pick which suppliers and which products you want to sell. You have to take the time to list the products with good product descriptions in place. You have to process the orders and get them shipped off to the right people. And you have to handle any issues or questions the customers may have.

As you start to grow your inventory more, you will find that doing this and keeping up with other things in your life can be really hard to handle. You need to keep doing the same process no matter how many products you add to your inventory. And you may find that it is easier to hire a team to help you do the work and manage things for you.

Before you jump in and do this, make sure that you make a high enough margin that it makes sense to hire others to help you. If hiring someone else is going to eat up all of your profits, then it doesn't make sense to hire someone to help. But once you have expanded out your products quite a bit and you have a steady customer base, then it may make sense to hire someone to help you out on occasion to free up some of your time.

Many people want to make a full-time income out of dropshipping, but very few people want to actually spend all day working on this business. Once your business starts getting to the point where you have trouble keeping up with it by working a few hours a night, then you are well on your way to scaling the business. Hiring some help can make sense to free up your time. This helps to ensure that you still get a nice income while only working part-time in the process.

As your business keeps on growing, you may find that you need to hire more and more to help the business grow. Your dropshipping business can grow as fast and as big as you would like. You just need to properly manage the business, handle customer issues properly, and work to grow the business in the right manner. As the business grows, hiring people to help manage your products can make a big difference while still helping you to make a full income in the process.

Chapter 9: How to Dropship with Shopify

There are a lot of different platforms that you can choose to use when it comes to starting your dropshipping business. One of the popular options that you can choose to use for this kind of business is Shopify. Shopify is a commerce platform that is going to help you start, grow, and even manage your business. There is so much that you can love about Shopify and how it can help your business to grow.

With Shopify, you get the benefits of creating and then customizing your own online store. Once you have that set up, you are able to sell in a bunch of different places at once. You can choose to work with selling online, mobile selling, social media, online marketplaces, brick and mortar companies, and even with some pop-up shops.

Shopify is completely cloud-based and hosted. What this means is that you are able to create your own e-commerce site and then not have to worry about upgrading at any time or maintaining the web servers and software along the way. This is great for many business owners who are not able to keep up with web hosting and all the maintenance that goes with running their own site. Shopify also helps you have all the flexibility that you need in order to run your business from anywhere as long as you have a connection to the internet.

Dropshipping on Shopify can be a great choice. It helps you to increase the market that you are able to work with. You simply need to pick out a Shopify plan and have some products that you want to sell. Shopify doesn't care if you are using products that you make or if you choose to dropship just as long as you are able to provide details on your products when you get started.

When you work with Shopify, you are basically setting up your own online store using web hosting and other services that this company is able to offer you. You can easily try out the company for a few weeks for free, even without a credit card. So even if you decide not to use this option, it is still worth your time to check it out. If you do decide to try out this option more permanently, there are a lot of paid options that help you to start your online store to sell unlimited products through many different sales channels based on your personal budget.

In addition to having a lot of different sales channels that your products will be available through, which can increase your reach, you will also get the benefit of 24/7 support and the security that your customers are looking for when it comes to keeping their personal and payment information safe.

Getting started with Shopify is pretty easy and many dropshippers find that this is one of the easiest and cost-effective methods to get their business started, especially if they want to go through the process of creating an online store. The first step after picking out your supplier and your products is to pick out which product you want to use through Shopify. There are a few options, and it depends on how much you want to spend a month and how much support and services you want. All of them offer an online store, unlimited products, 24/7 support, multiple sales channels, and free SSL certificate. Some of the more expensive plans allow you to pay less on credit card rates and can cost you less in commissions for each of the transactions that you do.

Once you have the right plan for your use of Shopify, it is time to pick out your template. Shopify can provide you with a lot of different templates that you can use. As a beginner, you may want to go with one of these templates because it makes things easier. You can also choose to pick out some of your own templates or create your own if you don't find one that works the best for your needs. Take your time to look through all the different options that are available. This will ensure that you find one that will be easy for your customers to use and one that works with the products that you sell.

Make sure to take the time to pick out a good template and go through and start to list out all of your products. All of the plans that are available through Shopify allow you to put unlimited amounts of products on the site, so go ahead and list as many products as you would like. Because of this, you will also be able to go through and use Shopify in order to scale your business because it is easy to add in more products later on.

If you already have your own domain name, you can use that along with Shopify. You will be able to connect your existing domain name when you get onto your account from the store admin. Or, if you don't have a domain name yet, Shopify makes it easy to get this all set up and working for your needs.

As you are adding in the products to your account, make sure to bring in excellent pictures. This is the first thing that a lot of people are going to see and these will help you draw in more customers as well. Each product posting needs to have a good description added to it, perhaps with a few keywords, to ensure that you are actually selling the product and that your customer will be able to find the product when they search for products like yours.

When you are creating your Shopify page, remember that it is going to be shared across a lot of different platforms. This is part of the benefit of working with this website, but it also means that you need to be careful about the work that you do. You need the products to sell across all of these platforms, so pick out high-quality pictures, good descriptions, and has all the information that the customer may need before making a purchase.

Shopify will work with a third party payment processor to help you handle the payments for all of your products. This ensures that both you and the customer are going to be protected during the process and can work the best since you are able to reach customers all over the world. Once you receive an order for one of your products through Shopify, you will receive a notification about it. The way you get the notification is going to depend on your settings. You can get an RSS notification, text message, or email after each order.

When you are looking for a method of selling your products in a multitude of ways and you want to reach your customers wherever they may be, then Shopify is the best choice to go with. There are a lot of options that come with it. It can help you to reach your customers through social media, online, in person, and more, and the plans are very affordable.

Chapter 10: How to Dropship On Amazon and eBay

Two of the biggest platforms that dropshippers will use to help sell their products are Amazon and eBay. Both of these platforms are household names, which makes them the perfect options for getting your products out there. There are times when competition may be an issue. But if you plan things right and pick out unique and high-quality products, it is still possible to make a lot of money with these platforms. This chapter will take a look at some of the steps that you can take in order to get your own dropshipping business up and running on eBay and Amazon.

Dropshipping on Amazon

Amazon is one of the biggest platforms that is used for dropshippers. It is usually pretty easy to sell items on the site, it reaches millions of people throughout the world, and the fees usually aren't too bad for most sellers to handle. Working with Amazon is pretty simple to use and almost anyone is able to work with this method as well.

To get started with dropshipping on Amazon, you first need to set up a seller account. You can choose to just start selling off your regular account or you can set up a separate one to help you keep things separated as well. At this point, you should already have your products picked out, so now it is time to list them. Just go to your seller account and start listing.

Just like with any platform you choose to use, it is often best to take your time when listing. You want to have high-quality pictures, ones that will show the customer the product well. Remember that the customer can't go to a physical store and actually touch and turn the product around. If you already own the product, consider taking your own pictures rather than using stock images. If you can find some unique way to showcase the product, something different than what the competitor is doing, then you should consider doing that as well to entice more customers.

Writing a good description is important as well. You want to make sure that the description is actually able to sell the product, that it is there to entice the customer to actually purchase that product. Using persuasive language, adding in some keywords, and showing the customer how this product can help solve a problem for them can all be great ways to write convincing copy to get more sales from the posting.

Amazon will usually charge based on the sale price of the item. You will have to give them about ten percent for most products that you sell. It is important to count this into your profit margin when you are picking out products. Only earning one percent on an item after Amazon takes their cut isn't really going to make this process worth your time.

Even though the fees may seem a bit higher with Amazon compared to some of the other options, there are a lot of benefits to working with this site. The biggest advantage is that you are putting your products with a brand that is really recognizable. Amazon is now a household name throughout the world, and you won't have to spend time telling your customers how its marketplace works. And since it is such a big company, you won't have to worry so much about some of the little things like SEO, marketing, and advertising just to get people to the website. When you sell your products in this manner, you can sell your products without having to pay for them ahead of time or having them sit around and not getting sold. You will only have to pay for an item once it is sold. Amazon is really good at making this process as easy and painless as possible. While there are a few fees, selling with dropshipping and through Amazon is a much cheaper option than holding inventory and spending for that.

In addition, Amazon makes it easier for you to expand with your virtual inventory. You can easily add in as many products as you would like to your store. Amazon doesn't have a limit to how much you can sell with them, which makes it easier to scale your business without having to worry about moving platforms or changing other things.

There are a few requirements that you must meet in order to sell on Amazon though. These include:

- You need to be the seller of record for all of the products.
- You need to identify yourself as the seller of the products on any information that is provided or included with the product.
- You need to be responsible for accepting and processions customer returns on all of the products for your customers.
- And you have to know all of the selling policies through Amazon and agree to comply with these terms.

The good news is that most of these are already going to be done for you when you sign up with your suppliers. As long as you stick with the rules and don't try to cheat the system, you will be able to get your dropshipping business up and running with Amazon.

Dropshipping on eBay

The next place we are going to look for starting a dropshipping business is through eBay. There are a lot of buyers who like to head over to eBay because it is a simple platform to work with and they can get some good deals. If you feel that your buyers are going to be in this area, or you feel like your product would be best suited for working on eBay, then this is definitely a place for you to start with your business.

If you would like to start your dropshipping business on eBay, the first thing that you need to do is create a seller account on eBay. When you get started on this site, you will have to create a seller account. When you post an item, you will have to pay a small listing fee. Make sure to count this listing fee in with your investment to the business so it doesn't surprise you later on. For those who get to this part and are still trying to figure out what they would like to sell, there are a few tools that you can use through eBay. You want to make sure that there is a high enough demand for the product but not too much supply before you decide to sell one product over another. Some of the steps that you can use in order to find out how good a product will sell includes

- Go to eBay
- Click Advanced Search
- Enter the product that you are considering
- Sort by Price highest first
- Select on completed listings only
- Click search
- From here you can take a look at the best selling products in the niche or for the product you are interested in.

Once you have chosen some of the products that you would like to sell, it is time to list them on eBay so you can start to make some money. Make sure to upload some images and good descriptions. Some beginners like to just copy and paste the description that comes from the supplier's website. This makes things easier but you need to take a look at the description first. Sometimes these are short and sometimes grammar and spelling are off. You want to really sell the product so you may want to rewrite the description using descriptive language and some top keywords for your niche.

At this time, you will also need to come up with the price you want to charge for the item. The price needs to find the right balance between being low enough that it can compete against some other items on the market but high enough that you are able to make a good profit margin, even after you pay for the listing fees for posting on eBay.

After you have paid the listing fee for that product, eBay will post the product online. You now can work on other forms of advertising in order to get more people to find your products and make the purchase as well. Once a customer finds your product and makes a purchase, you can take the payment and put that towards placing the order with your supplier. You simply give the supplier the customer's shipping address and they will take care of the rest of the work for you.

Since the eBay listing fee can cut into your profit margins a bit more, you may want to pick out a little higher margin when you choose a product you want to go with. This can help to cover the costs that you incur when you work with this site. You also can list more than one of the product to make the listing fees work more in your favor.

Both Amazon and eBay are great options when it comes to starting your dropshipping business. They can both help you reach a ton of customers and can do a lot of the advertising and work for you in the process. There are some more fees in the beginning compared to starting your own website and selling. But since these sites are well-known and do a lot of the work in the process, many dropshippers choose to at least get started with this method over some of the others.

Chapter 11: Creating a Personal Website for Your Dropshipping Business

Another method that you can use to help get your business off the ground is to create your own personal website. This method may cost a bit more in the beginning compared to the others. You have to pay for a domain name, get the website set up, and work on SEO. But once the website is up and running, it is a great way to build up a brand, and you can keep 100% of the money that you earn on your products.

Some beginners feel a bit worried about starting their own website. They feel that they would not be able to create a good website or that it is too much work. But if you are willing to put in just a bit more time and effort in the beginning, you will find that a personal website can work better than some of the other methods we have discussed so far in this guidebook.

In this chapter, we are going to take a look at how you can create one of your own personal website for this kind of business. We will use WordPress which will help keep things easy, but you can choose whichever hosting site that you are the most comfortable with. Some of the steps that you can follow in order to create your personal website to get your dropshipping business off the ground include:

Get Your Domain Name and Web Hosting

The first thing that you need to work on is getting your own domain name for the website. The domain name is going to be the unique address for your website. It is the name that a customer will type into the search engine in order to find you. Something like www.mystore.com is your domain name.

On the other hand, you also need to work with web hosting. This is a remote server that is going to store all of the data for your website and then makes that information accessible to anyone who decides to visit your site. You can think of the web hosting like a house that stores everything and the domain name is the address to that house.

There are numerous different domain names and hosting providers to help you out with this. But if you can, it is best to pick out the right one even if it costs a bit more. A good hosting provider and domain name can do a ton when it comes to how successful your website will be. When picking out a domain name, you may need to experiment around a bit. You may already have a good name in place for your business and that can help. If not, now may be the time to think about this a little bit. In addition, you may find that some of your first choices for domain names aren't readily available because someone else has chosen them. Being flexible and trying out a few different options will ensure that you are able to find the domain name that you want to work with.

Install WordPress

Once you have picked out your domain name and your web hosting, it is time to install WordPress. There are two different forms of WordPress that you can work with. These include WordPress.com and WordPress.org. Both of these can be great options and it often depends on the amount of freedom and work you want to have. It is best to work with WordPress.org because this allows you to use your own domain name which looks more professional and ranks higher in SEO compared to the other option. On the other hand, Wordpress.com can make things easier because a lot of things are automatic.

First, let's look at WordPress.com. This option is going to offer both the regular option and the Business Plan. If you are going with this choice, then make sure that you choose the Business Plan to help grow your dropshipping business. With WordPress.com Business plan, you will have a custom domain, premium hosting, the security that your customers need, and plenty of backups to make sure your information stays up to date.

With WordPress.com, you also get a chance to pick from hundreds of customized themes or you can install your own custom theme in some cases. It is also possible for you to share the page when needed to some of the more popular social media accounts you will want to work with which can make your social media strategy a little bit easier to work with. And as a business owner, you will find that there are a lot of graphing and statistical tools that you can choose to go with to make your website strong.

If you go with this option, the pricing can be a bit higher than some of your other choices. You will also need to register for an account through WordPress.com and have to abide by the Terms of Service that are there. But if you are fine registering for this and a few of the other kinks that come with this choice, you will have a great website that is backed by a powerful name in the industry. Most of the work will be done for you, too.

If you would like to have a bit more freedom with the website and get to control everything about it, then WordPress.org is going to be the choice that you want to work with. You will get plenty of security and you can either install your own custom themes or build your own with the help of CSS and PHP. You can also get the benefit of installing plugins into the plan, such as Jetpack, to help you get more functionality for sharing the site.

Probably the biggest benefit of this one is that you are able to really work with plugins. WordPress.com Business will allow you to have a few plugins, but you can pick almost any kind that you want with the WordPress.org option. Plus, you don't have to worry about registering with WordPress.org in order to use these websites.

Of course, these are just two of the options that you can choose from when creating your own dropshipping website. You can also choose to work with other platforms if you are interested in working with different features or if you think the way the platform is laid out will work better for the products that you are trying to sell. No matter which option you choose to go with, make sure that you have full control over your hosting and your domain name. That way, if you ever run into trouble with the platform, or you choose to switch, you can still maintain control over it all.

Set Up the Website and Pick the Right Plugins

Now that you have chosen the domain name, the hosting, and the platform that you would like to use for your website, it is time to get the website set up. Just like with the other options for your website, make sure that you take the time to list all of your products and write great descriptions to go with them. Since this is a standalone website, you will need to really work on the keywords that go with the different items to ensure that you can work on SEO and draw more customers to your page.

With the other options that we chose, you had a good name behind you, one that was well known and could bring in the customers for you. That company already did the SEO and a lot of the customer reputation work so you just had to deal with making your product stand out from the crowd. But when you work with your own website, you need to find a way to make the website stand out so people are able to find you and purchase the product. High-quality pictures, good descriptions, and even a blog tied to the website can all help you to rank higher with SEO.

Since this is a personal website, your template may not just include the items that you are selling. Many personal websites will have a contact page, an introduction page that talks about the company or the products a bit, and even an About Me page. If you have a blog or plan to create one, then make sure that it is linked to the website as well.

While creating your own website, you will find that plugins can be your best friend. You will need a few of them to make your website work better. You can consider a plugin to help with recommendations for the customer, ones that help hold on to the cart and sends reminders to your customers if they leave something behind, plugins for listing similar products the customer might like, and then plugins to help with processing payment so you can place the order and get the product sent out to your customer.

As you can see, there are quite a few more steps that come with creating your own website, and this can often turn beginners off form doing this method. But while it does cost a bit more and usually takes a bit more work when you get started, it is going to pay off on the long run. Once you get the website up and running and you get a good number of customers to visit your site, you can easily scale it and make more money without having to pay more fees or other investment costs to earn the money.

Chapter 12: Do I Need to Use Social Media for My Business?

As a dropshipper in the modern world, it is important that you figure out how to work with social media to grow your reach. If you forget to start up a social media presence, then you may as well just give up on the business right away. There are a lot of people who want to get into dropshipping and they are competing against thousands of other businesses out there in order to get ahead. Social media is a great way to get the word out there to help you reach as many people as possible and to help increase your overall business.

Social media has grown in leaps and bounds in recent years, and it seems like everyone is now online for at least a little bit of their day. This provides a lot of potential for a business to share their products and make some money in the process. The biggest issue you will have to consider when getting started is which site you want to get started with.

Since there are so many social media sites that you can work with, you may feel overwhelmed at first. The good news is that you only need to pick two or three to work with, and then ignore the rest. If you try to manage ten or more social media sites in order to promote your products, you are going to run into some trouble. Doing this may sound like a good way to increase your reach, but in reality, you are spreading yourself too thin and you aren't concentrating on where your customers actually are.

So, the first goal that we want to work on here is figuring out which social media sites are the best for reaching our customers. Spend some time learning more about your customer, thinking about the way that they like to shop and where they like to spend their time. Which social media sites do you think they would spend their time on? Pick two or three sites where you are likely to find these individuals, and then work on promoting good and valuable information on each one.

One note to consider is to try out some sites that aren't Facebook. Yes, we do spend some time talking about Facebook in this guidebook, and there are many benefits to using this site. But you shouldn't just automatically jump to this choice just because it is the largest and most well-known option. If your research shows that a few other social media sites are better for reaching your customers, then those are the ones that you should go with.

When working on your social media accounts, make sure that you concentrate on providing high-quality information and posts that provide value to your customers. There are plenty of other marketers you have to fight against on social media and your posts are going to get lost in the clutter and not get seen by anyone if you just post a bunch of junk. Find things that provide value, that are funny, and that can really get the attention of others in order to see more engagement from your posts.

Some of the other tips that you can follow in order to get the most out of your own social media strategy for your dropshipping business include:

1. Once you have been able to decide which of the social media sites you would like to use for marketing, it is time to work on ways to make your presence there effective. It doesn't do you much good to get on a site and then never have anyone see you.

a. For example, if you decide to use Facebook, you can start by setting up a good Fan Page for this business. You can then work on making this as good as it can be, using some of the free apps available to make the page amazing.

2. When you are on the social media site, make sure that you are always consistent. You should post fresh, valuable, and relevant content to the site on a regular basis. You should try to post at least once each day. It isn't going to work for you to build up a Facebook page or an identity on Twitter, and then abandon it forever.

3. Never use these pages for the personal stuff. You want to be friendly and give off more about your brand but never share your personal details such as that bad breakup on your business social media pages. This is unprofessional and it is going to drive a lot of people away from your business.

4. If you decide to work with Facebook for your marketing, make sure that you use the Facebook Insights that are provided. These are going to be analytical tools for your Fan Page, and they are free. You can take the time to look through them and find a lot of information about user growth, demographics, and any other information that you need to help grow your business even more.

5. If you decide to work with Twitter for marketing, be sure that you go on and update your content often. You can also follow people who would be the most interested in the products you are selling. Remember that quality is always more important compared to quantity when it comes to social media. Twittercounter can be a good free tool to work with because it will show you information about the growth, or lack of growth, that is occurring on your page.

6. Never purchase followers or fans for your social media sites. This is a big mistake that new marketers will try to do in order to help them grow their reach. But most social media sites are fighting against them and are starting to penalize marketers start to go with these paid followers and likes. If you go through and try to inflate the numbers using this method, you are going to be found, and it will end up penalizing your whole business.

Even as a dropshipping business, you will find that social media can be a very important part of growing that business. You have to find ways that are going to help you reach your customers and really get them to come into your business and purchase from you rather than from someone else. Follow these simple tips in order to really reach your audience when it comes time to sell the products that you have available.

Chapter 13: What About Using Affiliate Marketing?

As we have discussed a bit in this guidebook, there are many different ways to market and promote your dropshipping business. And as a new business owner, you need to be able to figure out which method works the best for your products and for your business. No one has an unlimited budget so you won't be able to try and get all of the different marketing avenues to help grow their business. You have to pick out the ones that are the best for you.

One method that you can choose to use that can help keep your budget on track and which ensures that you only have to pay out when a purchase has been made is affiliate marketing. Here, you let other influencers in the market take on the work of talking about and promoting your product. Then, when that influencer is successful at getting some sales for you, you can pay them an agreed upon amount.

This works out nicely for you. If an affiliate takes your link and doesn't make any sales at all, then you don't have to pay them. But if they do get a bunch of sales through their work, you earn a good profit, and they can earn an income as well. It is a win-win for both sides that ensures someone is working hard for you in the process as well.

Affiliate marketing is a pretty easy concept to get started with. The idea is that you will get other people to do the work of advertising your products for you. These individuals often own successful social media sites or blogs and they are looking for ways to monetize that. They already have done the work of building up a good presence online and they want to be able to benefit from that as well. They want a way to make money from their work and you want a way to sell more of your products. Both of you can work together to make this happen.

To get started, you will find influencers who are interested in promoting your products. There are different places you can list yourself under and then interested influencers can choose whether or not to promote your link. When you post in these sites, it is important to be as detailed as you can. Most affiliates are going to be a bit picky about the products that they are willing to sell. This is because they actually want to provide a product that their customers are going to want to use and want to buy. They don't make any money if they don't get their readers or followers to make a purchase. So the affiliate wants to make sure they are picking out the right product in the process.

During this step, take some time to really explain more about your product and what your company is about. The more details you can go into here, the easier it will be for the affiliate to decide if it is right for them and the more information they have at their disposal when they are telling their readers or followers about you. Try to think of any questions that the affiliate may have about the product or services, and include that in your description as well.

Next, you have to come up with an incentive that is worth it for your affiliate. Offering $0.05 per purchase is probably not going to get you any affiliates at all. Remember that these potential marketers have spent a lot of time on their blogs or on their pages, perhaps years or more. They want to actually make some good money in the process and they still have to go through and write posts that will showcase your product to their customers. If you place the amount too low, you aren't going to get anyone in the door to look at your products.

If you are unsure about how much you should offer as an incentive, you can do some research. Consider looking around at the competition and see how much they are offering for their affiliate links. You want to at least be competitive in this regard in order to get good affiliates to market your products. Remember, this is beneficial to you as well because you only have to pay out if you get sales from that affiliate. You don't want to short them during this time, or you won't make any sales.

Also, when trying to figure out how much you should offer, count this into your price margin. You are going to have to take that money out of the profits that you earn. So add that into the cost for the product and the shipping for the product, and then see what your price margin is in the end. If it is still in a comfortable range after doing this, then go ahead and use the affiliate marketing program to help you earn more.

Once you have determined what product to sell, gotten a good description up about it and your company, and decided how much you would like to offer as an incentive, you have to work on the links. Many affiliate marketing sites will help you with this. But the point is that each affiliate needs to be given their own unique link back to your product.

This is a very important step. You want to make sure that you can keep track of the individual sales that they bring in. Without these individual links, you have no idea who is bringing in which customers and how much to pay each person. And for a good affiliate marketing program, you want to have at least a few marketers talking up your product. Giving each marketer their own unique link back to the product ensures that you know where the customers are coming from and that you pay each individual the amount they deserve

When an affiliate signs up and agrees to market your product, you can simply give them the unique link and they will do the rest. They may talk about the product on their blog or on their social media page, and then they will provide a link to their readers or their followers. If one of the readers or followers is interested in the product, they can click on the link and choose to purchase. At the end of an agreed upon time, such as a week, a few weeks, or a month, you will pay the affiliate marketer based on how many of their readers or followers actually made a purchase on your site. If no one purchased through the link, then you will not have to pay anything.

Affiliate marketing can be a great way to promote your business. It is beneficial for both you and for the other person. The affiliate gets the benefit of earning an income on all the hard work they have put in on their site, and you get the benefit of only paying when the advertising leads to a sale while also reaching a much bigger group of people than you can do on your own. Set up a good affiliate program with your customers and you will see your business grow in no time at all.

Chapter 14: How Amazon FBA Can Help You Grow Your Business

Another way that you can grow your business is to use Amazon FBA. This is basically Fulfillment by Amazon, where the client companies are going to store their products through the fulfillment centers of Amazon. Amazon will then pick, pack, ship, and provide the customer service for these kinds of products. The success stories of doing this are circulating like crazy, and it is one of the reasons why this method is growing so much in popularity. However, there still aren't a lot of facts about how you can get started with this kind of business, or even how to grow and scale this kind of business.

The good news is that it isn't really that hard to get this kind of business running well. The real challenge with this method is to rise above the competition and learn how to expand out this kind of business. But if you do it the right way, you may be able to really grow out your dropshipping business while also making sure that Amazon is the one taking care of everything that your supplier usually handles.

Amazon is a name that most people know and trust. Working directly with them can be great news for your business. It can help you make your customers happy because they know the product is coming from Amazon's warehouse. And you get the peace of mind knowing that Amazon is taking care of all the work, even the customer service. As a beginner or even someone who has been in the market a little bit longer, you will find that dropshipping with Amazon FBA is the best option for you.

Amazon FBA

FBA is a fantastic way for you to make some more money on the affiliate sales that you may already be doing on Amazon, assuming that you are already selling a decent amount of the same products each month. FBA is when you will ship the products to an Amazon warehouse. You can then list the products on Amazon itself, and as the products are sold, Amazon will handle packaging and the shipping to the customers. If there are any returns, Amazon can handle these as well.

Once you have been able to ship the products over to Amazon, and you have taken the time to list them on the Amazon site, there isn't much to do. You have to make sure that traffic is being driven to your site, but Amazon will take care of the fulfillment for you.

This method works best if you have been dropshipping for some time. Many people who work with Amazon expect two-day shipping or at least shipping that is fast. You do not want to wait for an order, place it, have it shipped to Amazon, and then have Amazon ship it for you. Your customer will not be happy with that long of a wait time.

But, if you have been building up your business for some time and you know the approximate number of sales that you can make from one month to another, then this method can work. You can order many products at the beginning of the month, ship it over to an Amazon warehouse, and then Amazon will take care of the rest. And since Amazon covers the shipping in most instances, you will only have to deal with that cost once.

There are a lot of benefits that come with using FBA. In addition to enjoying the name familiarity that comes with using Amazon, some of the other benefits that come with this method include:

- FBA is reliable and fast: Amazon is able to process as well as ship order at really fast speeds.
- You do not have to take on any of the responsibility of warehousing, shipping, or even dealing with your customers.
- Amazon is good at converting, or turning traffic over to sales because it has a platform that others already trust and know.

While there are a lot of good things to enjoy when you work with Amazon FBA, there are also a few negatives that you should be aware of. Some of the negatives of working with this program along with your dropshipping business will include the following:

- If you use FBA, you will have to pay for the storage of your products. If you don't end up selling the products, this can end up being expensive.
- If you don't sell the items within a six month period, then Amazon will start to charge you more per month to store the items. This is why it is a good idea to wait until you know how much you are going to be able to sell before you get started.
- The backend of using Amazon is going to provide you with limited amounts of data on where the sales and the traffic are coming from. You will run into a lot of competition who are also using this program as well.

The biggest advantage of working with FBA for your dropshipping business is that Amazon is a large platform, one that a lot of people trust. And using Amazon can make the logistics and packaging of the products a bit easier. Amazon will handle all of the logistics, instead of you, and they are able to handle the products in a quick and efficient manner for your customers. This makes it worth it for a lot of beginners in this business.

The biggest disadvantage of using FBA with this kind of business is that you are going to have to pay to use it. Amazon is going to take a bit of the sales that you earn and they are going to charge for warehousing the products, for packaging, and for the delivery of the product. This can quickly add up and will make it hard to earn a good amount of profit in the process.

If you are able to find a product, or products, that have a good profit margin for you to work with, and you would like to make Amazon do the work after the business has grown quite a bit and you want to take a break from the work, then working with FBA is a great option. There are a few things that you should consider and remember when you are ready to get started with adding FBA to your dropshipping business including:

- If you want to compete on Amazon, you have to remember the pricing. Unless the product is truly special, which isn't likely, the price is one of the only things that will help you set apart from the other retailers out there selling the same product.
- Avoid a price war: It is hard to compete on the search results through Amazon. It is best to find ways to drive traffic over to your own personal landing pages with Facebook Ads and SEO.
- Targeted traffic is going to convert the best: If you are able to drive traffic to the product listing, it is going to work well for you. This is true even if you don't have the best

product or the cheapest product. Buyers who are searching for that product keyword are going to be ready to buy at that time. if you can capture them and make sure they get to the landing page for your products, you have a better chance of seeing conversions.

- If your margins are low, you have to sell a lot: It is best to find products that can make more money with each sale. This may seem harder to do, but the amount of time and effort that you put into the smaller and less expensive items are just not going to be worth your time. if you can, find items that will make it easy to earn $100 or more on each sale.
- Remember that some products are only seasonal. If you had a good month in July, remember that this doesn't automatically mean you are going to be successful in August. You have to learn what the different seasonal items are and then plan accordingly so you know when it will be a good month and when it will be a bad month.
- Don't run out of inventory. When you run out of inventory, it can take some time to restock depending on the supplier you used and other options. Each day you are not providing the item to customers, you are missing out on making money. But then you need to find a good balance with this because you don't want to keep around too much of the product or it will cut into your margins thanks to the cost of warehousing all the products.
- FBA can be hard. You have to put in the work to make this one happen. And for some people, even the benefits are not enough to convince them to go with it. If you do decide to go with Amazon FBA, realize that you have to go through and drive traffic to your particular page. There are a lot of other dropshippers and suppliers who are using this tool as well, and it is up to you to make sure that customers will find and use you, rather than relying on the competition.

Amazon FBA can be a great resource that will help you to grow your business. It can also take out some of the work that you end up doing when dealing with the customers and providing good service. But it is definitely something that needs to wait until you can build up the business and get enough orders to make it worth it since Amazon will charge a bit for using their services. You have to take a look at Amazon FBA and decide if it is the right choice for the business that you are running or if you need to try something else.

Chapter 15: Tips to Make Your Dropshipping Business As Successful As Possible

Now that we have taken some time to look into dropshipping and how to start your own business, it is time to take a look at a few tips that you can follow in order to get the most out of this business model. Dropshipping is a simple idea, but it does take some work to get things up and running. Some of the tips that you can follow in order to make your business as successful as possible include the following:

Focus on the Marketing

When you get started with your own dropshipping company, you have to take some time to focus on marketing. Even if you plan to list on Amazon or eBay, you still have to spend some time marketing your products in order to stand out from the crowd. There are many other sellers and dropshippers out there who are trying to compete for the same market as you. if you don't take the time to market your products and your page, you will end up getting lost in the crowd and won't make any sales.

We talked about a lot of different ways that you can market your products, and as a business owner, it is important that you learn about how each one can help you grow and scale your own business now. You may find that SEO is the best choice for you, especially if you do your own personal website to sell the products. You may find that spending some time on social media is a better option. Many new companies like to work with email marketing to see their results show with previous customers.

All of the methods can work well. But if you are able to think of a new method, one that has you go outside the box, rather than just using traditional methods, then consider that one. Dropshipping is an industry that has a lot of competition with it. Finding ways to stand out from the crowd can make a big difference in how successful you will be.

Do Not Underprice the Products

We have talked about this one a little bit, but you have to be careful about the pricing that you have with your products. There are some dropshippers who will try to beat out the competition by lowering the prices of their products by quite a bit. They think this is a surefire way to convince customers to work with them. While this may seem like a good idea, and some customers do like to look for a good deal, it can backfire on you on occasion.

Many customers know the price of other products, or they know how to search online and compare. If they see that the price you are listing at is too low, then they will be wary and assume that they are going to get a substandard product that they won't want, and you won't be able to make many sales in the process.

At the same time, you won't be able to earn as much income in the process either. The lower you make the price, the less profit you are able to make on that item. If you price it too low, the shipping costs and other costs will take up any profit that you make, and it is possible that you would owe money instead of making any money if you aren't careful.

Pick a Product That Makes a Good Profit Margin

There are a lot of dropshipping products that you can choose from when starting out your new business. But you need to make sure that you go with products that are going to earn you a good deal of profit in the process. If you are only going to earn $1 on each product, then it is probably not a good option to go with. You would have to sell thousands of those each month in order to make any profit at all on them.

The higher the profit margin on the item, the better it is going to be for your business. You can sell a good deal of the items, and make a ton more money in the process. Finding products that make at least 45 percent margin after you pay for shipping and taxes, can be great as well. And if you can find products where you can make a profit of $100 or more, that is even better.

How do you make sure that you are finding products that will make you a good amount of profit? First, go through your supplier's pages and decide which products you are the most interested in. Then you can take a look at how much each of those products costs for you to purchase them from the supplier. With that number in mind, go online and see how much other suppliers are charging for that same item.

The last step is important because you want to make sure that your products are priced in a competitive manner. You want to get the most out of the pricing, but you also need to be careful not to price too high compared to the competitors. If you look at the price that the supplier is charging and compare it to the price others are charging for that item, and you see the profit margin is too low, then it is time to move on to a different product. Take your time here and search around until you are able to find the right products that will make you enough money to make the process worth your time.

Find Ways to Bundle Items Together

As a dropshipper, it is your job to find ways that make your business stand out from the others. One way that you can do this is to bundle together some of the items that you are selling. This can be beneficial both for your customer and for you.

Many customers want their shopping experience to be as pleasant and quick as possible. They don't want to spend hours looking for items online that go together or will work together. If you are able to provide them with a bundle of the items they need in one spot, and if you can even provide it with a little bit of a discount, they are more likely to make that purchase.

This method is going to benefit you as well. When you get the customer to purchase the bundle, that means a bigger sale for you. If you are able to find a way to turn it into a subscription service, where the customer will purchase the same bundle or product each month so you can keep earning the same income from it over and over again.

Pick the Right Platform That You Like the Best

We spent some time talking about a lot of different platforms that you can use to start this kind of business. Each one has benefits and negatives that you are going to be faced with, and it is up to you to choose which one seems the best for your needs. Some of the bigger sites, like Amazon, Shopify, and eBay can be nice because they already have a lot of name recognition that goes with them, and you will already find a lot of customers to work with there.

But there are also some benefits that come with working on your own personal website to sell products. You get more choices with the templates that you want to use, you get the benefit of more options with how the website works. And, on the long run, these personal websites often end up being cheaper to use and maintain compared to the other options.

Always Provide the Best Customer Service

Customer service is always important, and it is definitely something that you need to pay attention to when it comes to selling your own dropshipping products. There is going to be a ton of competition out there, and one of the ways that you can make yourself stand out from the crowd is to provide the customers with the best service possible.

There are many different methods that you can choose that will help you to do that. You can make it easy for the customer to email or contact you and ask any questions that they may have. You can bundle your products and services together to make things easier and even cheaper for your customers. In some cases, sending along a little gift, a personalized note, or even some other special offer can help to provide great customer service that they are going to appreciate and will keep them coming back later on.

Order the Product Yourself Before Selling it

This can be a great method to get the same experience that your customer will when they order from you. It is also a good way to ensure that you are picking out the right supplier for your needs. If you have to go through the whole process just like your customers do, then you will see where the issues can be, and you can decide if that supplier is the right one for you or if you need to pick out someone else.

To do this process, simply go to the supplier page and order one or more of their products, the ones that you should like to sell to the customer. Fill in all the information and choose the shipping options that you will provide to your customers. Then sit back and wait.

When the product comes, note how long it took and whether or not that time frame is within the amount the company had promised. Take a look at the packaging and how professional it looks. Open the box and look at the product, determining if it is the right product, if it is made out of high-quality materials, and more. Basically, you want to consider whether or not you would be happy with this product and its speed of delivery if you had actually purchased and wanted this item for yourself.

If you are considering working with a few different suppliers, then it is best to do these steps with each one. If you want to see which company is better than the other when it comes to similar products, order at the same time from them and see what happens. You can compare shipping prices, shipping time, the price of the item, and the quality of the item when it gets to you.

If you find that there are any issues with the company you want to work with, then it may be best to pick out a different supplier. Don't assume that it is just a one-time thing that happened. You are the face of the business, and if a supplier isn't able to provide a good service and impress your customers, then you are going to be the one who is blamed. If there are any problems, consider working with someone else to ensure you give the best customer experience to anyone who purchases from you.

Starting your dropshipping business can be an exciting time. You have to figure out which products you would like to sell, which supplier is the best one to work with, and make sure that you are pricing and marketing the items so your customers are able to find them. When you are ready to get started with this new business model, make sure to check out these tips to make it a little bit easier to work with.

Conclusion

Thanks for making it through to the end of *Dropshipping E-commerce Business Model 2019*. Let's hope it was informative and able to provide you with all of the tools you need to achieve your goals whatever they may be.

The next step is to use the steps that we talked about in this guidebook in order to help you get started with your own dropshipping business today. There are a lot of different ways to make money in our modern world. Some require a lot of time and effort though, and most of them are not going to provide you with a reasonable amount of money for the time and effort that you put into it in the first place.

But when you get started with dropshipping, you will find that things can be different. You will truly run your own business without having to put a pile of money down and without having to hold inventory. A dropshipping business can easily have hundreds of products and you never have to touch a single one in the process. And with this business model, you can choose how big or small your business is at any given time.

This guidebook takes some time to look at the process of dropshipping and what it entails. We look at the basics of dropshipping as well as some of its advantages and disadvantages to getting started with it. We then moved on to some of the basics of getting your own business up and running, how to pick out a good supplier and good products, and how to provide good customer service each and every time.

From there, we moved on to some of the different platforms that you can use to help make that business grow. We looked at Shopify, Amazon, eBay, and even using your own personal website, and the reasons that you would choose to work with each one.

To finish off, we spent some time talking about how you can use social media to enhance your business and spread the word, how affiliate marketing can help you to see more with your business, and how to use Amazon FBA to bring it all together. There are so many ways that you can promote and work on your own business, and this guidebook will take a look at how you can use all of them together to get the most out of your business.

There may be a lot of different online businesses out there, but most of them are going to cost a lot of time and money and inventory just to get your foot in the door. Dropshipping is different. It is available for anyone who is looking to get started with their own business but who wants to be able to limit the amount of risk that they are dealing with for their own online business. When you are ready to get started in dropshipping, make sure to check out this guidebook to help you out!

Affiliate Marketing 2020

$10,000/Month Ultimate Guide—Make a Passive Income Fortune Marketing on Facebook, Instagram, YouTube, Google, and Google Ads Products of Others without any Customer's Complaints

By

Steven Sparrow

Introduction

Congratulations on downloading *Affiliate Marketing 2019* and thank you for doing so.

The following chapters will discuss all the steps that you need to know to get started with affiliate marketing. Affiliate marketing is one of the best methods that you can use to help you earn a good income from home. While it does take some time to learn how to make this kind of income work for you, it is a legitimate and lucrative way to make the income that you want.

This guidebook is going to take some time to look at affiliate marketing and what you need to do in order to get started. We will take a look at what affiliate marketing is all about, how to get started, how to find a good company and a good product to sell, and even how to set up your website so you can start to use that to bring in customers and making your profits.

We will then dive into some of the different vehicles that you can use in order to set up your affiliate marketing business. We will start with a look at using affiliate marketing in your website or blog, and then take a look at how you can work with affiliate marketing on Facebook, Instagram, YouTube, and even Google. Then we will explore some of the other unique things that you can do to really make your affiliate marketing endeavor successful.

We will end the guidebook with some more of the tips that you need to see success with affiliate marketing. We will look at how you can avoid some of the most common mistakes that beginners can make with affiliate marketing, how to turn this into a passive income, and so much more.

Affiliate marketing is a very effective tool to help you earn a good income in your free time, but you have to put in some work to see the results. When you are ready to get started, make sure to check out this guidebook to help you get started with affiliate marketing today!

There are plenty of books on this subject on the market, thanks again for choosing this one! Every effort was made to ensure it is full of as much useful information as possible, please enjoy

Chapter 1: What Is Affiliate Marketing?

Many people are interested in learning how to make money online or in their free time. They may already have a job or two, and sometimes even more, and they still find that they aren't able to pay the bills, or they aren't able to do the things that they want or have the freedom that they want. And with the way that our current economy is going, you will be able to find many different ways that you can make money online.

One of the best options that you can use to make money online in your free time, and a pretty lucrative income if you get it set up right, is affiliate marketing. With affiliate marketing, you are able to sell products from other companies and then earn a commission off each sale. You have to do some of the advertising for the company, but you are not in charge of the product, the customer service, the shipping, or anything else like that when it comes to the product.

Many companies like to do this method because it allows them to get more exposure to their products from some unique sources, without them having to spend millions in the hopes of selling even one product. With traditional forms of advertising, the company would have to spend a lot of time picking out places to advertise their products, doing customer surveys, and spending a lot of money to make sure they were getting sales. And there are no guarantees with this on whether they will get any sales and how many sales they will get.

For some big companies, it is possible to do this kind of advertising and then make some good money in the process. But for smaller companies or for those that are more local, it just doesn't make monetary sense to do this. They turn to affiliate marketing because they won't have to pay for any of the advertising until the product is sold. If one of their affiliates sells a product, the company will pay them a percentage of the sales. But if the affiliate never makes a sale, then the company never has to pay anything.

This works out well for the individual too. If they have built up a good blog or a good following on a social media site, they can use this to make money even when they are asleep. They can talk about and promote the product with a unique code that goes to the product. When someone clicks on the link and then makes the purchase from there, the amount is credited to the affiliate, and they get to earn some commissions in the process.

But the question here is whether you can actually make some money with affiliate marketing. The answer is it depends. If you have the right following present and you are willing to put in some work to promote the product, this can turn into a very lucrative way to make money. But if you just plan to randomly post links with no blog and only five people on your Facebook account, then you probably won't be able to make any money in the process.

The problem that can come with affiliate marketing is that, like with some of the other home business opportunities that you may hear about, there are tons of get-rich-quick programs and gurus who suggest that you can just start with affiliate marketing today and you will see results by tomorrow.

They will show that all these impressive numbers of people were able to make each month, and they show images of being able to just check in for a couple of minutes a day and that is it.

While affiliate marketing can be a great way to make some money online, and many people do see a lot of success when they choose to go with this method, there is an element of work that needs to be done. You will actually have to be an active promoter, you will need to go through and build up a following of people who trust you, and you need to showcase products that your followers are actually going to be interested in.

Does this all sound like work? Well, it is. You can make good money with this, but it isn't as simple as pushing a button and seeing the results. These get-rich-quick schemes may sound tempting. While it may seem like it is too good to be true, you can make money, but the get-rich-quick schemes are going to just take your money without showing you how to do a single thing. This guidebook will show you the actual steps that you have to take in order to get started with affiliate marketing and see some profits come in.

Just like with some of the other work at home adventures that you may try, there are going to be those who can make it rich, and those who won't make anything, and then everything in between. In most likelihood, you will be one of the ones who fall somewhere in between. Having realistic expectations about what is going to happen with affiliate marketing and how far your efforts will go can help you to know whether it is the right endeavor for you or not.

The biggest question here isn't whether you are able to make any income with affiliate marketing. It is more about whether you personally can make the processes and the steps that go with affiliate marketing work for you and your goals.

The Benefits of Affiliate Marketing

Now that we have taken some time to explore affiliate marketing and what it is about, it is time to look at some of the positives that come with this form of marketing. Affiliate marketing can be a great way to capitalize on some of the work that you have already done. If you have spent some time building up your blog with lots of followers, or you have a lot of people who listen to you on social media, then this is a great way to capitalize on the work with affiliate marketing and recommending products to your readers and followers. Some of the great benefits that you can get from affiliate marketing include:

1. It doesn't cost a lot to get started, in fact, most of the programs that do this are going to be free to join. So, if you incur any costs, this will usually come from the marketing and referral methods you choose to use, and you can have some control over these.
2. You don't have to be the one who personally creates the product or the service. You just need to market it.
3. You won't need to keep stock of the inventory or ship any products.
4. You can choose to work at any time of the day that you want, and you can choose where your office is, as long as it has internet access.
5. Passive income potential once you build up your business enough. This is going to depend on how you are able to market your affiliate programs.
6. You can add it to a home business that you already have in order to create an additional stream of income. This can be ideal for coaches, bloggers, information entrepreneurs and anyone who has a website.

The Negatives of Affiliate Marketing

While there are some great benefits that can happen with affiliate marketing, and it works well for many people, there are some times when affiliate marketing may not be the best option for you. It can be hard to work in affiliate marketing, and sometimes, you will have to put in more work than you had planned in order to see some results. Some of the negatives that can keep people away from affiliate marketing include:

1. It can take up a lot of time to generate the right amount of traffic that you need to bring in an income.
2. A process called affiliate hijacking can sometimes occur. This is when you aren't given credit for some of your referrals. Working with URL masking can help you with this issue, so you actually get paid for the clicks and referrals that you do.
3. A bad affiliate referral can do a lot of damage to your credibility. This is why you must do your research and pick a quick affiliate, so you won't have to regain your audience and their trust later on. You
4. You won't have any control over the product, the service that the business provides, or how this business treats their products and their services.
5. There are some companies out there who are known for not paying their affiliates. You must make sure that you screen anyone you want to work with to ensure you pick the right company.
6. There is a lot of competition. When you do find a good program that pays you well and has a good product, you will find that there are a lot of other people who want to join it as well.
7. The customer is going to belong to the merchant. Your stat is going to let you know how many sales were made of what product. But for the most part, you will not receive any information on who is purchasing the products. This makes it more difficult for you to go through and do any marketing for resale.

How Can I Become a Successful Affiliate Marketer?

Many people like working with affiliate marketing because they like that they can work from home, and it isn't going to require a lot of money to get started. You also don't have to be responsible for producing a product, keeping it stocked up, or shipping the inventory or deliver the service. You are pretty much going to be paid to refer new clients or customers to another business.

The idea behind the affiliate marketing process isn't really that hard, but like any business adventure, it does take some work and it requires some knowledge, planning, and a bit of consistent effort in order to make a significant amount of income. Here are a few of the steps that you can do in order to make yourself more successful with affiliate marketing:

1. The first step here is to learn about affiliate marketing and the different affiliate tricks to see success
2. Choose only affiliate products and services that are high-quality. You may even want to purchase the produce ahead of time, so you have a better way of checking out their quality before you promote to others. Remember that you will be judged based on the

quality of the products that you are promoting and checking them out ahead of time can ensure you are providing your followers the best possible.

3. Research the different programs to help you better understand how and when you will be paid. Take a look at some of the reviews that come with each company to see how other affiliates liked working with them or if it is the best company to work with.

4. Consider starting a blog. This is often seen as one of the most effective ways to work with affiliate marketing. You can do an informational, how-to, or a lifestyle blog that can gather some followers and then post your affiliate links on the blog.

5. Choose items to promote that match up with the niche you are in, or the content that is on your blog or website. So, if you write about figure skating on your bog, then you will find that marketing a new set of saddlebags won't go well with this kind of market.

6. Consider working with a few different types of products and ads. You will need to post the links more than once to entice customers, but the followers don't want to see the same ad in the same format and the same ad for the same product a million times. Mixing and matching will help you not overwhelm your customers.

7. Make sure that you disclose your affiliate relationship. Most visitors will already have an understanding that any graphic ads that show up on the page will mean you get paid. But if you write out a review and use a link in the text as a recommendation, let the readers know that this can lead to some compensation on your part as well. The FTC endorsement rules require that you do this so make sure it is present.

8. Marketing is your friend here. You do not want to rely on just going with social media or SEO to drive people to the link that you have. You need to learn more about your target market and the work to market your products to them to see the best results.

9. Start your own email list. The affiliate marketers who are able to see the most success with this endeavor are the ones who will use email to their advantage. Don't put this off because you will regret it. Email marketing is a great way to help you reach your followers a bit better, and it can increase the profits you get from affiliate marketing.

10. You may find some success with a funnel system and a lead page. This can work when you lure prospects over to the email list with a free offer, and then from there, you can send them over to your product page with the affiliate link. In the emails, you can even offer more free content and more offers from an affiliate.

11. Always take the time to monitor the success and how your affiliate program is going. If you are going with more than one program at a time, this can make it easier for you to see results and do well with your endeavor. Check on this on a regular basis and see if it is best to work more with one program or even dump one program in favor of another.

Before you decide to jump in with one affiliate program over another, or if you are considering whether you should add affiliate marketing to your current business, such as a blog or other website, you must learn what all is involved with affiliate marketing and what is required in order to turn it into a success.

If you do decide that affiliate marketing is the right choice for you as a sole business plan, or you want to add this affiliate marketing process to your own personal business, make sure that you understand that this process is not fast, automatic, and without effort. Just like with any other home business that you may work with, affiliate marketing is going to need some effort, some planning, and a lot of involvement on a daily basis to help you make money.

Chapter 2: Steps to Getting Started with Affiliate Marketing

Affiliate marketing can provide you with a great opportunity to earn some commissions simply by selling products and services to others. You are the marketing and advertising for the company. You won't have to make the product or even worry about inventory, shipping, or customer service when it comes to working with this form of marketing, which is part of what makes it such a successful thing for many people to do at home and in their free time. Many people decide to work with this method because it can help supplement their own income without too much work on their part, and you can do it at home in between your other job.

However, affiliate marketing is not always as simple as it seems. It can bring in a nice steady income, and there are those individuals who are able to join the market and make a full-time income. But these individuals are sometimes the exception, and they had to put in a lot of time and effort in order to earn this income.

The good news is that anyone is able to get started with affiliate marketing, they just need to be willing and able to put in the hard work, they need to have a good following, or a method to come up with this good following, a good product, and the time to market the products well. Let's take a look at some of the steps that you can take in order to start with affiliate marketing to bring in the income that you have been looking for.

Becoming an Affiliate

The first thing that we need to take a look at are some of the steps you can follow in order to become an affiliate marketer. You must always sell what you know. This means that when you are starting out, make sure that you sell a product or a service that you have some familiarity with. Online marketers are going to call this kind of process as 'picking your niche'. You are going to look unprofessional if you go into the market and try to sell something that you know nothing about. It is much better to pick out products and services that match up with the things that you already know so that you can reach the best audience, you can answer any questions that your audience has, and you actually know what you are talking about.

For example, if you are an interior designer and you have been doing it for some time, it makes sense for you to sell something like curtains or a comforter set. But it wouldn't make sense for you to sell something like car parts, even if these would provide you with a bigger check. Picking out items that have to do with the expertise you have will make it easier to sell and can take less effort.

The next step to concentrate on is starting a website that is dedicated and relevant to the niche you want to sell. This can help you in a few ways. First, it gives you someplace to send your customers when they are interested in the products you will advertise. And most affiliate marketing companies will want to see the URL of the website that you want to use for selling their products. This allows them to take a look and then they can ensure that the content is going to match up with the values and niche of the company.

You will find that it is pretty simple to set up a website. You can use a variety of options including WordPress.com. Be sure that the information that is on your website doesn't seem too salesy. You want to provide some value to the customer and to look like an authority in your niche.

Once all of this is set up, you can take your time to research the right affiliate program that you want to work with. Find an affiliate program that can offer you some products or services, ones that match up with your niche and interests. Amazon is a good place to start. Since this company sells almost everything and offers pretty good commissions, it is at least something to consider.

Another option to work with is Commission Junction which is another place to look because just by joining their site, you will be able to choose from many of the popular companies you know. You can search around and find the one that looks best or sells the products you are interested in. Or Clickbank is a choice of many affiliate marketers. This is because the commissions that are available for many marketers on this site are pretty high, helping you to earn more.

After you have had some time to do your research, it is time to join the affiliate program. Remember that most of these are going to be free to join, so be wary if one tries to charge you, especially if the amount is high. If you are being asked for your credit card simply to join the system, then it is likely that they are scammers and you should find another option to go with. However, keep in mind that the affiliate program is going to ask you for some information like a PayPal account or your bank account. This isn't so you can pay them. It's so that the company can come and pay you once you actually get some referrals and sales. You will also be asked for the URL of your website so that the company can check that your website is professional and that you won't harm their reputation in the process.

Marketing the Products

Once you have had some time to go through and look at the different affiliate programs that you can work with, and you have chosen at least a few different options for products to promote, it is time to actually start marketing these products. It isn't enough to just have a link and then just post it without doing anything else. There are millions of websites out there and thousands of other affiliate marketers that you have to worry about. If you don't put in the work, you won't be able to make a good profit from that link.

First, you should take the affiliate link that you are provided and then add it into your content. If you already have a blog or other content that you could just add the link to, this can really make a difference in the amount of success you will see, without as much work. You can add it to the content that you already have on your website, or you can choose to make a new piece that is dedicated to that link and that recommendation. This way, when someone comes to the page and clicks on the link, they will be taken straight to the company site. If the customer does end up purchasing the product, then you will earn commissions.

The good news here is that most affiliate marketing companies are going to make it as easy as possible to get a link to their site. They want you to be able to use these links because it means that they are making money as well. But the method in which you will get these links from the company will vary based on which company you are working with. Most companies will list the steps or will otherwise make it easy to get ahold of the link that you need.

Next, we need to include some kind of visual with any sidebars that we want to create. Your website, similar to what other websites will do, will have some kind of sidebar. This is a great place to add in some visuals for the product that you are trying to sell. Many times, the company you are working with will provide some high-quality images so you can find the right one for your sidebar.

During this time, you must make sure that you continue to produce content that is relevant to your niche. You don't want to just post about the affiliate links all the time. People are going to keep coming back to your website because they find useful information that they are able to use in their own lives as well. If you stop creating this content, they will stop coming back, and future affiliate links are going to end up on deaf ears. If you have to, make sure that you set up a schedule that makes it easy for you to post as often as needed, and always keep the information fresh and easy to read through for the returning followers.

Monitoring your success is so important when it comes to working with affiliate marketing. You will find that analytics can be so useful for this because it will show you how many people came to a site and clicked on your link, how long they stayed there, and even whether they purchased the item or not. There can also be a lot of other information for you to sift through as well, depending on the software and the analytics tool you decide to go with.

The good thing here is that a lot of affiliate marketing sites are going to offer you some great analytics. Remember, they are going to do well only if you do well too. They can provide you with a wide variety of analytics that may be helpful so that you can get an idea of what is working the best on your site.

1. If you find that there is one niche or one type of product that seems to sell well on your site, then you will want to start producing more content that will provide you a chance to market that product or niche more in the future.

2. Don't ever underestimate the power of Google Analytics. These can provide you with a good understanding of the demographics of your visitors. You can choose to tailor your marketing efforts to people who fit into this demographic, making your efforts more efficient.

3. Pay attention to the posts that you have and the ones that tend to get the most visitors. If you find that there are certain types of posts that seem to get more visitors than other, then you may want to stick more with the topics that go with these and consider adding some more affiliate links to them to make more money.

4. Focus on the things that work and get rid of anything that doesn't seem to work for you. The analytics that are provided to you, either your own or the ones provided by the company you work with, will tell you what is working and what you should change. As time goes on, you will be able to fine tune what you are doing, and this can lead to some great results overall.

How to Manage Your Business

Once you have the affiliate marketing all up and running, it is time to learn some of the steps that are needed to help you manage your business. First, we need to take a look at preparing for taxes. If you actually make some money on this, then you will need to pay some taxes on that income. At the beginning of the year, your partner companies are going to send you a tax form 1099. If they don't, this doesn't mean that you are off the hook; you will just have to do the taxes without this information.

If you are running this business as an LLC or a sole proprietor, you will need to report the income that is on the 1099 tax form on the Schedule C—Profit or Loss from Business. But if you choose to run the business as either an S or a C corporation, you will report this income on a Schedule K-1.

Another thing that you can consider doing is expanding your business. You want to strive to get more growth and to make more money in the process. There are a few ways that you are able to do this. First, look for some new products that are available that you think would be easy to manage and market online. Browse through a variety of affiliate companies and look for newer businesses that are getting on this program; they are likely to have some great products and have lower amounts of competition.

You also want to make sure that you are constantly promoting your business online. You can work with social media, email, and any other channel that you wish to help promote the business and to ensure that people will keep coming back and searching for the great deals that you offer.

And finally, after you have spent some time on your business and you have worked to grow it as much as possible, it is time to figure out how to automate as many pieces of the company as you can. There are several different digital marketing tools that you can choose from. Some are going to require you to pay for the use of them, but it does benefit you by providing you with some free time that doesn't have to be at the computer.

As we will discuss in this guidebook, there are a few different methods you can use for affiliate marketing. While setting up a website is one of the most popular options, there are also others that you can choose to work with as well. Some people like to do affiliate marketing on their Facebook page. Others may like to use their Instagram, their YouTube, or another popular page. We will show you some of the different things that you can do with these later on but be aware that there are many options you can choose from when it comes to affiliate marketing.

Chapter 3: Picking Out a Strategy to Use with Affiliate Marketing

Since it was first developed, affiliate marketing has seen a lot of changes. There are actually quite a few regulations that are in place. For example, SEO rankings can be hard on anything that provides low-quality content in order to get clicks. There is a lot of competition as others try to earn a lot of money in the process, and it is tough to get started and to try to stay ahead in affiliate marketing. Despite the fact that there are some challenges that come with affiliate marketing, having a good strategy in place and working hard can help you to earn a good income. There are actually people who will make millions through affiliate marketing.

As a beginner, you may be interested in finding out the best strategies that you can use in order to do well with affiliate marketing. This guidebook is going to take some time to discuss the best strategies that you can use to see results.

Stick with a Niche

Some beginners get excited and try to work with many niches all at once, rather than trying to find one or two that they can really work hard on. You should stick with just two or maybe three niches that are profitable and then work to increase your traffic there, which you can concentrate all of your attention on. Working with a few niches will help you to write high-quality content on a regular basis that will keep the followers coming back.

Sometimes, it is easy to think that having more niches to handle will bring in more customers since this will help you potentially reach a higher target audience. However, if you stretch yourself too thin, you will end up providing low-quality content on all the sites that no one wants to read. When this happens, your potential followers will be nonexistent, and you won't make any money. On the other hand, if you focus on creating some really amazing sites with just a few niches, you will bring in large numbers of followers and can potentially earn a lot of money.

Create Good Content

We talked about this one a bit before, but if you want to bring in the followers, you need to create content that they want to read. There needs to be something that will draw the followers back over and over again. It can be something humorous, something valuable, or some good advice that the people in your niche are interested in learning about.

In addition to writing high-quality content, you also need to make sure that you post new content on a regular basis. Your followers will get bored with your page, and your rankings will go down, if you only post information on a sporadic basis or you go a long time in between posting, your followers will quit coming back and you can lose out on potential earnings. Set up some kind of schedule for when you plan to post, such as an article a day or posting a few each week. If you get busy, you can write out your articles ahead of time and then schedule them to post at the times that you want.

Pick a Program with Recurring Revenues

Strategies that you do for affiliate marketing are going to be fluid and something that you do today may not work tomorrow based on a wide variety of factors. There may be cost cutting to the advertising of a company, a program that shuts down or some changes to how your website changes in search engines. It is a smart idea to ensure that the revenue you get is reoccurring, even if this means that you get paid in smaller amounts, but more often. While a one-time payment is great to increase your revenue, they are not going to offer you any protection against major changes that may impact your earnings in the future.

We will talk about this a bit more as we go through this guidebook, but if you can find affiliate programs that allow you to work with earning a revenue more than one time, you are going to see your profits really grow. These can be programs that allow you to make money every time that the person comes back and makes a purchase, you can earn the income from that. Or you can work with a subscription service so any time someone makes a purchase on one of your links and gets the subscription sent to them each month, you can earn some of the income as well.

These are much better sources for making money through affiliate marketing compared to working with some of the other options out there. You will put in a lot less work and earn more money compared to just working with a regular affiliate link where you only get paid one time for one sale.

Ensure the Traffic Comes from More Than One Source

If you choose to only go with one source for all of your traffic, you could be in trouble. What happens if a big change occurs or this source dries up? Your affiliate program will basically need to start again from nothing. To make sure that your affiliate program keeps doing well, make sure that your content is viewable from many platforms so that your traffic is diverse, and you won't be harmed as much if one single source happens to go down.

Affiliate programs that are the most successful are going to have customers coming in from a wide variety of sources. This means that the customers need to come from several different locations if you would like to see some results. We will show you a few of the different ways that you can implement more of these lines into your business, including Facebook, Instagram, Google, and even YouTube.

When you put all of these together, you will be able to bring in more customers. For every link that you want to work with, you will find that there are a ton of customers out there, but not all of them are found in the same place. Learning how to find them in multiple places can really make it easier to earn a bigger income.

Think About the Mobile Devices

We will talk about this a bit in a later chapter, but your website and your content need to be usable on mobile platforms. There are so many people who get their information from their phones and if you aren't meeting them there, you will miss out on a lot of revenue. Make sure that your website will work on most mobile phones so that you can reach your target audience.

You will find that many of the customers you are going to run into will also look at your pages through their mobile devices. This means that you need to take some time to make sure that any content you work with is going to work well on a phone as well. You don't want to put in all that effort on an amazing website and then find out that half or more of your viewers aren't even able to read through it at all.

The good news is that many of the websites that you use to help out with making your own website, such as WordPress, will have options that make it easier for you to optimize for mobile devices. This can make it easier for you to do the work, without having to come in with a lot of technical knowledge in the first place.

Prepare for the Seasonal Trends

There are a lot of new and even emerging trends that are always coming out, and a smart affiliate is going to ride on these trends and make as much money as possible before the trends are all done. It is important that you prepare for these breakout trends and then take advantage of them before your customers start to lose interest. Google Trends is a good place to check for this one because it always updates some of the trends that are about to break out.

Working with seasonal trends can be a little bit easier to handle because they are going to recur on a regular basis. For example, it is pretty easy to guess when the Christmas season is going to start and when it will end so you can work your content and your links to match up with this.

Make Sure You Use SEO

Google and other search engines are becoming more sophisticated with their SEO technology, and it is so important for an affiliate marketer to be able to sync their content with the changing requirements of these search engines. When you do well with SEO, it makes it so much easier to reach the right customers first because you will be ranked high on search engine results. But the rules are always changing. What used to be a concentration on just a keyword is now more of a concentration on what information is in the article that you write. This could easily change again in the future.

To rank better with SEO, you need to make sure that you pick out the top words that are on your website or your blog and decide if they are the ones that are most likely to be typed into a search engine by people who want to know the information you are sharing. If you do this well and provide high-quality content, you will find that your site is going to appear as the top link when customers are looking for you. This can take some research and some practice but learning how to do SEO is one of the best ways for people to find you.

Promote Things You Know

The affiliate marketers who do the best job are the ones who promote products that they have some familiarity with. If you work with products that you know and understand well, you will feel more confident in talking about them. And that confidence is going to show in the writing that you do, making people be drawn to your links and more likely to make a purchase. You will also know more about the product and what things your readers will be interested in when hearing about the product.

Some beginners will try to go with some products that they have never heard about because they may provide more money for each sale. But your readers are going to miss out on that confidence and that good selling that you could provide because you will stumble and miss out. Always stick with products that you know and are comfortable with and you will see better results.

If you get the chance, try promoting things that you already know about, and things that you can actually try out first. If there is a specific product or a digital item that you would like to promote, consider ordering it for yourself first. This will help you know whether you are providing and promoting a good product to your customers or not.

When you actually try the product or the service out, you get a better idea of the experience that your customer is going to experience as well. If something goes wrong, you can investigate it a bit and see if there are any ways that you can improve it or make it better. And if the product and service go well with very little to nothing to complain about, then you can rest assured that you are providing some excellent promotions to your customers, and this can make things much easier to work with.

Start a Product Review Site

One form of affiliate marketing that you can work with is known as a product review site. With this, in addition to your own blog, you would create a product review site and then you will always keep it updated with recommendations and reviews that you use on a regular basis. You can also leave up links to a website on the side or include it inside of the content that you are writing so that customers will go check them out and make a purchase. As long as your reviews are honest and pretty straightforward, you will see an increase in how much income you earn with affiliate marketing with this method.

There are a few ways that you can go through and work on this one. For example, you can just spend time reviewing the items that you wish to link with individually, you can do comparisons of a few similar products that you want to sell, you can compare to others and show how your product is superior to the others, and even write about specific hobbies and activities and then talk about how the product you are selling is able to help with this particular problem.

The goal here is to be as creative as possible. There are a lot of other people out there competing for the same market as you, and many people would love to make it rich with affiliate marketing. With all of this competition, it is important for you to find ways to stand out from the crowd and really make a statement. Finding ways that allow you to think outside the box can make a big difference and ensures that you will get the customers you are looking for.

There are a lot of different things that you are able to do in order to see your affiliate marketing income grow. The most important thing to concentrate on though is to create a really good website and work on providing great content for your readers. Some of the other things can then work with the good content and you will get the sales that you want.

Chapter 4: How to Pick Out a Profitable Niche in Affiliate Marketing

Now that we know a little bit more about affiliate marketing and how to get started with it, we need to take a look at some of the steps that you need to choose in order to pick out the right company, the right niche, and the right products for your needs. Everyone is going to pick out a different course of action when it comes to affiliate marketing. They will choose based on many different factors. But this chapter is going to take some time to look at the different factors that you should consider when it comes to picking out an affiliate marketing company to work with and the right product for your needs.

How to Pick Out Profitable Niche

The first thing we need to concentrate on here is finding a niche that is profitable. Affiliate marketing can be a great business model to make some money online. However, there are a lot of niches out there that just aren't profitable at all. If you are new to online marketing, then you may be confused as to which niche is going to be the most profitable when they get started. The key to picking out a profitable niche is to think about the needs of other people and then think of the products and services that could help them to meet or fix this need. Picking a niche can be similar to finding a target. You need to make sure that you pick a niche that is a good fit from the start. Otherwise, you will put in a lot of work and marketing, and nothing will result from it.

To start out with picking a good and profitable niche, you will need to take some time to ask yourself a few important questions along the way. Sit down with some pen and paper and take some time to answer these questions to help you get started. Some of the best questions that you can ask include:

1. What are you good at and what are some of your passions? Is it always wise to start with what you know and what you like?

2. Is there already a group of people that are already looking for a solution or a product to a particular problem, and can you come in and provide that solution to them? You will find that it is often easier to go out there and fulfill a need that is already there rather than trying to create a new need.

3. Are people willing and able to spend money on the product you want to advertise with? The way that people spend their money right now can give you an idea of what existing products and services they like and how you can choose the right stuff to work with in the future.

4. Is the market for the niche you like big enough to actually make some money? If the niche is too small, you aren't going to get as many profits, even if you put in a ton of marketing efforts. You can work with the Google keyword tool to find out how much search volume there is for that particular niche. This can also help you to get some other recommendations on similar niches if needed.

5. Are there other marketers that are spending money in this niche? If you can find that there are other marketers who spend money on advertising for a niche market, this means that it is more profitable. If there aren't any marketers out there in that niche, this may be a sign that this niche is a bad one to work with.

To help you get started, the three best niches to make a lot of money within affiliate marketing is relationships, wealth, and health. If you have a product or a niche that fits into this somehow, then you are well on your way to being in a spot to make some money. Of course, you will want to narrow down the niche a bit to help you target just a small segment of the bigger market, or you will waste too much time looking through things and doing the marketing that is needed.

How to Pick Out a Good Product to Sell

Each affiliate marketer is going to gravitate towards a different type of product that they want to promote. There are so many products out there to go with and make a profit with, that it can seem overwhelming. There are a few different ideas that you can stick with to help you get a product you feel passionate about.

First, consider picking out a product that you have used or are willing to use. You can then really talk about the product and explain the different features. You can even go through and talk about some of your own personal anecdotes about using the product and how it helped you. Whether the product is able to help you increase the conversion rate of your business or it helped you to lose weight, it can really enhance your affiliate marketing effort.

Another thing to consider when picking out a product to work with is to pick one that goes with your particular niche. This doesn't mean that you have to miss out on showing some of the brands that you know and love. But see if there are some ways that you can include them in with the niche you chose in a seamless and easy way.

There are a ton of products that you can choose to work with, and it is likely you will be able to find a bunch that will work well for you. But if there is really a certain product that you would like to promote, but it seems to not fit in well with your niche, then maybe looking at it from a different perspective can help make it fit.

And finally, you should try to promote products from companies you can stand behind. Make sure that the core values that you have align with the core values of the company. If you find there is a big disconnect between the purpose of the two brands, then it won't really fit with your audience well, and you won't get the clicks or the sales that you are looking for.

There are some bloggers out there who will mistakenly partner up with brands who had a bad reputation with the audience or the public as a whole. And then, when they started to promote this brand or company, it made the blogger's reputation go down and take a hit as well. The best way to ensure that you maintain your reputation while making money with affiliate marketing is to do some research about any company you are interested in. This helps to protect yourself and the personal brand that you worked so hard on.

How to Pick Out a Good Company

Once you have taken some time to pick out the right niche and the right product to sell, it is time to move on to looking at which company you want to sell with. The most obvious consideration here is whether they sell the product or the service you are interested in. It doesn't do much good to go through and do a lot of research about a company just to fall in love with them and find out they don't even sell in the niche that you are interested in. So, the first thing that you can do to prepare for picking out a company is to compile a list of your choices that offer the product you want to sell on your site.

After you have a list of at least a few different affiliate marketing companies, it is time to look at a few other things. First, take a look at the reviews that are out there for the company. Look specifically at ones that may have been written by former and current affiliate marketers of the company. You want to find out how the company does with taking care of customers, making sure that payments are on time and accurate, and look for any red flags that could raise some concern if you are not careful.

If you see that there are a lot of customer complaints, and the affiliates don't seem that happy with the product, then it may be best to take a step away and look at other companies. Remember that in addition to making money with these links, you are also putting your reputation on the line, along with the hard work that you already put in. It is much better to look for a company with a good reputation, one that is going to provide you with happy followers and a good commission.

The next thing that you can focus on is picking out a company that has a good commissions plan. Some companies are going to pay a better commission than others. You want to make sure to get the most out of your time so if there are two companies that offer the same product, but one offers a higher commission for selling it, it is at least worth your time to look into this and see if it is best for you.

While looking into the income, make sure to check the rules for when the commissions are sent, if the company is reliable with sending out the money, and whether there are any rules about minimums before you can withdraw. All of these things can help you to make a good decision about the product you are selling.

Picking out the product and the company you want to work with in affiliate marketing can be one of the best and most important decisions that you can make for your business. This can help you to make as much money on the endeavor as possible while maintaining your reputation and ensuring that you provide high-quality products to your customers. When you follow the suggestions and tips above, you will be able to do just that!

Chapter 5: Where Can I Place My Affiliate Marketing Links

There are several places where you can start to place some of your affiliate links. Having these in place ahead of time can make a big difference in how successful your marketing efforts can be over time. This chapter will take some time to look at the different places where you can place your affiliate links so that you can reach your customers and see the best results.

On Your Blog

The number one place where people will go in order to work on their affiliate marketing is to a blog. Blogs are fantastic places to put an affiliate link because they have a lot of opportunities and options when it comes to how you can advertise and the method you use.

After you have worked on your blog or website for some time, you should have a good following. This would be people who often come back to your blog over and over again in order to read the information that is there. These readers have started to trust your opinion and what you are saying. And as long as you do it the right way, you can convince others to click on your link and then choose to make a purchase based on the recommendations that you provide.

The first method that you can use when it comes to adding affiliate marketing to your website is to add it to the content itself. You would write an article either solely on the information of the product, kind of like an ad, or you can choose to talk about another related topic and then have a link to this product as a solution somewhere inside. If you go with this method, make sure that you let your readers know that it is tied to an affiliate link. It is required by the FTC that every business who is using affiliate marketing do this. The good news is that this is pretty common now and most of the time your readers recognize and understand why it is going on, so it's not a big deal.

Another option is to use banner ads. These are going to be visuals that show up on the top or the side of your website. The customer or the reader can take a look at the visual, and then they can decide whether it looks interesting to them and if they want to click on it, similar to what you can do with the link in your content. If they choose to click on the link and then make a purchase, you will be able to keep the profits that arise from all of that.

Facebook and Instagram

Facebook and Instagram, along with Twitter and other social media sites, are working with affiliate marketers more than ever. There are a lot of businesses that are turning to these sites in order to meet with their customers the best way possible, and you can definitely reach an advantage if you choose to work with this method of advertising.

On these sites, you will choose to post the link, and maybe some information and a picture on your profile. This is meant to show up to all of your followers, and then they can choose whether they would like to click on the link and make the purchase. If you have ever seen a friend selling health products or coffee or something else similar, then you are probably looking at a form of affiliate marketing.

The goal here is to make the posts stand out from the crowd. Even if you decide to do some paid advertising on the social media site, there are a ton of other advertisers out there, and finding a way for your product to stand out from the crowd, to really go viral and to spark something in others, and to not sound too salesy, can be hard. Posting good pictures, adding some stories, and really showing the benefit of the product can make a big difference in the results that you see.

YouTube

If you have a YouTube channel, then you have another method of affiliate marketing that you can work with. YouTube is great as a visual tool. And if you are able to come up with a video that can go viral, then you are going to be able to make a good amount of money on this method.

If you don't have a good YouTube channel, then now may be the time to create one. If you have a Google email address, then you can sign up for a YouTube channel. Then take the time to go through and work on the channel as much as possible. You want to keep it relevant to your niche. You want to make it interesting. And you want to look like an expert in your field.

We will take some time to explore using YouTube for your affiliate marketing and some of the different strategies and benefits of working with this channel. YouTube can really work well, as long as you can make some great videos and can really connect with your potential customer.

There are a lot of different benefits of working with each of these methods when you get started with your affiliate marketing journey. But finding time to work with each one can be a challenge, and sometimes you will need to limit yourself and find one or two methods that will work the best for you. We will spend some time looking at each of them a bit more as we progress through this guidebook so that you are able to get the most out of each method.

Chapter 6: How to Do Affiliate Marketing Through My Blog

The first place where you will want to work on affiliate marketing is on your own personal blog. Many people who have spent a few months, and sometimes a few years, building up a blog and gathering a large base of consistent readers, will choose to go with affiliate marketing to help them to monetize this blog. Since they already have the audience to do this, they can simply add the affiliate links into some of their content, and often they will get some clicks and some sales this way.

If you don't already have a blog, then now may be the best time to get one started. There are many different topics you can choose from, and you can easily be a way to create a blog, with lots of good content, based on the niche that you chose before. Of course, creating your own blog is not something that is going to happen overnight. It can take a lot of time and effort on your part, and you have to be ready to keep up with it, even once you have a good base of readers. Some of the steps that you can follow to do well with affiliate marketing includes:

1. Pick out the niche you want to use for your blog. You can choose from many different options. Remember that you will be writing on this topic for a long time to come, so make sure that you are able to enjoy the topic and one you won't be sick writing on within a few months.

2. Pick out a domain name and hosting. You want to go with a name that relates to your niche and is also easy for your readers to remember. This can help with some of the SEO that you will want to work with later on. The hosting is also important because it can help you to pick out the right platform, the right add-ins, and more.

3. Start writing. The best way to get a blog to gain more followers is to start writing. You should start a consistent writing schedule now and get the hang of it, so it sticks once more readers join the group. You can't just post on occasion or sporadically, or it becomes very hard to keep your readers coming back for more.

4. Set up the SEO. This helps your potential readers to find you online and through search engines. If you don't get this set up the right way and pick the right keywords, it could be very hard for the readers to find you, and you won't be able to grow your following.

Of course, this is a process that can take some time and effort to do effectively. You won't be able to write for just a week or two and expect to have 100,000 followers. But if you can work hard and consistently on your blog, the followers will come, and you will be able to turn this into a great source of income.

Now that the blog is set up, after a few months or more, you can start to work with affiliate marketing on the page. Some of the steps that you can take in order to work with affiliate marketing with your website includes:

Choose the Right Affiliate Marketing Program

The most important thing that you can do when you want to add affiliate marketing to your website is to choose the right program. Affiliate ads are going to be pay per action, which means that the reader has to actually click on the ad and agree to purchase or sign up for something before you can get paid. The more relevant your links or ads are to your content, the more clicks you will get, and the more money you can make in the process.

So that leads us to the question, what type of affiliate program is going to work the best for your page and lead to the most clicks? If you have a focused topic on your blog, then you want to find affiliates that can associate and meet up with that content. An example of this is if you have a photography business, you may choose to use affiliate links to camera equipment or someone who sells this equipment.

Many bloggers find that it works well to start on Amazon Associates. This is because Amazon already sells millions of unique products, and this provides the blogger with a lot of choices in picking out the thing that works the best for them. And since Amazon offers a commission that is somewhere between four to fifteen percent, depending on the product type and the volume, you can make a good amount of money on it in the process.

Of course, there are going to be a lot of other options that you can choose from when it comes to picking out a good affiliate link. The trick here is to find a balance between having a good company with good commissions and lots of products to choose from, and one that meets your niche but doesn't have too much competition associated with it.

An Affiliate Aggregator May Be a Good Idea

If you find that the topics on your blog are kind of diverse, then working with an affiliate aggregator, such as VigLink, a system that can automate access to 30,000 affiliate programs for you while monetizing the links that you place on your site, may be the right option for you. In addition, to help monetize some of the links that you already have on your block, this automation tool can also optionally insert new and ordinary links in your content if there weren't any links there before. So, if you have some content that calls out a certain product or store, the automation service would add in the link for you and make sure that you got paid for any clicks and purchases that may occur.

You will find that this is a great way to make sure you are getting the most out of your blog. Since it can take a lot of time and effort to go through and add in all of these links on your own, using an affiliate aggregator will ensure that you get the most out of all this, without having to put in all the legwork or worrying that you missed out on something along the way.

Create Some Content that Will Actually Sell

You don't want to work with content that is boring and will turn your customer away. Many bloggers will find unique ways to write information and content that helps to sell the products to their readers. For example, you may choose to write out a review of a product, or you can provide different solutions to your customers, or even do a comparison for a few different products. The more creative you can be here, the easier it is for you to make some money on that link.

The power that comes with a blog is that it is easy to collect a ton of fans for a niche and a specific topic. This lends itself really well to making recommendations and providing the links that go with those recommendations. But just adding in these links to a product, without any rhyme or reason behind it, can mean that you may get a lot of clicks, but quick exits with no sales.

Your job here is to write out some content that will actually help to sell the product. Don't just put up a list of books, for example, and then hope that people will click on them and make a purchase. Instead, write out a review of the books or write about them in some way, and then point the reader in the right direction if they are interested in purchasing it.

Integrate Affiliate Links in the Right Way

If you do decide to add these links to your site, make sure that there is some balance between the user experience that you provide and the monetization that you try to get. One way to do this is to still keep your content ad-free as much as possible.

There is nothing wrong with having a link in place on a few articles. But if you are doing this on each page that you have, and you add in a ton of links into each one, the reader is going to realize this and find the content less engaging. Your readers won't mind hearing about a product on occasion, but if you are doing it all the time, they will see that you just want money, rather than helping them, and they will leave.

Affiliate marketing can lend itself well to blogs. You already have a big market of people who are interested in what you have to say and the recommendations that you provide to them. When you take advantage in this, in a way that will still provide a good experience to the user, you will be able to see some amazing results with earning money off your blog.

Chapter 7: How to Do Affiliate Marketing Through Facebook

While most people head right to their blog when it is time to work with affiliate marketing, there are other ways that you can reach more people and earn money off your links. And the method we are going to look at now is affiliate marketing through Facebook.

Facebook is one of the biggest social media platforms out there with billions of profiles and people using this site each day around the world. This means that you get the benefit of potentially reaching a ton of people with your links, as long as you make sure you are doing it in the right way.

Before we get started with using Facebook on your affiliate links, you first need to set up the profile that you want to use. You can choose to work with your own personal profile, or you can choose to work with a business profile based on how you want to conduct your business. Make sure that it starts to show your brand and you only post things on the page, especially if it is your personal page, that lines up with the new brand and company that you are trying to work on.

Direct Facebook Traffic Over to Your Affiliate Page

Since most people already have their own Facebook accounts and know how to deal with opening up another one, it is time to move straight to the dirty work. You are able to use your Facebook audience in order to accumulate engaging likes until you have a ton of fans. But when you are working as an affiliate marketer, this isn't going to help you out until you are able to get some more of that traffic to head to your marketing page, so they make a purchase.

A good way to think about this is as a type of flirting that will help you to build up the relationships that you want, rather than going through with your guns blazing and sending out a lot of spam. Think of it this way, would you rather help out or look at a link from a close friend who showed the products, and actually talked to you on occasion without trying to sell you? Or would you rather have your inbox and page filled up with spam and messages about the product all the time? Your potential customer is going to feel the same way.

A good ratio for you to go with is about 80 percent entertaining content that has nothing to do with the selling (or at least a tiny amount of selling hidden in there), and 20 percent promotion. This ensures that you build up a good relationship with your potential customer without annoying them and putting them off from even looking at your page.

For Facebook advertising to work for your affiliate marketing, you need to make your potential customer genuinely like your page, using that 80 percent relevant and entertaining media. That way, when you do post some targeted promotions, they are more likely to at least take a look at it and maybe even consider purchasing the item.

What you should consider here is making sure that the thing you promote is the actual affiliate site rather than doing a direct sale. It is much better to turn the traffic into some new leads who are already familiar with the website that you are presenting, rather than trying to get more people interested in going to see your content, whether that is a blog post, or some special deal for them.

Once you are able to snag some new audience using an enticing reason for them to head back to your site, especially those who have been to the site in the first place, you can then send them back to the main affiliate or landing page, and even get them on your email list. This one thing is going to help you expand out the strategy that you have for affiliate marketing from just Facebook and your normal affiliate site. And if you are able to build up the email list that you have, you will really have some valuable customers who are highly likely to purchase from you in the future.

Facebook Advertising

Another option that you can work with is to not just focus on the people who are already on your page or profile but also work to get a portion of the very large audience base that is present on Facebook and get them sent over to your affiliate site. Facebook Ads is one of the best ways for you to do this. There are some different options that you can work with when you want to bring in Facebook Ads including pay per click advertising or paying per 1000 impressions. You can experiment with these to figure out which one is going to work the best for your needs.

Facebook Ads will help you to target the right audience for you because Facebook has information that can make your campaigns better. You can look up information about the age of users, their locations, where they work, what their interests are, and more. This can be great because you can highly target the audience you want to work with, and it pulls in traffic to one of your affiliates offers faster than before.

Setting up an ad on Facebook is pretty simple. You can go on your personal account or your business account and do the drop-down menu on the settings or from the small wheel that is right at the top right-hand side of the page. You should be able to see a lot of options on there that are meant to suit a wide variety of goals. If you want to make sure that more people see your page and can interact with it and engage, then you would go with the top option. Or for page Likes, you would select that option. To send these customers or audience members to your affiliate page you may want to try website conversions to help you track how many clicks are occurring and then converting to sign-ups for your email according to the plan.

If you want to use this campaign to get people to your offers or your content, you can try Clicks on Website. You can then go through and add in your website and some images to go with it. You should have more than one image in place here to really entice your customer base, but six is the amount that you should aim for and try to stick with the recommended size of an image that is about 600 by 315 pixels.

The next thing that you can work with is linking this new ad over to the Facebook page. The link will still make your customers go to your website when they click on it, but doing this option will make it easier to gain some more publicity in the process, and it builds up some links and associations between your site and your Facebook page. You can also work with adding in a call to action button to make things easier.

Make sure during this process you create a headline and a text in the bottom left parts. Keep the content snappy and to the point. You will be limited on the amount of space that you have for all of this, so make sure that it describes you and your business quickly so the customer can make their own decision about whether they want to go on your page or not.

When you are creating a Facebook Ad, you must make sure that any ad that you create is going to meet with the right people, otherwise, you will waste your time and your money. Think about the target market that you would like to see on your affiliate site. You can add in locations, genders, ages, languages, and even interests of the people you want to send the ads to. This ensures that the ad is specific enough that it will find the right people. You can even add in some more demographics with the drop-down box underneath languages.

Another thing to look at is the advanced connection targeting that will make sure that the only people you reach are the ones who are within a certain connection. The gauge that is on the top right and it will tell you how broad or specific the search is. If you are on a lower budget with this, you will need to be as specific as you can with the type of people you advertise to because this ensures that you will get the most out of your money.

Finally, you will need to get into the account settings and include some other information to help target the advertisement that you will do. You can enter some information like your time zone, country, and currency. Set your budget here for the amount that you want to spend each day. And you can set the ad to run on a continuous manner or set out the start and end on the specific dates that you would like.

Now, you will want to spend time learning which Facebook ads are going to be shown to your target audience and this is determined by a few factors. This can include how the ads are performing in the past, the target audience, and how much competition is in the marketplace. In the section that says Bidding and Pricing, you are able to do some optimization choices in order to make sure that your bid is perfect to get more clicks in the process.

Take some time experimenting with your bid, even if you are on a lower on a budget. It is so useful when you want to ensure your bid isn't set too low for your ad to get it shown. But there is also a benefit of making sure that you never pay more for an impression or any of the clicks that you are using than necessary.

While most people will spend their time just doing affiliate marketing on their website, doing this method on Facebook can be really important as well. There are a lot of potential customers you can work with, and you may find that you can really increase your reach if you work with Facebook in the proper way. Make sure to check out the tips above to help you see the best results with growing your affiliate market on Facebook.

Chapter 8: How to Do Affiliate Marketing with Instagram

Instagram is one of the most popular platforms for social media out there. It doesn't matter what niche you want to go with, business, money, beauty, blogging, and food, everyone is on Instagram, and the pictures and method of working with the platform can make it really a popular platform to use.

There are a number of techniques that you can use in order to use Instagram to help with affiliate marketing. Instagram is sometimes a tricky platform for you to monetize with affiliate marketing, and you may want to work with some of the other opportunities that are out there first and gain some more experience. One of the issues can come from not being able to add in clickable links like you can with other social media platforms. But there are a few different ways that you can maximize the results that you get with Instagram, even as an affiliate marketer, including:

Add in the Affiliate Links to the Bio

You are only allowed to put one link into the bio that you write for Instagram, so you need to make sure that it really counts. Instead of linking back to an affiliate product, website, or blog post, using one link that will point back to a number of links instead. Some of the cool ways that you are able to do this include:

1. Linktree: This is a tool that is easy to set up and free to use. You can work with the premium option if you need it, but most people are going to be happy with the free account because it can do plenty. Linktree is going to provide you with a short link that you can then place into your bio, which can then display your list of links to any follower to click if they would like.

2. Create a menu page on the website: If you don't want to work with a third-party tool, you can also go through and create a page on your website. You can simply create a new page on your website and list out all the links that you want to work with. You can choose text images, or buttons to do this. On places like WordPress.com, you can use the Elementor to build up a really stunning page.

Include Some Affiliate Links in the Stories that You Do

Once you get to the 10,000-follower mark on Instagram, you will then gain the ability to add these kinds of links with your stories using the swipe up feature. When your follower looks at your story and then swipes up with that story, they will be following the link automatically right to the service or product page.

Of course, if you don't have these many followers, you won't be able to use this swipe up function on your pages. However, there are a few other things that you can choose to work with. You can include a shortened and easy to remember link to the story by working with bitly or Pretty Links. Some people choose to work with sharing links with the followers by reminding the story watchers to click back on the bio.

Some people decide to take the extra steps to make their account verified. Once your account is verified by Instagram, you will then be able to have the swipe up feature, regardless of how many people follow you. Verifying your account doesn't have to be difficult. You just need to go to Settings and then look for the option to Request Verification, and then follow the steps that are listed. You will need to submit a relevant ID.

Use Vanity URLs or Short Links in the Image Descriptions

The link that is in your bio section is going to be the only place that Instagram allows you to add a clickable link. This means that if you add a link to the captions of your pictures, it can't be clicked on. This doesn't mean that you can't add this link to the caption though, it just means they can't be clickable.

When you are posting some pictures of the products you want to sell, or if you would like to write about the tools that you are an affiliate for, you can definitely include the affiliate link that you would like. You can use bit.ly or another site to help you to pick out a link that you can add, and then your readers can type it in themselves and get over to your affiliate site.

Try Some Personalized Coupon Codes

Some of the affiliate programs that you choose to go with are able to provide you with some discount codes or unique coupons that you can provide to your customers. There are two really big benefits that come from using these including:

1. They are going to provide some enticement to your audience in order to purchase the product that you are offering. They see the good or special deal, and they are willing to make a purchase.
2. Sometimes these codes are going to be tied back to your affiliate ID. This means that your followers won't need to actually click on a specific link in order to make sure you get the credit if they do make that purchase.

Instagram is a unique platform that you can work with when you want to increase your reach and really sell your affiliate links. The great platform with lots of visuals and other benefits are quickly bringing more and more people in, and this can help you to increase your reach and do more sales overall.

Strategies to Use with Affiliate Marketing on Instagram

If you are already on Instagram, there are a few steps that you can take in order to help you see some results with affiliate marketing. Some of the best tips that can help you do well with Instagram affiliate marketing include:

1. Create a page on your website to shop the Instagram and add it to the bio on Instagram. This is a great way to take your traffic and then convert it to your sales. If your Instagram is already full of lots of beautiful images, ones that your customers are already interested in, then letting them know how they are able to shop for these items can be key to your success. By adding information to the pictures and making them shoppable, the interested party can purchase right then and there.

2. Utilize coupon codes: Coupons have been a very effective way for people to purchase things. You can make up some exclusive deals and coupons that are just for your Instagram followers to help entice them more than ever before.

3. Sometimes focus on something other than selling. You don't have to go through and add a link to each picture. Sometimes it is nice to just place some pictures that showcase things you like and to get others interested, without having to sell something.

4. Don't forget to use Instagram stories. Since Instagram stories were first released at the end of 2016, it has been seen as a great tool to use for marketing and advertising for individuals and businesses all the time. Anything that gets posted in these stories will last for 24 hours. You can place anything you would like in the stories, but making them entertaining and engaging, and remember that these stories will only last 15 seconds each.

5. Work on a niche and then use Instagram to bolster the community. If you focus on a niche that has a very engaging following, you are more likely to see the success that you want. You can work on developing the niche that you want, and then work to build up that community and get more followers to take a look at your pictures and the things that you are posting.

6. Tie your blog post with the Instagram posts that you do. If you already have a blog in place, you can then have some complementing material in place to help you see results.

7. Consider working with a paid search: If you want to gain some more followers and really see your business grow, then you will want to work with some paid advertising on Instagram. You can do this with Google AdWords. Just make sure that you focus on the metrics that increase your conversion rate and also work with your budget. And always focus on doing the keyword research as well as you can to reach the right customers.

Instagram is a great option for you to work with when you want to grow your business and see more results out of your affiliate marketing. When you are ready to get started with your affiliate marketing with Instagram, make sure to check out this chapter and some of the tips that are needed to see success with this.

Chapter 9: How to Do Affiliate Marketing Through YouTube

The next thing that we need to look through when it comes to doing affiliate marketing is with the help of YouTube. You can easily make some money on YouTube with the help of affiliate marketing, which means that you will include links to your products, especially products that you review and also use in your videos. These links will then track the purchases that anyone makes after seeing your video. If there is a viewer who makes a purchase from that affiliate link, you will then be able to receive a small amount of commission from that sale.

YouTube is a great platform that you can use in order to get amazing results out of reaching a large audience. While some of the other platforms that we worked with used mostly words and content to help reach the customer, with a few visuals put in place, YouTube is going to be a bit different because it relies completely on videos that users post.

There are billions of hours of watched content on YouTube, and as a beginner, this may seem overwhelming. But if you can create some interesting and engaging content, and if you can create a video that is able to go viral, you will find that this is one of the best places for you to work on affiliate marketing and see the success that you want.

Setting up the account is pretty easy with YouTube. In fact, if you already have a Gmail account of some kind, you will already be ready to set up the account. But if you go to your YouTube account and you haven't done anything with it, then it is going to look pretty blank and boring. There are a few things that you can do to spruce it up and make sure that you will actually be able to see some great results from your page. Some of the steps that you can follow in order to set up your YouTube page, assuming you already have a Google or Gmail account, includes:

1. Access www.youtube.com and then use your Gmail credentials to log into the account. Then the main home screen of YouTube is going to show up.
2. Looking towards the upper right part of the screen, you should see an account profile picture if you set one up with Google. You can take some time to do it here. Click on it to see the Account Menu.
3. Click on the link for My Channel. You can then see the screen for Create Your YouTube channel will show up. From this screen, you will get a view of your profile picture, your username and more. You can click on the Edit link that is there in order to make some customizations to this part. You want to make sure that this part shows the identity of your business because it is part of the public information that people can see about you online.
4. From here, we want to take a look at the Activities you'll share on your channel heading. There will be four main options that you can pick from including Favorite video, Subscribe to a channel, comment on a video, and like a video. Add a checkmark to each part that you would like visitors to this channel to be able to do.

5. Click on the 'Ok, I'm Ready to Continue' button. From here, the YouTube Channel is created. You need to go through and start adding some videos to the page, ones that are engaging and will bring your viewers in. If you don't bring in viewers, then you won't be able to actually profit on the affiliate links that you post and talk about.

Once you have some videos up on your page and at least a decent sized following, you may be ready to add in some of the affiliate links so you can start making money on this process. But this brings up the question, how do you integrate the affiliate links into your YouTube videos in a natural way, one that doesn't look fake or too salesy in the long run?

One of the best times to do this is with a review video. This means that somewhere on your channel, you will need to do a review of a specific product that you would like to sell to your customers. You can then link that product in the video, and even in the description so that the viewers are able to actually go out and purchase that product as well.

These videos can be a great way to showcase the products that you are trying to sell. You can show your enthusiasm and love of the product through video in a way that you just can't do with other methods. This is one of the easiest methods that you can use in order to get an affiliate link into the video, and it makes it easier to monetize a video that isn't already sponsored.

So, if you are making one of these videos, you may want to find a way to make it unique and fun. You could have a favorite thing review, or you can just work on a review of one product at a time. Take a look at how you have set up the rest of the page and how the other videos are, and then choose from there. Then, at the end of the video, you can add in that affiliate link so that your viewers know where they can get the product that you talked about if they are interested in using it for themselves.

In addition to adding the affiliate link to the videos that you create, you also need to add in these links in the description. You don't want to add in too many of these links. YouTube doesn't want people to hope off the platform and go to other sites. It wants to keep them there as much as possible. If you add in ten links to each video that you create, YouTube may get mad and it can cause some issues to the ranking that you get.

So, the concern when it comes to an SEO perspective is that the goal of YouTube is to keep their viewers there as much as possible, watching a ton of content and engaging so that they can see more advertisements, and YouTube can make more money. So, if your video ends the viewing session for the video (such as what happens when they watch your video and then leave YouTube after clicking on the link), this may work out great for you because you made some money, but it is going to make YouTube mad. In the long run, it could mean that your video may not perform as well as it should because YouTube simply doesn't want people to leave at all.

This is the balance that you have to strike. Adding in that link, in the end, makes it more likely that someone will actually follow it and make a purchase. Often, even if you repeat the website ten times in the video, the customer is going to prefer to go to the description and click on that to make their purchase instead. Adding that is going to really help your business.

One way that you can make sure that you aren't making YouTube mad with conversions on each video is to not make each one about sales. You can have a few with affiliate links added in for good measure, but then make the majority of them focused more on something that is fun or entertaining. This way, your videos can still get some conversions and become successful, but you are still adding in some where the customer is going to stay on YouTube when they are done.

Another thing to consider is adding somewhere in the description of the video whether you are using an affiliate link or not. This is kind of like the FTC disclosure that you would need to add into your blogs. YouTube hasn't officially come out and said that you have to do this, so if you forget it is usually going to be fine. But it is a good practice to get into in case there are some rules that show up for this and to protect yourself.

The nice thing about affiliate marketing, especially on YouTube, is that you will get paid no matter what the customer purchases on the site (with more affiliate companies). When someone gets to your video and then clicks on your link, a little cookie is going to be added to their computer that will track what they do. If they go on the website and make a purchase, even if it isn't the specific product that you were advertising and promoting, then you will still be able to earn a commission on this.

This can be a great thing for many affiliate marketers to have with their chosen company. You can easily earn more commissions this way. Sure, they didn't purchase the specific option that you had been promoting, but if they filled up their cart with ten other items from that same website, you will still be able to earn a commission on it thanks to those cookies that were added to their computer in the first place.

Just like with the other platforms that we talked about, the commission rates that you are able to earn will depend on how many of the products that you are able to sell and which company that you will sell. Some may go up to 50 percent, although this is usually seen as high, and others are going to be as low as five percent. You should read up on the rules for commissions with your chosen company before you decide to get started.

YouTube is a fantastic platform to use when you really want to reach your potential customers in a unique and interactive manner. It is much different from what you are going to see when you are working with other platforms, and video can be really interactive and can lead to some good conversion rates. Make sure to follow the suggestions and tips above to help you see the best conversion rates possible when you use your affiliate links on YouTube.

Chapter 10: How to Do Affiliate Marketing Through Google

Another place that you can concentrate your affiliate marketing efforts is with Google. Google is one of the biggest search engines out there, and often when we are working with the idea of SEO on our websites and other platforms, it is based on the algorithm that Google presents, simply because it is one of the biggest throughout the world. While most of us just think about Google because of their email and their search engine, it is also possible to use this as a way to do affiliate marketing and grow your business.

This is another one that is going to line up with your blog or your website, so having one available, no matter what your other strategy parts are about, can be so important. If you already own a website or a blog, it is possible to earn money with the help of the Google Affiliate Network. This is a great program for blog writers and business dreamers to connect with companies who already match with the theme that you have on your website.

When you sign up with the Google Affiliate Network, you will be able to earn a portion of the sales if someone comes on your page and clicks on one of the ads, and then decides to purchase from that site. It is easy to make money with this program. But you have to make sure that you continue to produce high-quality content on the site, and that you find the right products to promote on the website as well.

So, first, we need to make sure that we are signed up with the Google Affiliate Network. This is pretty easy to work with. You can simply type this into your search bar, doesn't matter which search engine you are working with, click on the link, and then click that you want to join. To continue this process, it is necessary that you add in some basic information about yourself and the website that you are using and then click submit.

Now, it is time for a bit of a waiting game. It is often going to take at least one or two days before you are able to get the acceptance email back from Google. You won't be able to proceed through these steps until you get it back and can use that information to log in later on.

Once you have that confirmation email, you can log into your account. From here, you can go through and search the products and the different advertisers that are available, and see which ones are already going to be a good fit for the niche that you are working with. To get the most out of your affiliate marketing campaign, you must make sure that you are picking out the right offer and matching them with the right audience. You can find an amazing deal, but if it doesn't match up with what your customers want or need, then you are never going to get any sales.

For example, if you are working on a website that is all about camping, then it is in your best interest to find companies that will sell some camping supplies to your customers. You are able to do this by clicking the Products or Advertisers buttons that are shown prominently near the top of the screen while you are in your account.

After you have found some advertisers that interest you and show that they will do well with the audience that you already have, you need to apply to the ones that are of interest to you. You can click on the small box that is next to the name of the advertiser. Then you can click on the Apply to Selected button that will show up near the top of the screen.

The amount of time that it takes to get approved is going to depend on the advertiser. Some are going to be able to approve you right away, and sometimes the company will do a manual approval period, and this can take a bit longer before you hear back. Once you hear back from the advertisers, you can get your advertising code to place on the website. You can always take a look at the list of the advertisers who are approved with you under the Advertisers and then the Approved links.

Another thing that you should look at is the Action button, and then take a moment to scroll down to the Get Links so that you can see which ads are available to you from the advertisers you choose to go with in an earlier step that we did.

With that ad code, you will want to place it into the website so that it starts to show up in the right places. If you are working with a site like WordPress, you are able to put this into a text-based widget. If you are going with a website that is more of HTML, you must go back through and modify the code that you are working with in order to make sure that it fits with the rest of the code and to make it easier to properly show the advertisements that you want.

Once you get a campaign started, never just leave it unattended. You need to make sure that you are constantly monitoring the advertising campaigns that you work on. This way, if one particular ad isn't doing that well, you can quickly come in and pick out a different ad for the same company. If you do this a few times and the metrics don't seem to get better, then you may even switch it out for a different company instead.

Working with the Google Affiliate Network is a great way to get some more links to your own page. There are already many advertisers who are interested in getting onto pages found on Google, and you can make some good money in the process. Some of the tips that you should follow when you are working with this method include:

1. The more traffic that is already coming to your website, the more potential money you are able to make with this. If you are only receiving a handful of visitors to the page, then you won't be able to earn money, or at least not much. Consider building up your viewer and reading list before you start your affiliate program to help you earn more money right from the start of this process.
2. Don't try to limit yourself to using only the affiliate programs that Google offers. While this can be a way to get started, Google is going to take a percentage as well, which means that the amount you earn may be less. Working with some other affiliate programs can be a great way to be successful as well.

One thing to keep in mind when you are working with this method is that you may, at some point, be turned down by one or more advertisers. This is more likely to happen when you are new and still developing your skills. As time goes on, you will find that it is easier to get some good advertisers and companies who are more than willing to work with you.

Chapter 11: Other Unique Ways to Do Affiliate Marketing

This guidebook has spent a lot of time talking about the different ways that you can work with affiliate marketing. We have taken a look at some of the steps that you can work with to create a website and then turn that into an affiliate marketing source. We have taken a look at working with social media sites like Instagram and Facebook, and even YouTube. And then we took a way at how to use the Google Affiliate Network to help promote your affiliate marketing business as well.

But now, we are going to look at some of the other methods that you can use in order to really grow your affiliate marketing endeavors and can help you to really see some great results. The methods that are below can be used on their own, or in addition to some of the other methods that we have discussed. It is often going to depend on the strategy that you will decide to go with. Let's take a look at some of the other methods that you can use in order to help grow your affiliate marketing business.

Promote Some Social Media

We have talked a bit about using social media sites, such as Facebook and Instagram, to help you grow this business, but there are other options that you can work with as well. Becoming an affiliate marketer doesn't mean that you must own a successful blog or website, but you do need to have some sort of online presence in order to see success. Owning accounts on several sites, such as Twitter and Facebook can be a great place to start. But you should have at least a small following to help make this easier.

Of course, you will also need to spend some time building up an audience of people who will like your content and who may be more inclined to click on the links that you decide to post. You need to create a post that could have an impact on your audience.

A post that has useful content is going to be a good idea if you want to make sure that you build up the trust that is so necessary from your audience. You can go through and write some promotional posts, you must make sure that the whole platform isn't just promotions and there are other things put in there as well. So, any time that you post a new affiliate link into the content, make sure that it is powerful enough to have the trust and the attention from your audience in the beginning.

Make sure that you are posting content that actually has some relation to the niche that you are working with. If you spend your time posting a lot of irrelevant content to the niche on your site, it is going to drive some of your potential customers away. And remember to work with some images on these social media sites, especially if you are using a site like Instagram. Visual aids are going to do a great job when it comes to attracting your readers and picking ones that really catch the attention of your audience can make a big difference.

Creating an E-book

Another option that you can choose to go with is to create your own e-book. There is a large market for these e-books, and you have the option of making it free in the hopes of really enticing customers to look at your link, or you can charge a few dollars for the book and earn a double income here.

Although this option is sometimes seen as a little bit more difficult to work with, if you can create an e-book that is successful, you have the potential for long lasting results and a steady income that is easy to rely on. When you are writing this e-book, it is important that you go through and pick out a topic that you have some knowledge about. This doesn't mean that you have to spend hours writing hundreds of books, you just need to go out there and find a few good topics that your readers are interested in, and then start from there.

Make sure there is some substance in the book. If the reader gets through the book and feels like it was too short, that it didn't provide enough information about the topic, or that it was flimsy, they are going to feel like you pulled on over on them and they are less likely to actually even look at the affiliate links that you provided inside.

While your plan is to add in the links and make some sales, this is not the primary goal of what you are doing here. Instead, you need to provide some really useful and pertinent information to the reader in the book, and then add the links into the book in a way that shows you are trying to help them, not just make money from them.

You are not writing a new e-book just for the sake of writing it, and not as a way to get rich quick. The goal here is to provide your readers with some helpful information. Once the readers approve of the work, and they trust the information that you add to it, and you are then promoted to a legitimate source on the topic, then the affiliate links are going to be the bonus on top of it all.

Promote Through Some Communities and Forums Online

The next thing that you can consider working with in order to really move your affiliate marketing goals is to promote the link and your business through various communities and forums online. These types of online locations are found almost everywhere now, and you can use it to your advantage to promote the affiliate links that you have. But how are you going to do this?

The first step is to search around for a forum that already discusses the subject that you want to promote. Make sure that you take a look at the guidelines that are posted for that community or forum so that you have a good idea of what is allowed and what isn't when you post. After you have found a good community or forum to promote in, you should sign up and become a member. But you need to also make sure that you are an active member.

Don't go through and just look around and say comments like "I agree," "Yes," "No," and so on. You need to be actively on the board, asking questions, answering things that people may ask, and bringing in more comments. Don't worry too much about adding the link at this time. It is tempting to post all over and to make sure that your link is seen by everyone. But this looks really spammy and can turn a lot of people off from you.

Your goal here is to become an expert in the field that you are in with that forum or that community and not just someone who is there to spam others and make a few bucks in the process. Once you are an active and helpful member, others are going to start to trust you, and this trust is going to be so important to help you promote.

You can do this by interacting with others, answering some questions or offering some good solutions while adding your affiliate links into it. Over time, you will find that others are going to start trusting you more, and then they will be more than happy to click on those affiliate links that you choose to provide. If you can do this on a few different forums and communities along the way, you will be able to earn a good amount of income in the process as well.

Try Email Campaigns

We have brought this topic up a bit with affiliate marketing, but it is still something that we should spend some time looking into. Email campaigns are often seen as the best and most effective tool that you can use to know whether or not people are responding to the affiliate links that you are posting or not. Writing out one of the email campaigns that you want to use is going to be pretty similar to what you would do when writing a blog. The biggest difference is that instead of posting online where people have to come and find you, you will instead choose to send these emails directly to the people who have agreed to be on your list.

This means that you must make sure that you are engaging the customers and not just boring them or being annoying. Coming up with engaging copy that holds their attention, talking about a new product and how it can help them, and even adding in some coupons or discounts that are only available to your email list participants can all be good methods to use to start this.

In addition, spacing out your emails is important. Beginners can sometimes get overexcited and want to send out ten emails a day. But no one, even those who agreed to get emails from you to start with, wants to receive that many emails. You should make sure that you only send these out when you really need to provide the customer with some important information. Never send out more than one email a day at most though. Doing too many can put you on the spam list for even your most dedicated customers, and this is going to harm your overall ratings.

When you are working on your emails, make sure that the content and the information that is found inside is going to do a good job at engaging the reader. A good subject is a great way to help ensure that your consumers are going to actually read your emails. So, make sure that you think of a good subject, add in some great content to the email, and then include the affiliate links that you need. When you can do this, it is going to help you maximize the potential earnings that you can have in the future.

Article Websites

And the next option that we are going to take a look at is known as article websites. This is when you join a website and then write content for them. This doesn't require your own website, and there is the added bonus that this site already has a lot of potential customers who head there on a regular basis.

For this method, you will want to join some websites, at least one or two, that will allow you to contribute content to them. There are several types of websites that exist that will let writers register for their own account, and then they can contribute their own reviews or articles on a variety of topics. To find them, you need to go through and perform an internet search using some keywords like "article directory" so that you can find the free versions of these websites that allow you to publish the articles you want.

You need to take some time to search for review and article websites that already cater specifically to the niche that you are using with your affiliate. For example, if your affiliate link is going to sell books, you may want to search around for a website that does book reviews, one that will allow you to post the affiliate links that you have next to the book reviews that you publish.

Once you find a few websites that you want to work with, make sure you review the policies of each website you join. Some of the websites are going to limit how many affiliate links you are able to place into each of the articles that you are working with. Since you probably don't want to overfill your articles with too many affiliate links anyway, this isn't necessarily a bad thing. But always double check to see what the rules are with this.

After you read the guidelines and get set up with the article writing website that you want to use, make sure to start writing articles and reviews that are related to the affiliate so that you reach the right customers and can provide them with your link if they are interested. Internet users who land on the article page are going to already be searching for information or other products that they want or need, and this makes it a great resource for you if you do it right.

As you are writing the articles, you want to make sure that the affiliate links to your products are embedded in the article, before you go through and publish it live. Visitors who come to the website for the article will be able to read through it, and then click on the link to that product if they choose.

When you are writing these articles, make sure that they aren't too salesy or pushy. You want to still provide the reader with some useful information, something that they can take with them and not feel bad or like they didn't learn anything when they are all done. Make the information useful and helpful and even entertaining, and then add the affiliate link into it to add a bit extra to the mix.

These are just a few of the other methods that you can use when you are ready to promote your own affiliate marketing link. Using this properly can ensure that you are getting the products and the link out to the right people at the right time. Try out a few of these options, or consider which ones are going to speak to your customers the most and work the best, and then implement those into your strategy today!

Chapter 12: Things to Avoid with Affiliate Marketing to Get the Most Success

As an affiliate marketer, you are already going to spend a lot of time working on the marketing and promoting of a product. The more that you are able to promote the product, the more money you are able to make. But as a beginner, you may be worried about some of the things that you might be doing wrong, and the ones that are ruining all of the hard work that you put in. Some of the things that you can watch out for and make sure that you avoid when you get started with affiliate marketing include:

Selling and Not Helping Your Customers

Yes, if you look at the word affiliate marketing, you do see the word marketing there. But if you really want to be able to sell the product and make a profit, the job is to help the other person, rather than being pushy and salesy.

There are a lot of different marketers and companies out there who are trying to get the same market share as you are. This means that there is a ton of competition. And since most consumers are going to see a ton of advertisements in their life, they are very good at recognizing it and even being turned off from it, even when it comes from someone they know and trust.

Your job here is to not sound so salesy, and instead come in with a solution to a problem that person may have, in a way that sounds like you really want to help them. As a beginner, your impulse may be to create a landing page, or use your social media page, and then fill it up with words and links that said things like BUY THIS NOW! But when you focus too much on selling, you don't stop and provide the reader with any information on why they should purchase this product or why the product is so beneficial to them.

People are interested in hearing from other people when they are ready to make a decision on whether to purchase a product or not. This is why the review part of Amazon can be so powerful to your company. Those reviews are meant to provide the customer with genuine reviews and feedback about the product, and usually, this comes from those who gain nothing if the other person purchases the product.

For this, make sure that you keep the sales pitch down. If you listed that you were working with affiliate links to start, the customer or reader already knows that there will be something you want to sell. What they want to know now is whether this product is going to be able to benefit them or not. You need to step in and show the person how great your product can be in solving their ailment or the problem quickly.

Too Many

Another mistake that a beginner may make when they start is joining on each and every affiliate program that they could find. While it is fine to work with a few different companies in order to really enhance your income stream, there is a point when you may take on too much, and then you find the work is too hard to manage, and you won't be able to make any money in the process.

Always make sure that you choose the affiliate programs you want to work with wisely. Start with just two or three so that you can earn from multiple sources, but not end up overloading yourself in the process.

Not Testing the Products

Whenever you decide to promote another product, you need to consider testing it out. Put yourself in the shoes of your potential customer, and then test how the vendor will do. You want to make sure that the product is high quality, that the customer service is good, that you get the product in a timely manner, and more. And the best way for you to do this is to pretend that you are a customer and then make a purchase of the product to try out before any of your customers do.

Nothing is going to ruin your reputation or the trust that your customers have in you than when you lead them to a promotion that can cause a problem. Whether it is issues with the product, with customer service, or even with the company spamming your readers all the time after visiting or making a purchase, you will need to find this all out before you try to promote a product.

Not Tracking

Whenever you make a sale, you want to make sure that you know exactly where that sale is coming from. This is going to enable you to know which pages the sales are coming from and which ones are converting the best. This enables you to know how to grow and scale the campaign to be as successful as possible.

Taking the time to create a unique tracking ID, especially for Amazon, can be easy. Simply log into the Amazon affiliate dashboard. Then click on the Account Settings the top right. Then you can click on Manage Tracking IDs. From there, you are able to make a new tracking ID so that you can track which campaign and which web page sold what.

Yes, being able to make a commission on a product can be cool. But it is even better when you have a good idea of where and how you made that commission in the first place. This makes it easier to be a better marketer and it helps you to scale and grow your campaigns rather than just making guesses and working blindly on the things that you do.

Not Taking the Time to Compare

One of the best things that you can do when working with affiliate marketing is to compare the main product with some other products that are similar. When people are purchasing a product, they will tend to try to narrow down their options to two or three, and then they need some help to make the choice that is best for them. By comparing a few choices together, you can help your readers find the answer they need.

With this method, make sure that you track the page and see which product is gaining the most interest from your readers. You can then move the one that is converting the best to the top of the page. Not only do these comparison pages help your readers and are seen as very popular by them. They can also turn into some hefty profits for you as well.

Make Money Online Products

Perhaps you have been on a website and seen this one before. You are on a learning online marketing forum type site and then someone comes online and posts how they run into trouble making any money online. But then there is a signature that they post that says something like "I Made 50 Million Dollars with This" and then an affiliate link is attached to it. While this is something that can happen often, please don't be this kind of person.

If you are new and you want to be able to promote your products, even in the make money online arena, don't make any false claims that you were able to make money from that thing. In fact, you should never go online and make false claims at all. Sure, it is fine to talk about the benefits of the product or the training that you use, and you can even talk about why it all sounds good to you. But never go on and try to trick people because this will ruin all the credibility that you have.

Oh, Look! A Butterfly!

The biggest downfall that any affiliate marketer is going to have is this. It can even cause issues for someone who has been in this market for some time. It is all too common to work on something, and then there is something shiny that shows up in your inbox or is mentioned in a forum that you spend time on. Then you are off to chasing a new idea to make money, even if there is no proof that it works.

As an online worker and affiliate marketer, you must learn how to ignore these butterflies. There are always going to be more, and they will always be there to distract you. These are going to keep you away from your work and can make it even harder to earn the income that you want. One completed and profitable campaign is going to benefit you way more than 50 half-finished projects or campaigns.

Falling for a Scam

Affiliate marketing is a great way for you to make some good money online. And there are lots of people who hear about this method of making money and want to jump into the market. But because of all this interest in this is so high, there are a lot of individuals and companies who want to take advantage of this and will try to trick people into losing money with big promises that are never going to happen.

If you hear something about affiliate marketing that seems too good to be true, then you should take caution. You don't want to jump into something that promises big amounts of profits in no time, no work, and all of this for a fee. These are all signs that the party you are about to work with is a scam and you should run the other way.

First off, most of the legitimate affiliate marketing companies are going to be free to work with. This means that you will not have to pay any fees in order to join them. If some company is asking for money to get started, this is most likely a scam and it is best to look somewhere else. Another thing to look at is the promises that it makes. If they promise that you can make huge amounts of money, this is a red flag as well. This doesn't mean that you won't be able to make a good amount of money. But this takes a lot of time. There are those who can make a lot of money, those who can make a decent amount, and those who make nothing. If you work hard, you will be able to fall right in the middle and make a good amount of money.

If someone is telling you that you will be able to make $10,000 in your first month, then this is not the group you should go with. You may get there at some point, especially with the tips that we offer here, but if the claims say you will do this within a few days, then you are working with a company who is more interested in taking your money than one that actually wants to help you do well with affiliate marketing.

And the amount of time that you are told you have to spend on this is going to be another red flag. When you are starting with affiliate marketing, you will need to put in some work. As you advance this affiliate marketing process and business, you will be able to automate the process more and you won't have to spend as much time doing the process as before. But in the beginning, you do need to spend a lot of time with the various platforms and interacting with your potential customers in order to earn any commissions and sales on your affiliate links.

As a beginner in the affiliate marketing world, you need to be careful about falling for many of the scams that are out there. Many people, especially those who are new to the game, are going to fall for the scams that are out there. They are excited to make money online and quit their jobs, and they want to be able to go through and do it quickly. Be aware of what it takes to work with affiliate marketing and be skeptical about the different claims that you are hearing, and you will find that you can do well with affiliate marketing without being scammed in the process.

Using Copied Content

Always remember that when it comes to your affiliate link, content is going to be king here. If you are actually serious about this new affiliate marketing link and you want to make sure that you can make some profits and see success, then you never want to use the content from another website or content that someone else created.

Coming up with all of that good content for the links can be hard, especially if you are short on time or you don't consider yourself a good writer. But if you go over to another website and find some good content, and then you choose to copy it and use it on your own website, this is going to hurt you. Google is going to actively search for duplicate and copied content all the time. And if they find it, you are going to run into some problems and even get your website banned from the search engine, harming your chances of growing a business even more.

When it comes to creating a landing page or doing anything else with your content for an affiliate marketing campaign, you need to come up with your own content. You need to be resourceful and creative and find a way to reach your audience, without copying from someone else. If you don't have a way with words, and you are worried about this, then you may want to consider hiring someone to do the writing for you. Just never go through and actually steal the content from other places.

Buying Links or Backlinks

When you are working with ranking your website, the backlink is going to be an important part of the process. But this doesn't mean that you should go through and purchase 1000 backlinks for your website. It is common for many people, especially the beginners, to go through and purchase this kind of backlink for their website. And most of these are going to have nothing to do with spamming. But these are still worthless.

If you want to work with a backlink, then you need to go through and actually put in the work yourself. Purchasing these links is going to make you look like spam, and often you are going to spend more than it is worth. Many search engines out there will be looking for too many backlinks, especially ones that are done really closely together, and if they find them, it can harm your website and your other endeavors.

This means that you need to be careful about what you are doing with backlinks. In fact, it is mostly best if you don't purchase anything like this. You don't want to purchase likes to your page, view to the page, copy any content, or purchase backlinks. This is going to cost you a lot of money and can end up getting your page blocked and taken down.

Affiliate marketing is going to be a business that will require some focus and self-motivation on your part. For some people, they are born with these skills and can take them to the next level to see more profits. For others, these are skills that we need to learn along the way. Once you are aware of some of the biggest mistakes that can cause a lack in profits and in the profitability, you want, you will find that it is easier to grow your business and make more money with the help of affiliate marketing.

Chapter 13: How Can I Turn Affiliate Marketing into a Passive Income?

Affiliate marketing is one of the best options that you can choose to work with when you want to make money online. While there are other options to make money quickly online that you can choose to work with, none can provide the same return on investment or the same opportunities as affiliate marketing. While the tips that we have discussed in the rest of this guidebook can go a long way in growing your business and helping you to take home the income that you want, it is also important to remember that the ultimate goal of all this work is to turn the affiliate marketing into a full time and passive income.

A passive income is one that you can make with very little work. It is sometimes going to require a bit, such as writing a few articles a week to go on your website, but you won't have to sit down for 60 hours a week and try to make the income either.

Early on with affiliate marketing, you are going to have to put in some work. You will have to make a website, work to grow it, and try to find followers and readers who are interested in the product. After some time though and growing your business and building up the trust that is needed, you will find that the amount of work you need to do goes down, while the income you earn will go up.

The neat thing about affiliate marketing is that there are so many ways that you can grow this into a passive income source. Some of the options that you can consider include:

Working with Lifetime Links

There are many different types of affiliate marketing companies and programs that you can choose to go with. Some are just going to be a one-time income. They will provide you with a link to just one product for you to provide to your customers. If the customer clicks on that link and then makes a purchase, you will earn an income from that one time. You will have to reach that customer again and again with other offers if you would like to earn more commission from it later on.

Then there are those who will let you earn a bit more. They will allow you to earn a commission on anything that the customer purchases on the website. So, if they come to the site based on your link, but then they decide that item isn't right for them, you can still earn an income if they choose to go out and purchase another item instead. If they fill up their carts with lots of the other items on the website, but they got there from your link, then you will be able to earn a commission from that.

Another option that some companies and programs will offer is the ability to earn a commission on a customer for an extended period of time. The best option is one that is more of a lifetime, but even those that are for 30 to 90 days are better than nothing. This means that if the customer returns to the website any time in the next 30 to 90 days and makes another purchase, or that first original purchase, after clicking on your link, then you are going to be able to earn a commission on it as well.

If you can find it, working with a company who will provide you with a commission on the customer for a lifetime is really going to help you to earn a passive income in no time. This means that when the customer clicks on your link, any time that they come back and make another purchase, they will be able to send you a commission as well. This can work well for you because after you gain just one customer, you will be able to earn money over and over again as well.

Keep in mind that the companies who offer a lifetime link are going to be few and far between. Only a few companies offer this in the first place and the ones that do have a lot of competition. There are many affiliate marketers who want to work with this option because it provides them with the most money and can turn affiliate marketing into a passive and full-time income in no time. If you are able to find one, remember that it is most likely going to be really competitive, and you will need to find ways to think outside the box if you want to stand up from the crowd.

Another option that you can choose to go with when it comes to a lifetime income from affiliate marketing is to work with subscriptions. These are going to make it easier for you to reach a customer who is dealing with a need on a regular basis, say weekly or monthly, and then you can earn an income each time the subscription comes out. There are many different types of subscriptions that you can sell, and since most people will purchase these for a year or more, you will be able to earn a good amount of income in the process.

The best thing that you can do when you become an affiliate marketer is to make sure that you are able to find options that are going to keep you earning income over and over again throughout the years. Some of the options above are going to make this easier to do than ever before. When you are searching for opportunities to grow your business and make sure that you consider some of these options as well.

Article Writing Websites

Another option that you can work with when you are getting started with your own affiliate marketing business is to work with an article writing website. This is similar to what you will do with a personal blog, but you get the benefit of working with a website that already has a bunch of viewers and readers who are already looking for the information that you will provide to them.

You will have to take your time to find an article writing website that matches your needs and falls into the niche that you want to write or with the products that you would like to sell. This can be difficult at times, but you will be able to find some that are reputable and will help you to find the audience that you want.

With many of them, you may need to go through and apply to them. This shouldn't take too much time, but often, the websites want to make sure that you are able to provide them with some high-quality content, content that is important and going to provide value to the readers that they already get. Remember that they have spent some time on SEO and promoting, and they do not want all of that hard work to go to waste because some bad writers who only wanted to make money tried to publish.

Once you get on the website, make sure that your articles are useful and full of lots of information. The main goal on these is to provide the information that your readers are looking for. When they ask a question or search for a term or phrase through a search engine, you want to make sure that your article is one of the first ones they find in the results, and that they will actually read through the article and find the information that they want.

There is nothing wrong with adding in some affiliate links to your articles on these websites. In fact, it is pretty common that the writers on these sites will include one or two affiliate links in their articles. But you do not want to end up with ten affiliate links in each article, and you don't want to have it sound like an advertisement the whole time.

You will quickly find that the article website that you pick will have some terms and conditions that make you disqualified for posting with them if you do this. You need to be able to go through and provide value to your readers, not just an advertisement. Those who come to the page want to figure out something, not be sold something. The website you choose to go with will kick you off if you end up doing this.

You can come up with a lot of high-quality articles that can still include your affiliate links if you want. Instead of making it like an advertisement, consider writing an article that is informative, and then including a call to action at the end of it to help your customers find the solution that they want.

For example, let's say that you have a product that is a subscription box for receiving a few homecooked meals each week every month and you want to be able to sell it to those who want to lose weight, or who are looking to start eating more at home but just don't have the time. Instead of writing an article that just advertises the box and all the great things about it, you will want to write about something that is related, but which will still work in the end.

So, for this one, let's say that you decide to write about the benefits of cutting out fast food, or you can write about saving money, eating healthier, and better time management. After spending time writing about these topics and discussing some of the valuable tips that the customer and reader can use to make life easier, at the end of the article, you can list out an affiliate link to that meal subscription box.

Since you took some time providing the customer with some useful information, they will be more likely to at least check out the subscription box, and they are more likely to actually purchase it compared to just writing out the advertisement.

Another benefit of working with this method is that it can make it easier to get a lifetime income from the article. If you write an article that is high quality and has evergreen content, you will find that it will stay around and rank high for a long time to come. Someone who is looking for the information six months down the line or more can easily find your article, click on the link, and make the purchase as well.

If you are able to go through and do a few of these articles each week and you can come up with a few that work well with each of your links, you will find that the income is going to grow. It may be slow in the beginning, but if you stick with it, you are going to see some great results that can really push you towards your goals of a great income with affiliate marketing.

Your Own Personal Blog

Your own personal blog is still seen as one of the best ways for you to make a passive income out of all the work that you will do with affiliate marketing. This allows you to have the most control, and you will know the most about the customers that you are trying to reach, making it easier to promote your links to others, without having to worry so much about all the rules that other sites may try to impose on you.

You will need to spend some time working on your personal blog and really making it work. This is part of why a lot of people like to avoid working with a personal blog and would rather work with some of the other options instead. You need to take your time setting up a name, finding a place to host it, such as WordPress, and then setting up a schedule of consistent articles. You also have to keep at this for about six to twelve months if you want to be able to get a decent following and have any chance of being able to put affiliate links on it and see some great results.

But once you have that personal blog set up and ready to go, you will find that it can be really easy to set up affiliate links and see results in no time. You will already know your niche really well, and you have probably received a lot of emails and questions about certain topics. You can then use what you have learned and this knowledge to help you pick out products that can actually help your audience.

The one thing to make sure of when you work with these affiliate links is that once you start, don't make each article full of links. While your customers and readers are going to be happy to receive some recommendations on occasion, they do not want to find out that each and every article that you post is full of links and there to make you money. Also, make sure that you are letting people know about your affiliates and what you are doing because transparency is always the best.

Subscription Services

Another option that you can choose to work with when you want to see results with your affiliate marketing is to do a subscription service. This method works because it benefits your customers and readers with a product that they are able to use each month, and it gets shipped to them on time without extra work, and you get that same commission sent to you, without any extra work, each month that your customer agrees to the subscription.

If you are able to find an affiliate company that works with subscriptions, especially one that has a good reputation and provides a lot of value to customers, then you can make a good residual income in the process. And the amazing thing is there are a ton of these subscription services available out there, you just need to find the one that is right for your needs.

Think about the type of customer that you currently work with, or the type of follower or reader, and see if there is some kind of subscription service that they would be able to benefit from if you offered it. Would stay at home mothers enjoy having a service that allowed them to get a meal already done each week? Would teachers enjoy educational boxes that could make planning a bit easier? There are subscription boxes for everything, but the trick is to find the one that is going to speak to your demographics so you can get the most sales.

The ultimate goal that comes with affiliate marketing is that you can take all of the hard work that you have been doing, and then turn it into a way to make a passive income. Think about how nice it will be to turn around one day and be able to make some nice income without having to work so hard, and without having to chase down customers all the time. If you follow the rules in this guidebook and use some of the options that we have talked about above, you will find that it is easier than ever to turn your affiliate marketing goals into a passive income.

Chapter 14: Email Marketing to Make Your Affiliate Links Beat Out the Competition

One of the things that we have talked about in this guidebook a bit is the idea of an email list. You can get this list from the people who come and view your website or through links and other means. An email list is an amazing thing to have because it is going to include a list of people who have shown an interest in you, and who are willing to learn more, get some deals, and be kept in contact with you.

The email list is going to be one of your best resources as you work to grow your business over time. The bigger you can get that email list, the better potential you have when it comes to sending out affiliate links and actually getting people to respond to you. And as long as you don't send out too many emails, you make the emails interesting and valuable, and you don't come off as spammy, you will be able to talk to your customers and get them to click on your links.

So, the first thing that you need to do is make sure that you create a good email list. It isn't really worth your time to send out emails if you just have ten people on them. This is another place where you will find your website can be useful. You can ask people to sign up for more useful tips, exclusive deals, and so on based on what your website is all about. Visitors to your site can decide if they would like to join your email list and you will quickly start to gain an email list once your website starts to get more followers.

If you are working with an email list, you do need to be careful. No one is interested in getting twenty emails from you each day, especially if they are just about your affiliate links. They signed up to get useful information and some special deals that they would not get anywhere else. Yes, you can promote your links on occasion, but there needs to be some value with these emails, and they need to be spaced out enough that they don't start to annoy your customers.

Working on an email campaign can be difficult, but when you work with the email list that you create, you are already going to have some customers who appreciate your advice and your recommendations and who are more likely to at least check out your affiliate links because they trust you. Before you get going with that email campaign, make sure to follow some of these great email marketing tips that will make all the difference.

Add in Links that Are Obvious

The purpose of your emails, or at least some of them, is to lead your customers back over to your affiliate link, your website, or even your product page. Without setting it up so that people will go back to the website that you want, you are not going to be able to convert them to be customers. The key to do this is pretty simple. You just need to learn how to capitalize on each time when you think that the customer may feel compelled to click. You don't want to overdo this, but make sure that there are at least a few links along the way.

Honestly, your customer is probably not going to make it to the end of your email, no matter how great it is, especially if this ends up being a long email. Their attention span is going to be incredibly short and you don't want to end up placing the affiliate link only at the end just to have them miss it because they never made it to the end of the email. Placing the link throughout the email (some experts recommend doing it in every paragraph but concentrate on placing it anywhere that it makes sense), can make it easier for your reader to click when it makes the most sense for them.

In addition, make sure that your user understands that they are looking at a link. You do not want to work so hard on the email and then have your customers go away from the email because they didn't see any links for them to click on. So add the links into the email a few times and make sure that it is easy to see the links, and you will see some more conversions.

A call to action at the end of the email can be helpful as well. After you have provided the customer with some useful and valuable information, you can then add in a call to action, one that includes your affiliate link, for them to click on and check out the item and the solution to their problem. If you wrote some good copy in the email, it is going to be easier to convince them to make the purchase because they feel like they need it.

Don't Add Too Many Images

While some people like to add in a ton of images to their emails, this is not always the best option to go with. Many of your recipients may not even see the images because of the way their emails are set up, so this can be a waste of time and effort in the first place. And you should never send an email that has just one image or adds in messaging to your image to the customer because they may miss it inside of the email.

This doesn't mean that you can't go through and add in a few images to the email. This can make the work that you are doing more visually appealing and ensures that you keep the attention of the people you are sending the email to. With that said, you do need to be careful about how many images you are adding in. If the majority of the email is full of images with just a bit of text implemented in between, you will find that the email is hard to read through, slow to load, and many people will close out of it before they can even read it.

Also, when you are adding pictures, remember that a lot of the people who will receive your emails are going to do it through their mobile devices. The world of technology is changing, and we no longer just look at information on a computer or a laptop. Making sure that the content and the visuals that you have on your page can work no matter what device they decide to use to look at your emails and information.

Make It Easy for the Customer to Unsubscribe

This may not make much sense as a beginner (why would you want your customer to be able to stop seeing your emails), but it is actually much better than some of the other options. There are times when the user will get tired of seeing your emails or decide that they do not want to follow you any longer. If they become frustrated by trying to learn how to get removed from your email list, they will just go to their email provider and mark you as spam. Each time a user goes in and notes your emails as spam, it will count against your reputation, meaning that over time, your emails will start to show up in the junk folder rather than into inboxes.

This can obviously cause some issues. If your users are not able to see your information, they are going to miss out on your information. You may not want to have the unsubscribe button but make it easy to see so that when customers really don't want your services, they can just opt out of them rather than harming your reputation.

Make the Text Easy to Read

Remember that when you send out an email, you are sending it out to someone who will see this information on a computer or on their phones. Writing out a ton of text onto each paragraph is going to be hard on the eyes and can be tedious to handle. This means that you need to work on making your text as readable as possible.

First, make sure that your paragraphs are as short as possible. Keeping them to a line or two is usually the best bet. You need to make sure that there are some subheadings with the key points, you use some bullet points, and it is easy for your customer to find out the information that they need. While adding a lot of text is a great option when you are working on your website, this is going to make your customers to delete your emails and they may even send you to their spam filters.

Remember that you are sending out emails here, and the screens for each thing that you are doing can vary. Some people may even be reading your content on their phones and other mobile devices. This means that if the paragraphs are long and hard to get through, and the sentences go on for too long, it is going to be really hard for them to read, and they are most likely going to give up completely.

The best rule to follow here is to stick with about two to three short sentences for each paragraph. This may not be the way that you are used to writing out your paragraphs in other documents, but it makes it much easier on the eyes and can allow the customer or potential customer to actually see what you are sending to them.

Be Careful of How Many Times You Send Emails

As a beginner to affiliate marketing, you are probably really excited to share your information and your links with your potential customers. You see that a few people have agreed to join your email list and want to hear from you, and you are ready to get going. But the problem that some beginners will deal with is that they get so excited that they want to send out every thought and every link right away.

Your customers agreed to hear updates and important news and deals from you, not be harassed by you. You should only be sending out emails and information when it is something special. That means if you have already sent out an email to your list today, it is probably not a good idea to send out another one. Keeping yourself limited, perhaps to one consistent and regular email a week, can ensure that your customers don't get mad and annoyed with you, and makes it easier for you to not end up on the spam list.

The spam list is the worst place for you to be when you are growing your business. When you end up on the spam list, then this alerts the email providers that someone sees you as bothersome and as spam. When too many people do this, you are going to get blocked and then no one will be able to read the emails you send out anyway. Keeping your emails important and only sending them out when needed can be important to ensuring that your customers actually get the information that you are sending out.

Your email campaign can be a very important part of growing your online affiliate market. The people on your list are those who have already agreed to hear from you, and who have shown some interest in getting deals and more from you. If you are able to provide them with some extra value that no one else can get, then you are going to do just fine with this email campaign.

Chapter 15: Tips and Tricks to Get the Most Out of Affiliate Marketing

Now that we have spent some time looking at affiliate marketing and all of the cool things that you can do with it, it is time to explore a few of the tips and tricks that you can use in order to get the most out of your own links. There is so much competition out there for this kind of business, but this also means that there are a lot of opportunities that you can enjoy as well.

Affiliate marketing can seem scary and confusing and like a lot of work to someone who is a beginner. And it does take some time and work to make it a reality. But if you are able to go through the different tips that we have talked about in this guidebook, and if you are able to find a way to stand out from the crowd and the competition, and provide a good product to your customers, you are going to be able to see a ton of results in no time.

This chapter is going to take some time to focus on affiliate marketing and some of the tips that you can follow to get the most out of your work with this online money-making tool. Some of the best tips and tricks to try with affiliate marketing include:

1. Knowing what your audience likes: You can find the best product in the world to sell, one that seems really neat and can provide you with a good amount of commission, but if it has nothing to do with your audience and it won't benefit them in some way, then you are never going to make a sale at all. It is your job to know your customers and your audience. You need to know what their wants and needs are, what they struggle with, and what would make the lives of your audience easier. Once you are able to figure all of this out, you will find that it is easier to find the right product for your readers and then you can make the commissions that you want.

2. Actually, trying out the product: As you are picking out products that you would like to affiliate with, take the time to order one. This gives you the full experience into what it will be like for one of your followers or readers to get the product. You can test out the product and see if it actually works. You can see how long the shipping time was. You can talk to customer service and see how easy it is for customers to contact that company. If there are some major problems that come with ordering the product or the company in particular, then you should pick out a different product to sell instead.

3. Remember to work with some SEO: If you are working with a website or a blog, then you should consider working with SEO. Just because you make a website, or a blog doesn't mean that it is going to show up in search engine results. It would be nice if it would do that, but because of all the other websites and blogs that are out there, it is going to be almost impossible to get your website ranked in search engine results without working with SEO.

- SEO is search engine optimization. This is going to help you to reach a bigger audience. You can look at your page, and each article, and decide which keywords are the most important, the ones that potential readers would type into the search bar when they were looking for your website or the information that you provide.

- You want to be selective with the keywords that you choose to go with. If you choose too many, it is going to get expensive and be hard to rank. You want to find as many keywords that work with your particular website or blog, ones that have a high number of people looking for that information overall, and a low amount of competition. If you can find even one or two keywords that meet this requirement, you will be well on your way to ranking.

- Google Analytics and Google Keyword Planner can make this easier. It can provide you with all of this information so you can actually plan out the keywords that you would like to have on your website. You can choose how much you want to spend or bid to get these ranked as well, helping to increase your ranking and make sure that the right customers see your information.

4. Have more than one source for affiliates: It is usually a good idea to have a few different locations online where you are promoting the products that you want to sell. If you just focus on a website or just on social media, then you are going to find that you are missing out on a lot of the customers you could be reaching. Many successful affiliate marketers are going to focus on at least two different options, and in the beginning, this may be all that you are able to handle because that is a ton of work.

- Make sure that your plan includes at least two different places where you will promote yourself. You may choose to promote on your website and Facebook for example. Make sure that your plan also has room for you to expand to other areas later on once your resources and your time free up later.

5. Picking out some high-quality products: There are a lot of different products out there that you can choose from. But just because the product seems to be perfect for your audience doesn't mean that it is high quality. You want to go with a company that is reliable, and one that will always provide you with products that you can trust.

- This is one of the reasons why you want to test out the product ahead of time. Your reputation is going to be on the line in this situation as well. If you promote a product that is low quality, one that doesn't work, or you pick out a company that is horrible with customer service, it is going to be your reputation that gets ruined, and you will run into a lot of trouble promoting anything else in the future.

6. Remember that this does take time: One of the reasons that a lot of people give up on affiliate marketing is because they assume that they should be able to just do some work for a few weeks and then the money should start rolling in. While this is a nice idea to have, it is not realistic. And the fact that there are a ton of scammers out there who just

want to take your money after a bunch of promises doesn't really help the situation all that much anyway.

- If you are getting into affiliate marketing, realize that it may take up to six months or more of hard work before you are able to see all of the results that you would like. This doesn't mean that you won't be able to see results in the process. It simply means that you may only see a bit of profit until you put in the work and get to that point. Over time, with consistency and some hard work, you will see your profits grow and you will be glad that you stock with the hard work.

7. Be careful of the scammers: There are a ton of people out there who are looking for ways to make money. They want to be able to quite their normal day job and just work from home on their own schedule. Because of all this desire, there are a lot of scammers out there who are more than willing to take your money, after giving some big promises, and then running away. There are a lot of great affiliate marketing companies out there to work with, but then there are a lot of scammers out there as well. If it sounds too good to be true, then it probably should.

- If you are going through and the company is making big claims that you will be able to make thousands of dollars in a few weeks, then this is a sign that you should run away. If they say that you will only need to work for half an hour a day, or an hour a week, or some other silly claim like that, then it is time to look the other way as well. These companies are simply looking to part you with your money, and as soon as they have it, they will run away, and you will never be able to get ahold of them again.

- In addition, reputable affiliate marketing companies are not going to ask you for any money to start. They may ask for a bank or PayPal account, but this is so they can pay you once you get some referrals on your link. If a company is asking for this information because they want to charge you, that is a big sign that they are fake, and you should look somewhere else.

8. Doing link building is essential. Whether it is done through a natural link earning due to the quality of the content (always to be pursued) or with "a little more commercial" methods, so to speak, it remains a central issue. But we need to know how to get links without forcing the hand. Of course, you can proceed with great caution with link building only when the brand and the natural mentions (without link or link "branded") to the site are beginning to be evident. When you start having direct traffic or organic traffic for your brand key (ex. In our case "Bee Social"), then even the reception of incoming links becomes credible even for Google.

9. Before inserting affiliate links, test the yield of your page with Shortner URL (bitly or Google Shortner): open affiliate accounts, enter information, get approvals, etc., takes time. It makes sense to go step by step and test how many clicks generate the links that you put on your page with URL Shortner that count the number of clicks of users. It's

also a good way to do A/B testing and understand the most "profitable" positions and clicks on your pages.

10. A very valid tool is Social Networks. If you have a lot of followers and loyal fans or followers ready to click on what you are proposing, then the game is made—especially in subjects that are very suitable for social media, such as the world of animals. In fact, it does not matter where your visitors come from (whether from Google or from Social): what counts is how many they are and if they click. However, the click depends on how authoritative you are. A good ranking on Google or 100,000 fans (random numb. Unless you cannot position yourself in the very first search engine organic results, it must be a product, service, or action rewarded with wide margins. Read: the commission must be high. Because with a little effort, even if you're not in the best positions in SERP, you will be able to position yourself decently with long tail search keys, obtaining few results but well rewarded. If you do not get large margins from each commission, then you will need to generate a lot of traffic and focus on quantity, of course.

11. If you can find a niche topic that catches the interest of many audiences and makes them buy your product or service, then you will have more chances of getting clicks (and, therefore, commissions—by a large margin, maybe). Main topics, with widespread affiliate programs and high advertising interests such as online insurances, forex, and similar issues, are very well guarded by affiliation professionals. Here, you have to be very "armored" on the SEO side and be able to have important investments.

These are a few of the tips that you can follow when it comes to seeing success with affiliate marketing. It is going to be something that you do have to put some work in order to see the results that you are looking for. It isn't going to be something that you can accomplish overnight, and you must realize that it will take at least a few months before you really start to see the results. But if you can maintain the hard work that you are doing and you make sure that you don't give up because you aren't seeing results right away, you will be able to reach customers and make sales in no time.

Conclusion

Thanks for making it through to the end of *Affiliate Marketing Playbook 2019*, let's hope it was informative and able to provide you with all of the tools you need to achieve your goals whatever they may be.

The next step is to get started with some of the tips that we talked about in this guidebook and use it to grow your affiliate marketing campaign in no time. This guidebook spent some time talking about affiliate marketing and why it is such a good way to make money at home in your free time. In addition, we also took a look at some of the places you can start affiliate marketing, and not just on your own website, the things that you should avoid when you want to be an affiliate marketer, and other things to consider when it comes to making your own affiliate marketing goals work for you.

There are a lot of different methods that you can use in order to make money online with affiliate marketing and to see the results that you are looking for. When you are ready to start your own affiliate marketing business and see it grow, make sure to check out this guidebook to learn all the tips, tricks, and the information that is needed to make this business successful for you.

Finally, if you found this book useful in any way, a review is always appreciated!

Amazon FBA E-commerce Business Model $10,000/mo Ultimate Guide

Foolproof step-by-step method for beginners to create your E-commerce that Generate Passive Income almost in Autopilot

By

Steven Sparrow

Chapter 1: What is Amazon FBA?

Imagine this scenario. You've done your market research, get your products, and have two hot items listed on Amazon, all recording massive sales. Your business is gaining momentum and surging forward. As a smart entrepreneur, at this point, you will probably begin to consider increasing your stock so you can maximize your profit, but one problem you may face is the issue of a store to accommodate extra shares. There is also a chance you may find it hard to maintain your fast delivery records with more stocks.

Does this mean you should bin your hope of expansion? No, not at all. This is where Amazon FBA comes in.

FBA stands for Fulfillment by Amazon. It is a program that lets you, as an online seller, make use of Amazon's many considerable warehouses to store and ship the products you sell through the Amazon website. It is one of two major fulfillment options offered by Amazon to sellers on their platform. The other is known as Fulfillment by Merchant (FBM)—a program by which the seller (you) handles packing and shipping of orders directly to customers. FBM sellers only make use of Amazon to reach potential consumers and generate demand.

Fulfillment by Amazon, on the other hand, basically involves sending your products to an Amazon fulfillment center. These products are then stored in warehouses. When a customer places an order for one of the products, Amazon physically picks, packages, ships and tracks the order for you. They also take charge of returns and refunds. This makes the burden off you and gives you more flexibility in your selling practices.

The FBA program is so streamlined yet powerful that when customers buy your product from Amazon; they will not know that they are purchasing from a third-party seller using Amazon FBA! They will think they are buying directly from Amazon. It is difficult for them to realize any difference between purchasing from a seller through Amazon FBA and from Amazon straight. They will see similar delivery options, the same return and refund policy, and the same stellar 24/7 level of service. Your product will also have access to one of the largest and most advanced fulfillment networks in the world without having to spend thousands of dollars on storage facilities and staff.

As an Amazon seller, the FBA offers a very profitable solution, and can certainly take off your neck, a lot of time-consuming tasks. Amazon sums up FBA pretty well in Seller Central: "You sell it, we ship it."However, the solution is not a magic bullet, and it requires a concerted effort to get started.

Vital Stats to put in mind

As online shopping becomes increasingly popular, more and more people are turning to Amazon for everything – from purchasing seasonal gifts to everyday groceries.

Since launching in 1995, Amazon has transformed the way and manner the global retail industry operates. Similar to the familiarity between the word "search," and "Google," "Amazon" has become the face of "online shopping," and no one can dispute that.

It has given online users access to different products in less the amount of time they would take or spend on a physical store or a mall. Despite its many features, Amazon continues to scale by incorporating advanced features, acquisitions, products, and services. The company is not only doing an excellent job but also excelling in all angles, setting a massive benchmark for other brands out there. And thanks to the brand's remarkable reputation across the world, its customer base continues to grow every year to accommodate as many audiences as possible.

Amazon is reputable for concealing its customer tallies and entire sales figures from public scrutiny. This points to how massive and enlivened the Amazon Marketplace is. The statistics can also come handy if you're looking to make some critical decisions with regards to your Amazon store.

The statistics listed here will give you a clear overview of Amazon's size, usage, and fame throughout the world.

So, let's get started.

Amazon Seller Statistics

Amazon is, by a large margin, the most visited eCommerce platform in the world.

During February 2020, Amazon.com had over 2.01 billion visits (both desktop and mobile). This is a reduction from 2.73 billion trips in December 2019.

As of 2019, Amazon has over 2.5 million active sellers offering different products on the platform. Among these sellers, an estimated 25,000 Amazon sellers make over $1 million worth sales, and 200,000 Amazon sellers make over $100,000 worth sales.

Amazon.com, on its own, has over 300 million active users.

According to Tech Crunch, Amazon takes an estimated 49% of the total eCommerce market share in the U.S.

Amazon currently operates at 13 different countries worldwide.

Homeowners constitute about 80% of shoppers on Amazon.

Females take up about 51.1% of shoppers on Amazon, of which 45.9% of them are married.

Millennials are the biggest customers out of all the generation of users on Amazon. They spend and use twice the amount of time and money Baby boomers spend on the platform.

Over 300,000 third-party sellers began selling on Amazon in 2017.

Over 140,000 third-party sellers have exceeded $100,000 in their annual sales.

Amazon recorded total revenue of $42.75 billion from third-party sellers in 2018 and $31.88 billion in 2017.

According to Statista, third-party sellers on Amazon sold 54% of their units in Q2 2019.

Revenues from retail Product sales, seller-service, and Amazon Web Services account for some of Amazon's revenue segments.

60% of the best-sellers focus on selling products from the Home & Kitchen category.

According to Statista, in March 2019, Amazon app ranks as the most popular shopping app in the U.S. with 145.2 million active mobile users.

According to the 2019 Statista reports, there are approximately 103 million Amazon Prime subscribers in the U.S. alone, which has increased by 95 million from June 2018. Only FBA brands are accessible to Prime buyers.

According to Statista's survey in February 2019, 20% of Amazon prime users shopped on Amazon every week, whereas 7% claimed they made purchases almost every day.

Prime subscribers average more spending on Amazon than the regular Amazon customers. The average Prime users spend an estimated $1,300 per year on Amazon, while the typical customer averages $700 per year.

Amazon Product Statistics

There are over 12 million products, media, and services featured on Amazon.

As of April 2019, Amazon.com has 119,928,851 products in total on its listing.

According to a survey of 2000+ American customers conducted by Feedvisor, 89% of online buyers are more likely to trust Amazon to purchase their goods than any other online marketplace.

Jewelry, shoes, and clothing make a combined revenue of 33.4 million.

In 2018, over 11.1 million home improvement tools were sold.

Each year, Amazon records approximately 64 million Home & Kitchen products.

Books are by far the most extensive product category on Amazon. There are over 44.2 million products in the group.

The most popular product categories amongst Amazon Prime subscribers in the U.S. are home improvement, apparel, electronics, and kitchen goods.

A CNBC report reveals that Amazon recorded over 100 million product sales during its Prime day sale in 2018.

Based on an official report released by Amazon, SMBs (Small & Medium Businesses) record an average of over 4000 products sales per minute.

23% of online shoppers visit Amazon when they want to make a purchase but are confident of a specific product.

Amazon Net Sales: Yearly

- In 1995, Amazon recorded a total net sales of 511,000 million U.S. dollars.
- In 1996, Amazon recorded a total net sales of 15.7 million U.S. dollars.
- In 1997, Amazon recorded a total net sales of 147.8 million U.S. dollars.
- In 1998, Amazon recorded a total net sales of 609 million U.S. dollars.
- In 1999, Amazon recorded a total net sales of 1.6 billion U.S. dollars.
- In 2000, Amazon recorded a total net sales of 2.7 billion U.S. dollars.
- In 2001, Amazon recorded a total net sales of 3.1 billion U.S. dollars.
- In 2002, Amazon recorded a total net sales of 3.9 billion U.S. dollars.
- In 2003, Amazon recorded a total net sales of 5.2 billion U.S. dollars.
- In 2004, Amazon recorded a total net sales of 6.9 billion U.S. dollars.
- In 2005, Amazon recorded a total net sales of 8.5 billion U.S. dollars.
- In 2006, Amazon recorded a total net sales of 10.7 billion U.S. dollars.
- In 2007, Amazon recorded a total net sales of 14.8 billion U.S. dollars.
- In 2008, Amazon recorded a total net sales of 19.1 billion U.S. dollars.
- In 2009, Amazon recorded a total net sales of 24.5 billion U.S. dollars.
- In 2010, Amazon recorded a total net sales of 34.2 billion U.S. dollars.
- In 2011, Amazon recorded a total net sales of 48 billion U.S. dollars.
- In 2012, Amazon recorded a total net sales of 61.09 billion U.S. dollars.
- In 2013, Amazon recorded a total net sales of 74.75 billion U.S. dollars.
- In 2014, Amazon recorded a total net sales of 88.99 billion U.S. dollars.
- In 2015, Amazon recorded a total net sales of 107 billion U.S. dollars.
- In 2016, Amazon recorded a total net sales of 136 billion U.S. dollars.
- In 2017, Amazon recorded a total net sales of 177.9 billion U.S. dollars.
- In 2018, Amazon recorded a total net sales of 232.9 billion U.S. dollars.
- In 2019, Amazon recorded a total net sales of 280.5 billion U.S. dollars.

Amazon FBA Statistics

According to a report published by Statista, FBA users make up 73% of Amazon sellers in the United States. The results vary according to the size of the sale. For merchants with purchases above 1 million dollars, only 10 percent use the services for all articles, 12 percent do not. They are putting all the traders into consideration, almost half of traders who use FBA for between 70 and 100 percent of all orders.

Prime users spend about $1300 every year. This means that you will likely gain more visibility and sales with Prime buyers when you use Amazon FBA.

Amazon makes use of the FIFO (First In, First Out) model to estimate the charges for storing your products in its warehouse.

When FBA was launched in Australia at the end of February 2018, it had a 33% adoption rate relative to other popular marketplace sellers by the end of the year.

How Amazon FBA Works

Amazon takes control of all the hard work for you within FBA, so the way it works is pretty straightforward. Here is a step-by-step guide on how Amazon FBA works:

> **You send your product to the Amazon warehouse.**

Amazon has around 100 warehouses across the United States, many of which are over a million square feet. You inform them about the products you're sending and tell you which warehouses to send the products to.

> **Amazon sorts and stores your products.**

Once your products are received in any of the Amazon warehouses, they will be sorted and added to the inventory. The products are then stored safely in the warehouses. If any of the products get damaged by chance in the warehouse, you will be reimbursed fully by Amazon.

> **Amazon takes care of your orders.**

Once a customer places an order for your product, Amazon takes control of the entire transaction for you. They accept payment on your behalf and automatically update your inventory.

> **Amazon ships your product.**

The ordered product is picked from the storage by one of Amazon's warehouse workers or robots. The product is packed into a box and shipped to the customer.

> **Amazon takes care of customer service.**

Once the product is delivered to the customer, Amazon follows up to ensure the client is satisfied with the shipment. Amazon also takes control of returns or questions from the customer. However, you're to take charge of responding and taking actions on the feedback you receive on your product listing.

> **Amazon pays you**

Every two weeks, Amazon adds up all your sales, deducts your seller fees, and pays your profits directly into your bank account.

Benefits of Using Fulfillment by Amazon (FBA)

The FBA program allows you to grow whatever business you do and lets you get your products in front of millions of potential customers. Amazon has a legion of loyal shoppers, which can translate to increased sales for you. Some of the top benefits of using Fulfillment by Amazon include:

1. Simple logistics and shipping.

Managing your fulfillment can be challenging, especially if you're a newbie. It can take up a large chunk of your time and yet still bring forth loss. It can even get worse when you start receiving more orders as this would mean spending more time packing and shipping, or more money hiring more employees for the job. FBA makes room for outsourcing to Amazon while taking advantage of their experience and expertise.

2. Reduced shipping prices.

Amazon makes use of major shipping companies that give them steep discounts on shipping costs. As an FBA user, you will enjoy those discounts in the form of subsidized shipping rates when shipping your inventory to Amazon. You will be paying less in shipping than if the items were being sent from your individual's account. You can also take advantage of the free shipping if any of your orders fall into the Amazon's open super saver shipping category. And most importantly, Amazon offers Prime members free two-day shipping on all FBA products – a huge incentive that can translate to higher sales for FBA businesses.

3. Management of returns.

Managing and processing returns can be a pain in the ass for many business owners. But with FBA, you transfer all the entire processes to Amazon, from handling all of the administrative issues to dealing with unsatisfied customers and overseeing returns and refunds. Amazon also takes charge of attending to customer inquiries, reversing logistics, and returning shipping labels. Though you get charged to enjoy all these, you'll agree with us that the price is far less than the amount of work they take off your shoulders.

4. Excellent Customer service management.

If there's one thing Amazon is well known for, it's its fantastic customer service that continues to get better each year. By registering as an FBA business, Amazon completely takes over your customer service management, easing the stress of attending to a series of inquiries and complaints. One great benefit is that they continue to attend to your customers even while you're asleep, thanks to their 24/7 support services.

5. Fast delivery.

Amazon boasts of hundreds of fulfillment centers around the globe. This means your products can be comfortably delivered to your customers within a short period no matter where they are located. Once a shopper places an order, Amazon automatically figures out which fulfillment center is nearest to the shopper and ships it there.

6. Shipping Standardization

Amazon handles and processes all FBA orders precisely the same way it treats its merchandise. This implies that when a buyer orders for your item, Amazon will pick the item from their inventory, pack it, and ship it to the buyer. However, you can feature a product on your website, and, through the FBA service, still have Amazon take control of all of the heavy lifting.

7. Earn Consumers' Trust

Amazon is an average American's delight. Americans don't just love the company; they trust it. They know that whatever they order with two-day shipping, they can sleep soundly knowing that they will receive their orders in 48 hours. When you join FBA as a seller, your product listings will prominently display "Fulfilled by Amazon" for all shoppers to see. Buyers appreciate this quality, making them more likely to patronize you. Potential consumers, who expect excellent customer service, will trust you. Shoppers will automatically trust you more, thus increasing your sales.

8. Potentially unlimited storage space.

FBA gives you access to unlimited storage space for your products. This relieves off you the worry of the size of storage space you need for your products. You don't also have to worry about paying for a warehouse, as it is taken care of by Amazon. The good thing is that there is no minimum amount of inventory you can send so that you can send in as little as one product without any issue. And if your list performs excellently well and your products sell quickly, Amazon will give you unlimited storage.

9. Fulfillment of orders from other channels.

The FBA shipping app lets you automate Amazon's Multi-Channel Fulfillment (MCF) service, which allows you to handle and ship inventory that is being sold on other channels (e.g., BigCommerce) while still getting Amazon to fulfill those orders. The service automatically delivers orders to your Amazon store from your BigCommerce store for fulfillment. It also sends data such as tracking information and order updates to your customers from your BigCommerce store.

10. More Time to Grow Your Business

With Amazon FBM, you take care of all the inventory, the labeling, packaging, the shipping, the tracking, and the customer service. If you're just starting your eCommerce business, you most likely won't have room for all of these. But with Amazon FBA, you will be handing off those responsibilities to Amazon which gives you way more time to concentrate on other things like market research, keyword research, product development, SEO, online advertising campaigns, partnerships, and more that are also vital to the growth of your business. Not putting enough time and effort into these practices may affect your business.

11. Automatic Access To Prime Audience

About two-thirds of U.S. households use Amazon Prime. Close to 85 million consumers use the premiere service. It is almost impossible for someone subscribing to Amazon Prime to buy products that aren't Prime eligible. Apart from having access to a larger volume of products, Amazon Prime users also enjoy faster delivery than other shoppers. When you use FBA, your product will carry the Prime logo, allowing your brand to use Amazon Prime to take advantage of the premier buyers. You also get the opportunity to reach new and existing customers who are looking for free one- or two-day shipping, targeted at Prime-eligible items, and only convert if the Prime badge is visible.

12. Access to the Coveted Buy Box

It has been found that 82% of Amazon desktops purchase use buy box or mobile. The buy box is seen as the white box located on the right-hand side of a product details page where the "Buy Now" and "Add to Cart" buttons are located. In short, it's where the bulk of the money is made on Amazon. The Amazon algorithm automatically determines which seller is represented in the buy box and for how long. Though the algorithm works uniquely, FBA is one of the factors Amazon likes to see within your shipping methods, so it is highly likely that you will get access to the buy box on your other product listings.

13. Increased visibility

As an FBA business, your product will gain better visibility and rank higher in the search results. Additionally, your items will be listed by price only instead of by total price (the price of the product plus shipping costs) done for non-FBA products, thus increasing your chance of being one of the first items in the search results.

14. Reduced overhead costs

As an FBA business, you don't have to bother about administration storage costs and employees. So you'll be able to concentrate on selling more products and increasing your profits!

15. Opportunity to run your business anywhere

Being an FBA seller allows you to sell your products from anywhere in the world. You can be anywhere in the world and still be generating consistent sales. Amazon will take charge and manage all your orders 24/7.

16. Ease of Use

One of the most significant benefits of FBA is its overall ease of use. If you've been spending way too long elbow deep in dealing with customer complaints, spending hours in post office queues or in preparing deliveries, imagine never having to touch a product, dispatch order, or deal with a return ever again. This is what FBA offers you. FBA allows you all the essential time you need to focus on other crucial aspects of your business, such as creating brand awareness and sourcing new inventory.

Disadvantages of Using Fulfillment by Amazon (FBA)

These benefits are indeed fantastic, even perhaps too good to be real! But is FBA without any disadvantages? Amazon, undoubtedly, has an intimidating reputation and so it would be easy to think that their FBA service is perfect for all businesses. However, this is not entirely the case. Amazon FBA isn't a celestial bounty of warm hugs and good times. Though Amazon FBA is an excellent resource for any business, it is not without its drawbacks. Having explored the many benefits, it's only right that potential disadvantages are highlighted so those intending users can make informed decisions.

1. FBA is expensive.

As you may have noticed from previous sections, Amazon FBA costs money. Amazon charges a lot of fees for its FBA service, including storage fees and fulfillment fees, and these costs can run pretty high. Vendors also have to pay removal fees for damaged and defective inventory as well as disposal prices to get rid of unsellable products. Although firmly believe that these costs are ultimately worth it, we understand that your business may not be in a position to take them on alongside other vital expenses like marketing and manufacturing, especially if you're just starting your business. Moreover, these fees can pile up quickly, particularly with oversized or slow-moving products. You may need to understand how instantly your inventory moves in; you intend to reduce storage fees. It may also take some extra cautioning to ensure your products remain profitable after paying all these fees. You'll need to ensure that your products are still cost-effective after taking into account your FBA fees.

2. Long-term storage fees.

Storage fees are reasonable since Amazon would be storing your products on your behalf. However, if your items sit for over six months, you incur long-term storage fees, which may affect your profitability. Amazon deals with selling products, not storing them. So they make sure you pay sky-high storage fees if you let your inventory sit too long.

3. Risk of increased returns

Amazon takes over the major business processes, including ensuring seamless and easy returns. One drawback to such an arrangement is that buyers are likely to make more returns without a concrete basis. This issue can be managed in some way by always ensuring you supply only quality products, and your customers do not feel the need to seek returns when they receive their orders. However, there will still be those buyers who do impulse and test buys, have buyer remorse and return an item. Amazon's simple return policy FBA does make it easy for this to occur. There's also the possibility that Amazon might deem a returned product unsellable, and you may have to incur extra cost for the product to be removed from your inventory. This should not necessarily discourage you from using FBA, but you should prepare your mind for such situations.

4. Prepping your product for Amazon FBA can be tricky.

Amazon has strict guidelines when it comes to preparing and shipping items to their warehouses. Apart from correctly entering all details into Amazon's database, the products must be properly labeled before being shipped to the right warehouses. Failure to follow all the guidelines may lead to your inventory being rejected at the warehouse leading to frustration and delays, not to talk of the extra work. The truth is following all of the instructions isn't that easy and may take some practice to get used to if you're just getting started.

5. Tracking inventory can be hard.

You may find it quite challenging to keep track of what products you have available, what items you need to order, and what is not selling when you are not the one in charge of the sales. Out of sight is out of mind. It can even be more challenging if you have to keep inventory changes in unison if you sell on multiple channels. The good thing is that apps like the ByteStand app let you automate the management of your inventory between Amazon and BigCommerce.

6. Product packaging is not branded with your logo.

Amazon sells your products using their name. This means that when a buyer receives their order, dispatched by Amazon FBA, the packaging will carry Amazon's logo. This can make it more difficult if you're aiming to establish your reputation as a brand long-term as your identity is not visible on your packaging. If brand awareness is one of your business goals, be sure to evaluate its significant a disadvantage to your business, against the many other advantages Amazon FBA offers.

7. Sales tax can be a problem.

Tax collection in the United States varies across states. Each state operates based on different rules and guidelines. While it can be pretty straightforward if your business operates in just one state, it can be a bit complicated with FBA because of the different fulfillment centers. Inventory is shuffled continuously between these fulfillment centers, making it hard for sellers to determine where to pay their sales tax. Do you only collect state sales tax for where your business is registered or situated? Or for every state where your inventory is stored? There's no straightforward answer. You can talk to tax partners to you help only and automate complex tax rules and guidelines for different regions.

8. Commingling merchandise can be scary.

Amazon offers sellers the option of commingling or pooling their products with the same products from other vendors. This is usually done to boost efficiency as the option lets you save time on labeling and preparing your products. But the problem is that your products may be pooled together with others that are counterfeit and damaged. The chances are that you will receive negative reviews or be banned from selling on Amazon if your products are reported as fake or damaged.

9. Product Handling Issues by Amazon

Like every other business, Amazon is not without its challenges. There have been complaints of inventory getting damaged or lost while in the fulfillment centers. Though Amazon takes adequate responsibility and ensures sellers are reimbursed accordingly. However, seeing some cases go undetected is common, which leads to a loss on the sellers. To avoid such issues, sellers are advised to keep adequate inventory records right from the point of shipping.

10. Precise Product Guidelines

Certain products like bubble wrapping and poly bagging fall under Amazon's particular product guidelines for ensuring the safe arrival of inventory at Amazon fulfillment centers. It is not to get precisely right if you do not have the experience. Amazon can, however, come to your rescue in this regard, but you would have to pay the preparation fee per item.

11. Lack of Control

If a lack of control and personal oversight makes you feel vulnerable, you should probably reconsider your decision to register for Amazon FBA. As an FBA business, Amazon controls most of the legwork for sales, payments, inventory, and returns. Generally, you will not know the minute details of your associated account's fulfillment and customer relations. As a result of this, you may fall victim to wrongful FBA charges, which could add to a high figure of losses. Moreover, the chances are that the likelihood of misappropriating charges will increase with an increase in yearly sales. Though Amazon has a system in place to look after these errors and refund sellers when necessary, with significant sales volume detecting all the misappropriations is almost impossible. The good thing is you're totally in charge of your profit margin and don't have to depend wholly on Amazon as you always can seek reimbursements owed to you.

Chapter 2: Steps to creating an FBA Account

Now that we have understood what Amazon FBA is all about and how it works, you probably are excited about taking advantage of this excellent opportunity to improve your earning potentials. Now that you're warmed up, let's concentrate on how to set up your FBA account. Below are seven actionable steps with plenty of practical tips on how to get your FBA account up and running.

1. Create an Amazon Seller Account

It's impossible to set up an FBA account without having an Amazon seller account. While it's possible to do this step much later, you should commit yourself to do it once and for all from the onset. Here's how:

- Log on to Amazon's official website and scroll to the bottom of the page where the page footers are situated.
- You will find the "Make Money with Us" tag on the second bold column from the left.
- Below the tag is a link labeled "Sell on Amazon."
- Click on that link and follow the instructions.

2. Choose what type of account to create - Individual or Professional.

The next step is to make an upfront decision as to which type of account you want to create. There are two options – individual or professional. Here is how both differ:

- An individual account is free. You do not have to pay any monthly subscription fee. However, the 'freeness' comes with tons of limitations. On the other hand, a professional account will cost you $39.99 every month, but the first month will be free to allow you to get your account set up. This option comes with all the premium features.

If you do not intend to take the FBA seriously, or probably you're just trying it out, then you should do just fine with the individual account. But if you're someone who wants to go into the FBA business full-time and have access to all the features, the professional account is easily your best bet.

3. Choose Your Niche

Choosing a niche is very challenging because it could determine success or failure. However, being excited about an opportunity may cause you just to want to sell everything your mind can think of. The best approach to choosing your niche includes the following steps:

- Consider the areas that you are most passionate about and list them out on a paper. These things may consist of special interests, hobbies, professional experiences, something you have done extensive research on, or read about, etc. Ideally, you can consider just anything you're comfortable with.

- Consider all of the likely products and product lines that are available in each of those areas. Make a list of those products and product lines under each of the regions you earlier listed.
- Narrow down those lists to particular niches. For instance, if you're passionate about gardening, niches such as "garden weeding tools," or "designer flower plots" may be much more suited for marketing than "gardening supplies."
- Reduce your list of niches to 3 - 5 subjects that you are familiar with. The idea is to ensure you go for products you won't have issues with coming up with advertising copy, blog posts, product listings, or podcasts. Once you narrowed down your list, proceed to the next step.

4. Research Products

This is the point, whereas they say, "the rubber hits the road." Even though the niches you chose align perfectly with your passion, offering those products to consumers is entirely different. This is why you need extensive product research to ascertain the marketability of those products or niches. Below is a detailed guide on how to conduct product research:

➢ General Product Searches

This involves conducting general searches to better understand the performance or standing of your niche in the e-commerce world. To do this, conduct random searches for products in your niche on online marketplaces like eBay, Alibaba, and even Amazon. Use Google search to see trending products in your niche and the retail outlets reputable for such products. For best results, you should go for products that fall within the range of $10 to $50 in prices as they tend to be impulse buys. This could help you turn in a reasonable volume of sales within a short period.

➢ Automated Product Searches

Tools like Similar Keyword, Jungle Scout, and Merchant Words can help you in determining the potentials of a particular product. These tools work by giving you an idea of how often the specific product you are researching appears in keyword searches. This allows you to have a sense of whether such a product is in demand or not.

In reality, the success of your product will depend on supply and demand forces. If your chosen product is in high demand, it will most likely sell at a higher price depending on the quantity available in the market. Ideally, your chosen product should be in high demand, but with less competing suppliers.

➢ Amazon Best Seller Rankings (BSR)

Though not reliable, Amazon BSR can give you an idea into which products or niches tend to attract the most buyers. However, it should not be a priority for deciding whether you sell a particular product or not. Examine the first three to five products on the BSR within your preferred niches. A higher BSR number implies that less of that specific product is selling than its competitors. On the other hand, a lower BSR number means the more of the product is selling than its competitors. If there is a vast number of products with low BSR in a particular niche, then such a niche is most likely to be extremely competitive. Ideally, you should target niches with higher BSR ranking, as they are a lot easier to break into.

Additional Tools for Market Research

There are several other exceptional tools you can use for conducting in-depth market research, which can offer insightful data and ways to interpret it. Some of the most popular and useful market research tools include:

- Jungle Scout
- AMZ Scout
- AMZ Base
- Sonar
- Watched Item (tracks items on eBay)
- Unicorn Smasher.

BONUS: Additional Product Research Tips

With the steps above, you should have been able to have a clear idea of the kind of product you will be offering for sale. Usually, you should be aiming for the next stage, but there are some tips you might want to consider if you are yet to ascertain the kind of products that suit your business objectives. Here are they:

- Stay clear of competing with products from established and highly reputable brands. Competing with the big boys will hurt your business, especially when you are just starting. You might find it impossible to match or even compete with their marketing strategies and budgets.
- Consider clearance or bulk products from retail stores. This lets you leverage established brand names to build up your business in the short-term. However, it can be challenging to keep a continuous supply of these products, so be sure not to depend entirely on such a strategy.
- You can also visit local retail stores around you to have an idea of the kind of items in demand.

By following all of the steps listed and the additional product research tips, you should be able to come up with the specific products you want to lead off.

5. FBAFees

After you have conducted your research and decide upon a specific product or product list, you will want to explore Amazon's resources to determine the type of FBA fees associated with such a product. The fees usually depend on variables such as the product's shape, weight, size, need for special handling or storage. Ideally, you should keep these fees to the barest minimum.

Below are there several categories of fees FBA businesses are subjected to:

> ## General Fulfillment Fees

These fees are typically for all FBA businesses. The general fulfillment fees are estimated based on two factors: the size of the product and the total shipping weight. Based on this, products are divided into two, namely: standard products and oversize products.

- Standard products are items shoes total shipping weight is a few pounds at most. Common examples include a tea kettle, a book, a wallet, a sweater, etc. Standard products are further divided into four sub-categories: small standard, substantial standard, larger standard, and most extensive standard.

Sub-category	Average product weight	FBA Fee
Small Standard	< 12 oz.	$2.41
Large Standard	12 oz. - 1 lb.	$3.19
Larger Standard	1 lb. - 2 lb.	$4.71
Largest Standard	2 lb. - 20 lb	$4.71 + $0.38 / lb. over 2 lb.

- Oversize products include items such as TV, microwave, large tea kettle, and so on. This category is also further sub-divided into four: small oversize, medium oversize, large oversize, and special oversize.

Sub-category	Average product weight	Long side + Girth	FBA Fee
Small Oversize	20 lb. - 70 lb	130 in.	$8.13 + $0.38 / lb. over 2 lb.
Medium Oversize	70 lb. - 150 lb.	< 130 in.	$9.44 + $0..38 / lb. over 2 lb.
Large Oversize	70 lb. to 150 lb.	< 165 in.	$73..18 + $0..79 / lb. over 90 lb.

Special Oversize	150 lb.	165 in.	.$137..32 + $0..91 / lb. over 90 lb.

How to calculate shipping weight under general FBA fees

For standard products weighing (Small standard and medium standard categories) under 1 lb. And unique oversize products (weird grouping), the product shipping weight is the sum of the product weight and the packaging weight, i.e., *shipping weight = product weight + packaging weight*.

For every other category of products, the shipping weight is the product weight or the dimensional weight (whichever is greater) plus the packaging weight, i.e., *Shipping weight = product weight (OR dimensional weight) + packaging weight*.

To calculate the dimensional weight of a product, multiply the length by the width and the height. Then divide the value by 139 i.e. *Dimensional weight = (length x width x height) / 139*.

For instance, if you're offering a lunch box that weighs 2 lb. for sale with dimensions 12 six by 6 inches. The item will be categorized as a "largest standard product" with a total dimensional weight of 3.1 lb. Since the dimensional weight is more than the product weight, Amazon will use the dimensional weight when determining the total shipping weight of your product. Consequently, a packaging weight of 0.19lb plus a dimensional weight of 3.1 lb will equal a total shipping weight of 4lb (0.19 lb + 3.1 lb). Because the product falls into the category of a "largest standard product," the general fulfillment fee equals $4.71 + ($0.38 per lb x 2 lb). The lunch box is 2 lb. more than 2 lb., thus the total shipping cost = $4.71 + ($0.38 x 2) = $5.47

  ➢ **Storage Fees**

The storage fee is simply the amount Amazon charges you for using space in its warehouse. It is calculated based on the volume of space (in cubic feet) your product occupies and is charged per month. For example, you're charged your July storage fee a week or two into June.

The good thing is that calculating the storage fee is a lot easier than the general price.

Month	Category of Products	Storage Fee
January - September	Standard Products	$0.69 per cubic ft.
	Oversize Products	$0.48 per cubic ft.
October – December	Standard Products	$2.40 per cubic ft.
	Oversize Products	$1.20 per cubic ft.

To calculate the volume of a given product (i.e., how many cubic feet it takes), divide the amount (length x height x width) by 1,728 (12 x 12 x 12). Thus, if your item measures 16 x 10 x 10 inches, the volume equals 1,600. Divide that by 1,728, and you have 0.93 cubic feet (or 64 cents).

If you notice, it is costlier to store smaller products than larger ones. According to Amazon, this can be attributed to the fact storing smaller products in the right fashion is more complicated and more expensive.

➤ **Removal Order Fees**

Removal order fees include the fees you pay to Amazon to return some (or all) of your inventory to you. The fees may also include the payment for the disposal of whatever items you haven't sold or do not intend to sell going forward. Either option is charged on a per-item basis.

Category of product	Return Fees	Disposal Fees	
Standard Product	$0.50	$0.15	
Oversize Product	$0.60	$0.30	

➤ **Miscellaneous Fees**

This category of fees includes:

i.   Unplanned preparation fee: This is the fee charged when you send an inventory to an Amazon warehouse without labeling or preparing correctly. Amazon does the fixing and charges you accordingly.

ii.   Returns processing fee: This is the fee Amazon charges in a situation in which a customer returns an ordered item that qualifies for free returns to Amazon. Amazon will, in turn, charge you a returns processing fee equivalent to your original fulfillment fee.

iii.   Long-term storage fee: This is the fee Amazon charges when your inventory stays in their warehouse for more than six months without being sold. Ideally, you should request returns if an item seems likely to remain unsold for six months. You will only be charged the removal orders fee, which is much less than the long-term storage fee.

The other kinds of fees you can expect to pay Amazon as an FBA member include:

- **Standard Seller Fees**: Amazon charges an estimated 15-18% of the product price as a seller's fee when a product is sold. How much will depend on the product? Although Amazon says they take only 15%, there are other hidden charges such as refunds that are typically not fully charged back, which increases the amount of charge a seller pays to Amazon as standard seller fees.

- **Fulfillment Fees**: The fulfillment fees are charged per unit and vary depending on whether the item is a standard size or oversized. The fees also include picking and packing, shipping and handling, product returns, and customer service.
- **Inventory Storage Fees**: These are fees Amazon charges FBA sellers every month for storing their inventories per cubic foot depending on the calendar month and daily average volume. These fees also depend on the product size category. Like we said earlier, Amazon also charges long-term storage on items that have been stored in an Amazon fulfillment center above 365 days.
- **International Shipping Fees**: Amazon has incorporated the Global Export service into its delivery option, which lets sellers deliver their inventory to customers all around the globe.

6. Establish Your Product Sourcing

After deciding on your first product and product line, it is time to establish the sourcing of your product before you can start listing and offering your products for sale. Product sourcing lets you solve the issue of what to sell. Put in mind that this step can be a long, time-consuming process as it can take a lot of time to get a reliable supplier with the highest quality of products available.

➢ Product Testing

Payless attention to this step, if you intend to sell a product, you have already made use of over and over again. However, if you want to offer generic market items for sale to cut your expenses, you should ascertain the right mix of quality products to provide to your customers. As such, you will want to test different samples of the products to ensure you are getting quality product sourcing.

➢ Search for a Supplier

Usually, the cost is the primary factor most sellers use to determine which supplier best suits their needs when sourcing for products. Below are the several different ways of finding a supplier for your products:

i. Overseas Suppliers. Many FBA business owners use suppliers outside the U.S., especially suppliers on Alibaba. This can be attributed to the fact that most of these suppliers allow bulk purchases of items at 25 percent or less than the retail market price. Moreover, getting your products from a supplier outside the U.S. lets you gain a broader profit margin.

ii. Local Trade Shows: Local trade shows allow you to meet and negotiate with industry leaders that provide the products you will be selling at a wholesale price. Trade magazines and newspapers are a quality medium to get updated about such shows in your neighborhoods.

iii. Bulk and Clearance Items from Local Retailers. This provides an excellent opportunity for short-term product sourcing.

iv.   Local manufactures. If you intend to be selling an item that is produced locally, then making use of local manufacturers is by far your best approach to sourcing your products. Moreover, they will most likely appreciate your efforts.

Irrespective of how you source your product, be sure to foster a good relationship with your suppliers, mainly if they offer additional products that might align with your more extensive customer base. The truth is, you will need more products as your FBA business expands. So be sure to establish a positive, long-term relationship with your suppliers.

> ### Research Shipping

A high shipping cost can eat deep into your profit margin irrespective of how lowly your wholesale prices are. Make sure you consider shipping costs in your overall analysis when you are choosing your supplier. It will also do you a lot of good to get yourself familiar with the several rules, taxes, and regulations guiding shipment of goods from overseas in your country.

Another factor you should factor into your decision is the shipping duration. Fast shipping can make a huge difference when it comes to items that are always in demand. Running out of stock for such things and not being able to restock it promptly is not only going to impede your sales but also hurt your reputation among your customers. Be sure to ascertain that timely shipping is another positive feature of whatever supplier you will be patronizing. Also, familiarize yourself with governmental rules and regulations that can delay shipments, so that you're able to plan and time your shipping wisely to prevent running out of stock.

> ### Ship Your Product

Once you have decided on the supplier to source your product from, you can then order and ship your first order of items. Ideally, you should ship the products to yourself before sending them to the Amazon Fulfilment Center. But if you want your expenses to reduce, you can have the items shipped directly from your supplier to the Amazon Fulfilment Center. However, be sure to abide by Amazon's specific guidelines on how to prepare and ship your orders.

7. Establish Your Brand

The next step is to establish your brand. Although this step could be carried out earlier in setting up your FBA business, it is still well in line to do it once you have received your first batch of products and are ready to offer them for sale. Establishing a great brand that is not unique but attractive to prospective customers isn't a day job. But with the steps listed below, you should be able to go through the process without much hassle.

> Naming Your Brand

Your brand name is one of your major selling points. A weak, dull, and unattractive name will discourage prospective customers from patronizing your products. As such, you must be very careful when choosing a name for your brand. For best results, do not limit your brand naming to a specific product if you intend to expand into other products later. Factor what your FBA business will look like in five years into your plans. Consider a brand name that can stay valid for several years to come. The following ideas below will help you pick a great name for your brand:

- Come up with random names. Be sure to limit your options to names that align with your broader business perspective and your long-term objectives.
- Use search engines, notably Google, to see if your choice of names is available. Online tools such as Namechck also allow you to check the best titles available for your brand.
- Factor availability of domain as well. You might love a name so much, only to find out the name that another person has used to register a domain. Your best bet is to go for brand names that are available to be used as domains.

➢ **Design Your Brand Logo**

This might be the perfect time to put your creativity into the test if you possess top-notch graphic design skills. Ideally, the logo should align with the brand name you chose. Without graphic design skills, you can leave the job to a professional graphic designer. Freelance sites like Upwork and Fiverr gives you an abundance of options to select from. For optimal results, keep the logo simple. You also want to ensure that the logo does not have too many colors and intricacies. A complicated logo speaks very little to the mind of potential customers and can be expensive to print.

➢ **Choose a Brand Theme and Tag-line**

Your brand themes and tag-lines are also some essentials you need to decide to make your brand stand out from competitors. Below is a list of 10 top company slogans to inspire you:

- Nike: "Just do it."
- Coca-Cola: "It's the real thing."
- Apple: "Think different."
- De Beers Consolidated: "A Diamond is forever."
- Cheek-Neal Coffee Company: "Good to the last drop."
- Subway: "Eat fresh."
- McDonald's: "I'm lovin' it!"
- Maybelline: "Maybe she's born with it, maybe it's ..."
- Tesco: "Every Little Helps."
- Wheaties: "The Breakfast of Champions."

For the best result, your slogan should be kept simple and concise. For instance, the De Beers iconic four-word slogan "A Diamond is forever" perfectly aligns with the brand's business goal: to nurture relationships eternally like diamonds. The slogan didn't just increase De Beers' reputation in the diamond manufacturing industry but also won AdAge's best slogan of the century in 1999.

➢ **Register your brand name and logo**

After creating your brand name and logo, it is time to set up your business as an LLC (limited liability Company) and register your brand name and logo with the U.S. Patent and Trademark Office department.

8. Start Listing Your Product

After you've successfully established the identity of your FBA and your products are with the Amazon Fulfilment Center, it is time to set up your product listing. This step requires to be very creative. You have worked very diligently at establishing up your FBA business to this stage. Make sure that you come up with product listings that will not only be attractive to your potential customers but will also avail them with plenty of information to make an informed buying decision. Your choices at this stage will determine your income level. Below are tips to guide you in making a quality decision regarding your product listing:

- **Use quality product photos**

Quality product photos that highlight the vital features of your product are of undeniable importance. Unprofessional product photos can whittle down all of the efforts you put into setting up your identity and your image. Low-quality product photos do not adequately communicate the value of your product to potential customers, because they find it hard to express the value you place in your products. While you can get professional photos from your supplier, note that the case is at all times. In case you're unable to source pictures from your supplier, hire a professional photographer to capture professional images of your products to use as product photos with your product listings.

- **Use Detailed Product Titles**

Product titles are the primary way to capture the attention of a potential customer to your product from their Amazon search. For optimal results, make sure your product titles contain clear, concise, and unique information to attract potential buyers to your product listing. One great way to get inspiration is to randomly search for similar products in your niche to get an idea of how they wrote their product titles. You can then decide on the part of the titles you feel is too much or a turn-off, and is vital to capturing attention.

- **Write Your Product Descriptions**

Your product descriptions should be succinct and clear. However, it should contain as much information as possible. Here are some tips for writing product descriptions that sell:

- Define your buyer persona: Your buyer persona is a generalized, fictional representation of your ideal customer. To create your buyer persona, consider the following questions:
  - ✓ Where do they live?
  - ✓ What is their educational background?
  - ✓ How old are they?
  - ✓ What is their gender?

- ✓ What is their marital status?
- ✓ What do they do for a living?
- ✓ What sort of personality do they have?
- ✓ What are their goals in life?
- ✓ What do they read, watch, browse, and listen to?
- ✓ What are their hobbies?
- ✓ What kind of home do they have?

- Research for templates: Read product descriptions from other vendors within your niche and different niches. Evaluate which of the stories appeal most to you. Then create a model combining the best features of the various styles.

- Choose your tone: Product descriptions can be written in different tones. Depending on what you think is most comfortable to you and your customer, the report can be friendly, lighthearted, professional, and informative. For best result, incorporate highly sensory words and actionable verbs that trigger imagination and interests.

- Highlight only the best features and benefits of your product.

- Include answers to the various questions your customers might have about your product in the description.

- Use bullet points for description listing, so it does not bore the readers.

- Incorporate bold titles and some white spaces between paragraphs when setting up your product descriptions. This makes it easy for customers to scan through the story and then focus on specific features and benefits that they are most interested in.

- Include all necessary information: When filling the Amazon's product description form, be sure to include all relevant details, including the weight, color, sizes, installation guides, expiry date, warranty, safety guide, etc. This information will not only allow intending customers to make an informed purchase but can also set your products apart from a competitor.

9. Product Marketing

Having an attractive and professional product listing may only bring you a few sales within the Amazon marketplace. You will need to incorporate aggressive marketing into your sales strategy if you want to turn over inventory and ring up sales. The idea is to bring your product to interested buyers wherever they are rather than waiting for them to visit the marketplace before finding your product. One FBA expert recommends that you need to "advertise the hell out of your product." That's necessarily the truth. Below are some of the best approaches to marketing your products:

> ### PPC Advertising

Pay Per Clicks (PPC) advertising is a cheap yet effective way to advertise your FBA products. It offers you a pretty simple and cost-effective approach to gaining a broader audience for your products. Pay per Click, in a nutshell, is a model used to drive traffic to a particular website or landing page, in which an advertiser (you in this regard) pays a publisher when the advertising link is clicked. Typically, the publisher is any of the first-tier search engines, including Google Ads, Microsoft Advertising, and Amazon Advertising. When an individual clicks on the ad link, and it brings them to your product listing page, you will pay a small fee "as a referral" to whatever PPC company your choice. The best thing about the PPC is that you are sure that every dollar you spend on your ad brings a potential customer to your product. We recommend you use Ad companies related to your product, e.g., the Amazon Ad, which lets you target only qualified buyers for an even higher ROI.

> ## Take advantage of reviews.

What other shoppers say about a particular product plays a significant role in helping a prospective buyer on the fence about buying to make an informed decision about the purchase. Product reviews are proven ways for generating organic recommendations for your products. People prefer to go for a product with great reviews. Be sure to encourage and elicit your buyers to drop their studies through your fulfillment documents anytime they make a purchase. You can also try to invite individuals to test your product at a particular discount or for free and write a review on it. The idea is to increase the credibility of your products to get more customers to patronize you. The more reviews you have for your products, the more attractive your products become potential buyers.

> ## Use Platforms such as JumpSend

JumpSend is excellent if you're looking to get more sales, improve your product rankings on Amazon organically, and increase reviews for your products. The platform works using automated email campaigns and setting up giveaways, discounts, and coupons. It lets you get your products to the more than 100k shoppers on JumpSend, which boosts sales velocity to your product and improves rankings for specific keywords that you're aiming at on Amazon.

> ## Social Media Advertising

It is only sensible to make use of social media marketing to advertise your products because it is where the vast majority of your would-be customers spend their time online. Follow the strategies below on how to incorporate social media in your marketing strategy:

- Avoid chasing your tail. Instead, focus on one platform at a time. Using all the channels at once when starting can affect the effectiveness of your social media marketing. Start with one, generate leads, build your reputation until you start getting returns from your efforts, and then expand to the next one.
- Open a page: A social media page gives your brand the visibility it needs. Make sure the page is opened using your brand name and post curated content targeted at making the page fun and exciting. The primary goal is to let more people know about your products, trust your brand, and become regular buyers.
- Use influencers: Social media influencers are individuals who have built a reputation for their knowledge and expertise in a particular niche. Influencers are great if you're looking to launch and promote your product because they usually have authority in their niches and with large followership. However, expect to be charged some bucks if

you are hoping to hire influencers to promote your product. You also have to offer them your products for free to add a review to their content.

- Try paid ads: Advertising on social media can be pretty high if you aim to target a specific interest group or demography. Paid ads let you place your product listings right in front of qualified buyers. Social media can be pretty fickle, so we do not recommend that you focus all your advertising efforts on it. In short, do not rely upon it as your only marketing strategy.

➢ **Content marketing**

While setting up your website isn't necessary when you're just beginning, content marketing can be an effective way to market your products to your customers in the long-term. Though there are different facets to content marketing, including blogging, vlogging, and podcasting, your objectives can be the same as anyone you choose. Below are some tips to help you set up your content marketing strategies for optimal results:

- Make your content informative and easy to read. You can make use of a professional writer if that would mean getting it right.
- Streamline your content to align with the best parts of your product, including its use, tips, and advantages over competing products.
- Be sure to build up the value of competing products when writing product comparison, but don't hesitate to focus on why your product is better.
- Leverage on bigger competitors by linking your content to their content and websites. This is related to what we discussed with incorporating influencers in your social media marketing. Your primary focus should be to get their followers to become fans and buyers of your product.
- Post regularly and purposefully. Bombarding your audience with daily content might not be valid. Two to three solid posts every week that are useful and relevant to their daily lives should do the trick.
- Focus more on building strong relationships with your audience rather than selling your products to them. Avoid hammering them with marketing posts all the time. Your posts should serve the best interests of your audience and let them yearn for more. Once they trust your brand, you won't even need much marketing to get them to buy your products.

➢ **Make use of Email Marketing.**

Email marketing is a powerful marketing strategy available to any online business, and you should leverage its power to get your brand off the ground. A significant key to an email marketing campaign is building an email list. Your email list contains people who already know and love your brand, your product, or both, making it relatively more comfortable for you to market your products. Below are essential tips to help you get the best of your email marketing strategies:

- Treat your email subscribers, in the same manner, you treat buyers. This is a vital approach if you are looking to build your email list successfully.

- Make sure you collect email subscriptions from existing customers.
- Make use of popup boxes, email subscription landing pages, campaigns, invitations, giveaways, promotions, drives, and incentive programs to foster email subscriptions. The more aggressive and creative you are with securing email subscriptions, the more success you will get with your email marketing campaigns.
- Provide your email list with regular updates, discount offers, tips, and new product announcements. Never leave your email list to rot.
- The content of your emails needs to align with your website content. Make sure your email content provide purposeful and useful information or service at all time. Don't disturb your customers with sales flyers. Doing that will baldy affect the reputation of your brand.

> **Use Coupons and Special Deals**

It is probably hard to see a rational shopper that would ignore a discount offer. Coupons and exclusive deals have proven to be an effective way to drive sales for a long time. You can incorporate either or both of the tools in your FBA business settings or utilize promotional sites or bargain hunter sites.

The "Amazon Buy Box"

Aside from the fact that Amazon FBA saves you a lot of time and effort, you also get the chance to fight for the "Amazon buy box." The buy box is the shopping cart that appears beside the Amazon product pages, which carries the "Add to cart" button. The majority of Amazon customers simply click on this button without even looking below, which has links to other providers who sell the same product. Amazon uses a largely secret algorithm, which decides which dealer gets the buy box advantage in the shopping cart. Nonetheless, your most important objective as an Amazon FBA seller is to fight for and win the coveted buy box

To achieve this, there are two essential factors. One, you have to qualify as a seller. This involves registering as a seller for at least 90 days. Secondly, you must have secured some sales and have exceptional reviews. Though Amazon will not notify you if you won or qualify for the buy box, you will notice it by increasing your sales.

One of the most critical criteria Amazon considers, if you are a reseller, is the price. However, winning the buy box goes beyond undercutting a competitor by a few cents, factors such as customer satisfaction, current stock, and cancellations are also considered.

If you can secure the buy box, you can easily win against a competitor offering an item at the same price. And that can broadly impact on your sales volume. As you can imagine, sellers under different product categories compete for their category's buy box status. If you are the only one offering your product, you do not have a competitor for the product listing. But still, winning the buy box will let you stand out from the competition.

Is Amazon FBA Suitable for Your Business?

Despite its many advantages and extensive coverage, Amazon FBA, like anything, isn't perfect for all businesses. If you run your business primarily as an Amazon seller, FBA presents an excellent option for you especially if you are stuck between an expanding full-time brand and a kitchen table business, as it can help you upgrade to the next level and focus on sourcing new products and generating sales, rather than becoming bogged down with time-consuming and monotonous fulfillment tasks. Using Amazon FBA can be a lucrative and worthwhile venture. Nonetheless, you need to do your homework and learn about all the relevant rules and regulations, and most importantly, understand your target market – and customers – to decide if the model works for you and your business. Your success or otherwise as an Amazon FBA business to a large extent depends on your products and business objectives. Ultimately, for a lot of Amazon sellers, Amazon FBA is an easy way to outsource many of the tasks associated with running an eCommerce business. Still, then, you must make sure the benefits outweigh the extra cost involved.

Tactics to Successfully Sell on Amazon FBA

- Start small: You don't need hundreds of products to get started on Amazon FBA. You can start with just a few products and take it from there. Beginning with a handful of products, let you quickly set up an organized, streamlined process. Once such a process is in place, scaling up to as many products as you want shouldn't be an issue.
- Research competitors to discover profitable products: A great place to start is to look at Amazon's best sellers. As a newbie, it is advisable not to enter into straight competition with the best sellers in your category, but you can take a look at the best sellers to get an idea of the kinds of products in demand. Then plug those products into a service like Unicorn Smasher or AMZ Scout to understand various types of juicy data such as the estimated volume of sales, competitor Intel, and fee calculators.
- Being careful of the kinds of products you sell is essential: Consider the sales rank. High ranking items sell quickly, but there's a lot more competition. On the other hand, low ranking items can be slower to sell and, hence, have a higher likelihood of resulting in long-term storage fees. However, due to the limited competition for those listing categories, it's easier to become the dominant seller. The truth is knowing the sales rank lets you know what you're really up against.
- Build a brand: If you want your business to stand out from the multitude of sellers on Amazon, you'll need your unique brand. This involves having in-depth knowledge about your target market, positioning your brand to prospective buyers, and creating attractive product titles, images, and descriptions. Set up your online store to streamline the customer experience to complement Amazon sales. You can also make use of unique packaging and inserts to ensure your brand personality stands out upon delivery. Proper packaging is also a good starting point if you're looking to get your customers to sign up for your email list or follow your social accounts.
- Try bundling products: It can be challenging to win the buy box if you're competing against hundreds of sellers on the same listing. A proven way to get around this is to

create a new bundled listing. For instance, you can combine a popular board game with an extra dice bag. This allows you to create a specialized listing that still pops up when buyers search for the main product. You get more sales as there's no competition and you can charge more since you're offering extras.

- Incorporate good SEO practices: There are thousands of sellers on Amazon, so it can be a challenge to get your products in front of prospective buyers. Similar to Google, however, Amazon puts different factors into account when determining which products come up for any given product search. By incorporating good SEO practices through keywords research, you can improve your ranking in the search results.

- Use quality product photos: One of the critical requirements for FBA sellers is the use of product image that displays only the product (no people, text, etc.) against a white background. Sellers are also allowed to add as many as eight more photos (depending on the product category). Since your product image is the first thing a prospective buyer will see, be sure to use only quality and detailed photos. Ideally, let the pictures highlight the different parts of the products from different angles, show close-ups of various features, explain the products in action, and show a person holding it for scale. If possible, create 360-degree images and videos to make your product pages more attractive.

- Optimize your product titles: Ever notice how most products listed on Amazon have long, detailed titles? Well, that's sellers attempting to stuff their keywords in. Amazon allows as much as 250 characters for titles, but that doesn't mean you've to use all the 250 characters. Amazon's algorithms don't favor product listings with excessively long titles. So your objective should be to be as descriptive and straight to the point as you can while still inserting your main keyword optimally into the title. For the best result, consider following this format: Brand name, product name, essential features like color, weight, or size.

- Optimize your bullet points: One of the major highlights of your product listing is your bullet points. A lot of buyers go straight to them whenever they find they click through a particular product. If those bullets don't contain the details they need or don't answer their questions, they're likely to bounce. So be sure to include all necessary information in your bullet points. Provide answers to popular questions, and ensure your product's benefits are well highlighted. Like we said earlier with titles, you do not want to go overboard when highlighting all these points.

- Create a detailed product description: If you are the type of person that hates boundaries, this is your chance to go overboard. Your product description can contain as many instructions as possible. You can also add as many product photos as you want and even throw in a few videos. Some sellers also use the opportunity to tell their brand stories; you can consider that too. Use the chance to say to your customers all the essential details so they can know precisely what they are getting by purchasing your product.

- Take advantage of the question and answer section: The question and answer section is one of the features you should take full advantage of. The feature allows anyone to submit random questions about a product, whether they've purchased it or not, and anyone to provide an answer, whether they've bought the product or not. You should not wait for customers to post questions before you answer them. Getting the ball rolling yourself even increases your engagement. You can ask a friend to post a subject that's likely to be asked about your product. Then you can provide the answer, so prospective customers can see that you're a helpful seller.

- Get reviews: If you are unable to do anything on this list, make sure you do this. It's a no-brainer that the average customer prefers to buy products that have positive reviews that those with zero or negative reviews. When people have doubts about something, they resort to looking for other people's opinions. If 50 buyers say Product A is excellent, and no one's saying anything about Product B, even though it's cheaper, guess which one people are going to buy?

- Select the right repricing program: Though the lowest price doesn't guarantee to win the buy box, it is nonetheless a significant factor. Amazon lets sellers change the costs of their products as much as they want. Many sellers take advantage of this by using repricing software to change their prices throughout the day – most times in response to competition. Most sellers use rule-based repricers, but that occasionally ends up in a race to the bottom, with the risk of prices going so low that there's little or no profit remaining. Algorithmic repricers are much better due to their advanced systems and often lead to higher profits. But then, you don't have to go the automated lane if you've got only a few products for sale – you should be able to tweak the pricing manually easily.

- Consider the Amazon Marketing Services (AMS): Do you notice the "Sponsored products related to this item" section? Those are ads set up using the Amazon Marketing Services. This marketing tool lets you set up ads for your products and target them based on similar products or keywords. It also offers performance analytics so you can optimize your ads.

- Use the FBA Calculator: The FBA Calculator can help you in many ways. It provides you essential insights such as your purchase and sales price, the dimensions and weight of your product, and more. It also offers you the opportunity to optimize your profit margins by providing you with a detailed financial report. You can also consider Seller Central tools such as Inventory Event Detail and Inventory Adjustments. They can also come handy for your FBA business in different situations. You should also be consistent with checking your reports. If possible, check all the stories like that can be vital if you intend to cover every error—failure to make use of all these tools as at when due can lead to a knotty situation. Finally, do not forget that the cutoff for Amazon's reimbursements is 18 months, so if you are considering a month of data, keep this in mind.

So, is Amazon FBA worth It?

Answering these questions depends on three factors: how significant your profit margin is, how much you're shipping per month, and how niche your market is.

1. Your monthly shipping rate: To enjoy the benefits of FBA, you need to ship at least 40 items per month. If you're struggling to reach that minimum threshold, listing as an FBA business may not be worth the hassle and the numerous fees involved in preparing your inventory according to Amazon's strict guidelines. You should be better off handling those responsibilities or through a smaller fulfillment company that's cheaper and more flexible.

2. Profit margin: FBA isn't a great model for sellers with low-profit margins. If you're struggling to make much money on your sales, it's a no-brainer that FBA fees drag your margins down to zero or even negative. Although many of the fees are reasonable given that Amazon is doing a lot of things on your behalf, we think you're better off focusing on boosting your profit margins first rather than incurring more expenses in the form of fees.

3. Your niche: If you're a seller of super-niche products like vintage zines geared towards old-school Goth music fans, it's really of no point using FBA. Remember that one of the things you enjoy as an FBA user is the eligibility for Prime. If an Amazon customer is shown a list of similar products, and only a few of them are eligible for Amazon Prime, it is more likely that they will write off those that are ineligible and choose one of the eligible ones. But then, not everyone who sells '70s Goth zines use Amazon. The buyers searching for your niche product probably don't care about Prime eligibility; they will just be okay with finding what they are looking for.

If you're a vendor in a competitive market who ships tons of products every month and make sizeable profits, then yeah—FBA is an excellent investment. It's a guaranteed way to gain prospective buyers' trust, free up your schedule, and get more sales on your product details page.

Several countries rarely use the FBA service. Firstly, they do not know about it and the others because they are not willing to lose control. There is also some set that has never dealt adequately with Amazon FBA to see how enormously the program can contribute to its growth. If you've been into online trading for about ten years, then you unquestionably must have come in contact with your fulfillment strategies even before the birth of the FBA. In such regard, you may feel it is useless to change anything, even if this is an error. And you also cannot imagine that it can be more favorable to hand over the management of your business to another company. But it is the case in Amazon FBA services.

Chapter 3: Most Profitable Products

In this chapter, we're going to take an in-depth look at the most profitable products/product categories to offer on Amazon FBA. Before then, we will consider essential factors to consider before choosing a product to sell on Amazon FBA.

Factors to consider when choosing a product to sell on FBA

1. Profitability

The number one reason for joining FBA is to make more money. So, there's no point specializing in unprofitable products. Determining profitability isn't just down to selling your product for more than you bought it. You also need to factor the account seller fees, marketing costs, packaging and shipping fees, and the time you invest in all of these tasks, not to mention the tax you'll incur on your income. The key to making a profit is to know how much it will cost you to sell a particular product and then calculate your profit margin based on those numbers.

You can use SaleHoo Labs to calculate the average price that a given product is selling for on Amazon and other competing marketplaces. You can also do your market research online.

If you have excellent negotiation skills, you can leverage on that to get the best deals from your suppliers to increase your profit margins.

2. Price point

Profitability is essential, but it's not all that matters. For instance, if you managed to source an attractive shoe for $0.50 per item, and you put the price at $1.50, then you will make a good profit. However, you need to sell a lot of shoes to make a good income. That's why you should be careful when deciding your price point. Your best bet is any price between $15 and $200. Anything less than $15, and you might struggle to make enough money. On the other side, anything above $200 is difficult to sell.

We'd recommend choosing a price somewhere in the middle - around the $50 mark should be okay. That allows you enough room to pay for all of the additional expenses you have to cover, especially if you are getting the item for a great price. Your buyers also won't have to bother excessively about handing over their money.

3. Competition

The hot retail online is tempting, but it mostly doesn't end well. Often, a trendy product means a highly competitive product, and even when that is not the case, it doesn't take long for such products to be rushed by sellers. And the more saturated a market is, the lower the price, and the more difficult it is to sell in it, especially for those that are just starting.

Ideally, you should target products that have low competition, which can quickly secure a considerable portion of the market. Another option to search for a trending product or niche and offer something similar, perhaps different or better. That way, you enjoy the best of both worlds: A hot market and less direct competition.

4. Size & weight

It can be challenging to sell products like surfboards and table tennis tables on FBA because of the cost and logistics involved in getting such items to your customers, primarily if your supplier is based in a foreign country like China. As such, it's better to go for lightweight products that you can easily package and ship. The rule of thumb is that your product should weigh less than 2kg (or 4.4lbs) and should be small enough to fit in a shoebox. While large, heavy items can be profitable, the chances are that you will encounter logistical issues, and you want to prevent such as much as you can.

5. Durability

The other factor to consider before choosing your product is the durability of your product. You want to ensure you specialize in highly durable products. For instance, you don't want to run the risk of shipping handmade clay pots from Bangladesh to the United States or ordering remote control cars with lots of complex components. Though both can bring you a reasonable profit margin, they seem like too much risk.

6. Seasonality

Certain products such as Halloween costumes, Christmas trees, and Inflatable pool toys only sell at specific times of the year. While they can bring some good bucks, you're better off avoiding seasonal products, especially if you are looking to sell all year round.

Top 10 Profitable Products to Consider for your FBA business

1. Books

What better product to offer as an FBA seller than what Jeff Bezos started with when he launched Amazon back in 1994? Books! And when we talk about books, we mean the usual ones, including the books made of paper and ink, and digital ones commonly referred to as Kindle books. Interestingly, books' popularity continues to grow even several years later. Amazon successfully leveraged on this to become a giant in the online market; you can do so too.

Apart from being a highly popular niche, books also offer a huge profit margin. You can pick up books in bulk for as low as a dollar, and offer them for sale on Amazon at 1000% of their original price. While this isn't a guaranteed formula all the time and you probably should base your entire business strategy on such premise, if you are looking to maximize revenue, it most definitely deserves a spot in your list of considerations.

2. Babies' items

As long as humans are procreating and the population continues growing, the market for babies' stuff will always be in demand. And because babies don't stay the same size for a long time, they will need plenty of things. An added advantage is the low cost of most of the items. They are also durable and lightweight. This makes them excellent for storage.

Pro tip: Target first-borns because parents have shown overtime to spend more on them.

3. Kids Toys

Kids love gifts, especially toys. So selling kids' toys can be your ticket to success if you offer the right products.

Pros of Selling Kids Toys

- Toys are timeless.
- Easy to make a bulk purchase.

Cons of Selling Kids Toys

- Unfavorable competition for new entrants due to the presence of big brands

Shipping and packaging issues due to varied sizes and weight

4. Jewelry Items

Baubles, gems, precious metals, and other jewelry items are consistently in hot demand. This can be attributed to its superb store of value and durability. From watches to earrings, bracelets, pins, necklaces, and more, you're guaranteed to find jewelry for every potential customer. Moreover, the profit margin can be as much as 50% or even more. But to succeed in the niche, your marketing strategies have to be top-notch as the market is pretty saturated with a lot of sellers. You also have to be at your best regarding taking advantage of unique long-tail keywords. You will struggle to make sales if you intend to describe your items using only single generic keywords. The competition will drown you.

Pros of Selling Jewelry

- All-year-round demand
- Easy to sell
- Easy to store as they don't have much weight

Cons of Selling Jewelry

- Highly competitive
- Packaging and shipping can be stressful

5. Workout Clothing

If you have close ones that are crazy about fitness, you will understand how passionate working out can make people be. Workout clothing has been one of the top-selling niches for years, and you can easily leverage the trend. The good thing is that most of these people prefer to buy their clothing new (a used sweatpants sounds awful right? Eww!), so you can quickly increase your profit margin.

6. Electronic gadgets and Accessories

Tech is the new cool, and many people don't mind spending their last buck to buy their favorite tech gadget or accessory. Little wonder why Amazon charges sellers in this niche a lower commission fee of 8% versus 15% for most of the other categories. Another great thing about tech gadgets is that you have many choices and subsets to choose from, including a plethora of new releases now and then. The advantages are limitless!

7. TV Accessories

TV accessories are one of the best niches to consider, given the number of new video game console systems emerge every year. Many game lovers don't mind spending a vast amount on getting accessories for their choices.

Pros of Selling TV Accessories

- High-profit margin potential
- Passionate buyers
- Easy to specialize or niche down to a specific brand

Cons of Selling TV Accessories

- High prices
- Packaging and shipping can be a challenge due to varied shapes and sizes.

8. Beauty Products

Many people wish to be pampered. You could leverage that by specializing in the sales of beauty products.

Pros of Selling Beauty Products

- Accessible to ship and package
- Easy to market
- A plethora of sub-niches to choose from

Cons of Selling Beauty Products

- High competition, especially with big brands.

9. Video Games

Ever met hardcore gamers? If you haven't, you're missing out on a unique set of customers. They can spend any amount to get the best deal on video games (as well as gaming systems). Though a lucrative niche, you need to be careful if you intend to go for it as you may struggle to match deals and prices from top gaming stores like GameStop, RadioShack, etc.

Pros of Selling Video Games

- Game producers do most of the marketing for you.
- Packaging and shipping are pretty straightforward.

Cons of Selling Video Games

- Can be challenging to beat the competition
- Sourcing popular games can be tough, while less known games might not sell.

10. Women's Boutique Apparel

Not to sound cliché, but there's nothing that gets a woman excited while shopping than discovering the next best outfit! By specializing in the sale of women's apparel, you can supply what could turn out to be the next favorite among women. You also have the chance to incorporate a lot of accessories such as hats, scarves, hats, sunglasses, and more!

Pros of Selling Boutique Apparel

- Potential high returns if you can get the right supplier
- Universal appeal to women

Cons of Selling Boutique Apparel

- Buyers might prefer established brands
- Huge startup costs because you need to stock different sizes and colors of apparel.

Chapter 4: Product Listing

The truth is that every product is unique. For this reason, you may need to learn how to fill extra fields when you are listing a different product. However, this guide will attempt to cover all the primary methods for listing your product on Amazon successfully.

How to set up your product listing

Before the end of this article, you ought to be able to make your own Amazon item posting. For instance, I'll be making a posting for a water bottle, and because this is certainly not a genuine result of mine, I won't endure all the transportation arrangements.

First Step (go to 'Add a Product' or 'Add Products via Upload')

After signing into your Seller Central record, click on 'Include a Product' under the Inventory drop-down menu. (Note: You can likewise transfer items by tapping on 'Include Products through Upload.' This strategy is valuable for different sorts of things, yet If this is your first posting, the spreadsheets in question might overpower you.)

Second Step (go to 'Create a new product listing')

On the 'Add a Product page,' you may browse three techniques. To begin with, you can include an item that is as of now on Amazon. You can do this via scanning for the item by name or item ID. Second, you can tap on "Make another item posting" just underneath the pursuit box. This is to be utilized If you are transferring a fresh out of the box new item that isn't as of now selling on Amazon. Third, in case you need to move different items without a moment's delay, you can utilize the "mass transfer" highlight to one side of the screen.

Third Step (Pick an Amazon Category)

Once you've tapped on "Make another item posting," you'll be approached to dole out your new item to an Amazon classification. You may discover the ranking one of two different ways: utilizing the inquiry include or by perusing the classes. For simplicity, I like just to use the web crawler work.

After composing your item into the search bar, you'll be given the entirety of the potential classifications for that particular item. For my example, I am given 12 unique decisions in which my water jug will fit. Select a proper for your item. For my water bottle, I'll pick the fourth alternative, "Sports Water Bottles."

Fourth Step (fill the listing)

On the following page, you'll notice that your posting data is separated into seven tabs: Vital Info, Variations, Offer, Images, Description, Keywords, and More Details.

I'll walk you through the significant fields of every tab, except how about we start with the principal cost - Vital Info.

Vital info

1. Product Name: This will be the title every client sees on your posting. Fundamentally, you pack whatever number keywords and highlights as could be expected under the circumstances into your title. Rather than just utilizing "Water Bottle" as my Product name, I used "Lightweight Insulated Water Bottle, 18 oz., for climbing, outdoors, biking, and work". What's more, my title could proceed as long as I remain inside the 250 characters limit.

   For more bearing regarding how to make your title, look at our other article, "How to Optimize Your Amazon Product Title."

2. Producer and Brand Name: In case you're selling your private-name item, you'll just utilize your image/organization name for both of these fields.

3. Producer Part Number: You won't need this except if your item is a new part for another Product.

4. Product Quantity: Since I'm not selling a 2 or 3 pack of water bottles, I'll enter one here.

5. Material Type: Snap inside the field to be given a rundown of materials to look over. I'll imagine my water bottle is made of plastic.

6. Shading and Color Map: I enter the shade of my product. However, I leave the ColorMap field unfilled. In case you're anticipating selling different hues, you'll clarify when we go to the Variety tab.

7. Shape: If this doesn't have any significant bearing to your item, leave it clear. I utilized "Round"; however, I figure most clients would think that.

8. Color of the Lens: You can leave this clear, too, except if your product has a shaded focal point.

9. Size: Here, I could utilize either 18 oz. Or then again X-Large, contingent upon what I need to underscore.

10. GTIN Exemption Reason: Most items are required to have a GTIN (Global Trade Identifier Number), which is by and large something like a UPC or (for books) an ISBN. Be that as it may, you can be given an exclusion relying upon your Product classification.

11. Related Product ID and Type: If your item is connected to another Product, you ought to enter the other Product's ID here. For instance, If my water bottle were just perfect with a particular bike, at that point, I'd connect my water jug to the bicycle's UPC here. If your product is independent, leave these fields vacant.

12. Thing Display Dimensions and Weight: Here, you'll enter the length, width, and weight of your product.

13. Shaft Length: Depends on the type of product you are listing. So we are proceeding onward.

14. Product ID: As I expressed over, each product will require a Product ID to be sold on Amazon. This ID (for the most part, a UPC) will recognize your product from each other product. You can check with the producer for this data, or If you've made a private mark

Product, you'll need to buy a UPC for your new product. There is an assortment of sites that sell UPCs in different groups (simply scan for modest UPC scanner tags).

Variations

If your product arrives in an assortment of hues or estimates or some other unmistakable assortments, you'll have to demonstrate that here. Navigate the drop-down menu and choose the kind of variety that accommodates your product.

After you've picked a variety, more fields will be uncovered to give an additional explanation to your Product posting. Just fill in the various types you have inside that topic; at that point, click Add varieties.

When you've included the varieties, they will show up beneath. Presently basically fill in the suitable data for every type, and you're finished!

Offer

1. Import Designation: Do not fill in this tab, yet If it will enable you to pick a suitable assignment.
2. A nation of Publication: Skirt this except if your product was distributed.
3. Vender Warranty Description: If you offer any sort of guarantee or assurance on your product, enter it here. I composed, "If in any way, shape or form you are discontent with the water bottle, we offer a full, unconditional promise."
4. Discharge Date: If you wish clients to know when you discharged this product, do as such here. Most merchants will leave this clear.
5. The nation as Labeled: If your Product was not made in the USA and your name uncovers the starting point nation, you can incorporate that data here.
6. Availability of Gift Wrap: In case you're not utilizing Fulfillment by Amazon and need to consider blessing wrapping and blessing messages for your product, you can do that here.
7. Assessment Code: If you are utilizing Amazon charge assortment administrations, you can enter your code here.
8. Satisfaction Latency: In case you're not utilizing Fulfillment by Amazon, you can demonstrate the time it will take for you to launch the product once it has been requested.
9. Restock Date: You can leave this field vacant.
10. Legitimate Disclaimer: Mine peruses, "As usual, if you don't mind peruse and agree to all marks and warnings."If you don't know about the specific wording of your disclaimer, counsel your maker or look for a legitimate guide.
11. Begin selling date: Basically, pick the date on which you'd like your product to be accessible on Amazon.
12. Marked By: If an individual marks your product, you can incorporate that data here.

13. Satisfaction Channel: Now, you'll pick whether you need to satisfy the sets of your product or permit Amazon to meet them. I healthily suggest utilizing Fulfillment by Amazon, assuming there is any chance of this happening.

Images

On the Images tab, transfer the suitable pictures for your product. Make sure to agree to the rules given by Amazon on this page.

If you need more courses for your Product pictures, make sure to look at our other article, Four Photo Fails to Avoid on Your Amazon Listing.

Description

The Description tab is separated into two segments: Key Product Features and Product Description.

A — Key Product Features

The Key Product Features fields will turn into your visual cues of situated close to the highest point of your posting, similar to this water bottle posting:

There are two realities you have to think about your Product includes:

- Though Amazon claims it doesn't, numerous master dealers have confirmed verification that Amazon positions your product dependent on keywords inside your Product, highlight visual cues. I suggest pushing the same number of extraordinary Keywords as you can into these highlights.

- Amazon says they constrain you to 100 characters for every field. Be that as it may, If you utilize more, the words despite everything show up on your posting (they don't shorten the sentence). Presently, Amazon may, in the long run, start taking action against lengths of your Key Features, however starting at now, they don't appear to mind. My suggestion? Use as much space as possible and occupy that space with catchphrases.

B — Product Description

The Product Description is one higher chance to offer your product to your client.

Utilize this field to sell the client on the advantages of your product. Don't merely discuss the highlights; however, plan to clarify how your product takes care of your client's issues. You will be restricted to 2,000 characters.

Keywords

Your Keyword tab is a crucial piece of your Amazon posting. Albeit no client will observe the data your contribution here, Amazon will utilize this data at whatever point clients scan for your Product or related Products.

A — Search Terms

Fill each search term field with the same number of one of a kind Keywords as you can, and separate every watchword with a comma. Note that you don't have to repeat keywords , so If you've utilized a keyword in your title or visual cues, you won't have to use it again here.

This is the reason exceptional investigation into your Keywords is so essential. You need to have enough Keywords to use in your title, visual cues, and in these pursuit terms.

B — Platinum Keywords

You are not a Platinum Seller, so move along.

C — Topic, Other Attributes, Intended Use, and Target Audience

The following four segments are, for the most part, fields dependent on drop-down menus. Just snap on each area, and you'll be given a drop-down list of related decisions.

You might be enticed to avoid this piece of the procedure since it takes some an opportunity to finish (and by tab #6, you're tired of it). Be that as it may, recall, Amazon utilizes the entirety of this data to index your product for client look. Why not give them however, much information as could reasonably be expected?

More Details

I'm not going to stroll through the More Details blog for three reasons:

- This tab is redone dependent on your Product classification. In case you're not in the water bottle class, it won't help you to tell you the best way to round this area out because my fields will be unique with yours.
- It's quite apparent. You stroll through each field and fill in the most considerable number possible. A few areas will have nothing to do with your particular product. However, others could be useful for Amazon to think about.
- This is the most extended tab out of all! In any case, I do need to bring up this is the tab on which your cost is resolved. You ought to have two explicit spots to enter a value:
- Maker's Suggested Retail Price: This isn't the value your client will pay. It's just the value you decide a client could pay If you weren't so liberal. In your real posting, it shows up as the rundown cost. In the model beneath, the merchant entered $35.95 into their Manufacturer's Suggested Retail Price field.
- At long last, this cost turns into a "stay cost" for your product. It gives your client a feeling of examination and brings out the impression of a decent arrangement. Pick this carefully. Deal Price: The Sale Price is the genuine value your client will pay on your

posting. In the above past model, it's the $11.97 underneath the List Price. If you'd like more bearing on finding the correct cost for your product, follow my three-advance procedure in our article, Follow These Three Steps to Determine Your Pricing, Sweet Spot.

- As I said previously, the remainder of the fields ought to be genuinely illustrative and modified to your areas. Recollect that enormous numbers of these fields are discretionary, so If you don't get them, you can likely skirt them.

Conclusion

When you've strolled through every one of these means and filled in the fundamental data for your product, it's an excellent opportunity to tap on the "Spare and Finish" interface at the base.

If the connection is as yet concealed out (not permitting you to tap on it), this is because of a missing bit of fundamental data. Glance back at the tabs and check whether there are any that are labeled with an alert outcry symbol. Assuming this is the case, go to that tab and fill in the field that is featured in red.

If you are as yet experiencing issues, don't spare a moment to utilize Amazon support by opening another program window and returning to your fundamental Seller Central dashboard. Snap-on the "Help" connect in the top, right-hand corner of the page, at that point, follow the suitable advances.

Chapter 5: Four Elements of a Product Listing

As a dealer on the Amazon commercial center, you most likely know a smidgen about how promoting on the web-based business platform works. From Sponsored Products to Prime Day bargains, there are a vast amount of approaches to give your image an extra 'help' and get before more customers. One thing merchants probably won't understand, in any case, is that it's conceivable to boost your natural posting highlights without going through extra money – If you realize how to do it right.

What is SEO on Amazon

While Search Engine Optimization (SEO) is used to help organizations and brands rank on huge web indexes like Google, for makers, it can work a similar route on Amazon, which is a gigantic web crawler for Products. Toward the back, Amazon servers read every product inclining to coordinate list Products with purchaser inquiries accurately. While paid to publicize and posting highlights may assist brands with appearing in the 'supported' segment of the indexed lists, improved posting substance can assist Products with positioning higher in list Products naturally.

The most effective method to Optimize Your Amazon SEO Strategy

Improving your Product postings boils down to understanding your purchasers and what they're searching for in your Products. There are a lot of thoroughly considered pioneers there regarding the matter, however here are a couple of the fundamental components for any triumphant Amazon SEO technique that will help kick your group off today:

Keywords

The most significant thing to recall with regards to building Amazon Product postings is explicitness. Amazon SEO works basically off of organized substance, which means it possibly checks for keywords If they compare to explicit fields. Toward the back of your Product postings, ensure you are amazingly exact with what search terms you need to rank for. The more Keywords you incorporate, the better – it kills any opportunity of passing up an extraordinary pursuit. A best practice here is to do some exploration to perceive what buyers are looking and how they're expressing sure Keywords so you can be confident you aren't feeling the loss of any basic search terms.

Product Images

This presumably doesn't come as any shock. However, a great many people settle on purchasing choices on Amazon dependent on a specific something: the photos. Without extraordinary Amazon Product photography, potential purchasers will avoid directly over your postings. Make a point to upgrade your assignments by following Amazon's picture rules, indicating various Product edges, and including meta-labels the back-end. A higher Product active visitor clicking percentage causes you to rank higher in Amazon query Products, which makes Product pictures so significant.

Variations

Varieties are another approach to help support your Amazon SEO system. Having various hues, loads, or size alternatives featured in anProduct posting is a piece of the Product depiction, and every one of these varieties tracks as a remarkable catchphrase toward the back. These various varieties additionally help balance out Product request, say If one variety is doing great in search yet another isn't. With types, the two hues will rank together on Amazon in a solitary posting.

Product Descriptions

Product portrayals are a blend of keywords, pictures, and buyer decisions, however primarily designed in a way that is satisfying to your shoppers. Most Product portrayals incorporate a sentence or two of watchword filled data followed by simple to-peruse visual cues that go into subtleties on Product highlights and realities. To boost every Product posting, track which portrayals are positioning admirably in Amazon SEO and which aren't, and afterward utilize these outcomes to set benchmarks.

While upgrading natural postings for SEO is necessary, it can require significant investment, persistence, and assets. Working with a solitary outsider dealer can dispense with this weight all together

The Best Amazon Product Description Template

If getting guests to discover your Products upon a vast ocean of contenders is a large portion of the fight, the other half is convincing them to purchase at this moment. Also, that is where you need some skills in Amazon Product Copywriting

It is the way you put words and phrases to interface with guests and impact their purchasing conduct. Much like legendary dim craftsmanship, incredible copywriting adequately control individuals' buying choices in support of you.

As driven FBA vendors, knowing how to compose incredible Amazon Product portrayals and copywriting aptitudes are an enormous resource. You've endeavored to get your product observed, don't those let potential purchasers sneak away at this point!

How to Write an Amazon Product Description

From doing Productexplore a few times over, I've seen that many, numerous vendors don't invest a lot of energy into their Product depictions. This is a slip-up. You could be leaving essential deals by not taking advantage of each pixel of Amazon Listing land conceivable.

So how about we plunge into probably the best ways to deal with composing that ideal, changing over Product depiction.

1. Know Your Customer

How might you hope to interface profoundly, manufacture trust, and convert guests into clients? If you don't know precisely what their identity is?

Before you can even beginning composition, you must accumulate enough information on your intended interest group. If you can recognize and comprehend your purchasers, you can address them all the more viably. Start by thinking about the accompanying:

Segment Trends: Gender, salary, interests, ways of life and so on – Search Google for sites, online journals, discussions and Facebook gatherings

Client Reviews: Wants, concerns, what they like/don't care for – Look at the audits from your rival's Product postings

Client Experiences: How individuals utilize these Products? – Search Youtube and websites

The data you accumulate here will be reflected in each segment of an enhanced Amazon Product posting. It's hands down the ideal approach to construct trust, conquer complaints, and at last, convert guests into clients.

2. Understand the Buyer's Mindset

As advertisers and dealers, it very well may be hard to see things from a customer's perspective until the kingdom comes. That is the reason this is such a valuable exercise to do before making your Amazon Product depictions

If it helps, really go out on the town to shop on Amazon at that point, consider back the accompanying elements:

- What did you like, for what reason did you click it?
- What things pulled in you, what stood apart from the rest?
- For what reason did you wind up getting it?

The odds are, your purchasers will be experiencing a fundamentally the same as an experience when perusing your Products. So this knowledge will assist you with understanding their accurate purchasing procedure and choices.

3. Study Your Competitors

Regardless of whether different Products have all the earmarks of being selling amazingly well, this doesn't mean they should be the most beneficial postings.

A significant number of the apparent "smash hits" or most noteworthy checked on Products could be losing loads of cash each day with horrible changes.

Consider the reality they could be running gigantic rebate coupons off-camera, parting with Products for audits, and pretty much to flame out of after their launch battle.

You generally have the potential for success to have out among the group with a remarkable Product posting. Improving your depiction could be one tremendous advance towards removing deals from those contenders.

4. Research Keywords

Keywords are high-volume, significant search terms guests use to discover products they need to purchase. Intensive watchword inquire about is substantial because you should mesh them into your Product portrayal as well.

Best Practices For Writing Amazon Product Listings

1. Titles

The key reason for your title is to get consideration and snaps from guests. Recall this should be composed of people and not only for robots!

Try not to Stuff Keywords: Creating a muddled title that is stuff with Keywords won't help much with SEO, and it will diminish your Click-Through-Rate altogether. It is anything but a keen play. Concentrate on making an appealing Title with 1-2 top keywords.

Consider Title Length: Guests on better places and gadgets will see titles, and they will show up at various lengths. Guarantee your title gets consideration at all distances and positions: 35, 76, and 155 characters.

Keep the Rules: Amazon sets out a style manage for every classification. Ensure you are not disrupting any of the norms (even though many do appear to negate each other now and again).

2. Use Bulleting

Projectiles' focus ought to give stable highlights/benefits in brisk fire progression. Attempt to concentrate on one of a kind points of interest and don't be unclear.

Make Powerful Bullets: Bullets should be as explicit as could be expected under the circumstances. Rapidly express your Product key highlights and advantages without an excessive amount of promotion. Contingent upon the classification, between 150-200 characters is a decent length to focus on.

Bid Directly To Customers: Craft shots to rapidly conquer guest's protests. If different models or comparative Products have issues, get them out, and clarify why yours is better or unique.

Identify with Their Lifestyle: Another stunt that functions admirably is getting individual. Consider utilizing the language they use and demonstrating how your product would fit in their way of life consummately.

3. Product Description

The Product depiction is the place we go further, conquer any last complaints, lure guests, and advise them to purchase now.

Think of the best infomercials. They make you feel like the client utilizing a superb Product or experiencing a sub-par one.

Show how your product is unique or superior to the others. In any case, do this as the type of account, take them by the hand and assist them with envisioning the experience of utilizing your product.

Note: Amazon just permits 2000 bytes of information, around 300 words, or 1,900 characters with spaces to do this. Recount to a story, however, be brief and hustle your central matters and keywords inside this cutoff.

4. HTML Formatting

With regards to arranging your Product portrayal, Amazon is very prohibitive and doesn't offer a lot of help. You've even got the chance to enter the HTML code physically; else, you'll end up with a major square of content that is not peruser cordial by any means!

TOS Disclaimer: Technically, Amazon expresses that you are not permitted to utilize any HTML to design your Product portrayal like this. Be that as it may, numerous venders do this (counting me), and it's never been an issue. It essentially makes your depiction simpler to peruse for customers, and that improves their general understanding.

Here's a speedy glossary of a portion of the HTML codes you can use to make your portrayal stick out and more uncomplicated to peruse:

- Strong Text Style: Insert Text
- Line Break:
- Addition Text
- Paragraph: <p>Insert Text<p>

HTML Restrictions: Amazon has additionally confined the utilization of section styling, including italics, content shading, focusing, text dimensions, textual style family, foundation pictures.

If you endeavor to include any limited HTML, you'll be indicated a mistake when you attempt to spare your posting:

The Product Description you gave was invalid. It will be ideal if you check that it doesn't contain any unique characters.

The simplest method to work out your HTML depiction is to:

- Compose your portrayal content first
- Include your HTML labels and code

- At that point evacuate all spaces and line breaks between your duplicate and HTML, to keep your depiction inside as far as possible

So there you have it! All that you have to get making an extraordinary Amazon Product Description that effectively changes over guests into clients. Simply recall, consistently center around talking legitimately to YOUR guests and tending to their inclinations or concerns. Presently go get composing!

Chapter 6: Product Launch

As an originator, there's nothing all the more energizing (and upsetting) than launching your product. You've relaxed for a couple of rounds, watched the game get played, and now you have a triumphant hand and are all set all in. In any case, wagering with even the best chances is as yet a bet. Furthermore, without a healthy Product launch plan, you're leaving a lot to risk.

In this guide, you will learn:

- How to do a successful pre-launch(Pre-Launch)
- How to utilize the launch day to make more sales (Launch)
- How to scale your business in the coming days, weeks, and months that follow. (Post-Launch)

Product Pre-launch

Some time ago, organizations used to contribute crazy measures of time and cash into a "Huge explosion" launch. They'd go into covertness mode, construct a product, structure their point of arrival and advertising pipes, and set up an elaborate PR plan. Be that as it may, after such a large number of gigantic launches transformed into flops (hello, Segway), we realized there was a superior way.

Today, a "launch" is not, at this point, the vital turning point of your product. It's only a little occasion for your product's course of events. What's more, the best way to guarantee an effective Product launch is to begin early and get however much genuine input as could reasonably be expected before you launch.

1. Offer early and frequently with some of your clients

You launch when you realize the thing won't tumble down. In any case, you ought to test with clients a long time before that. When you have a variant of your Product individuals can utilize and get some an incentive from, you ought to be out there getting criticism and repeating. This could be weeks, months, or even a long time before you expect to launch

The number of early clients you need will rely to a great extent upon your product. In any case, in case you're selling a B2B SaaS apparatus, I've seen the sweet spot as clumps of 20–30 clients. Along these lines, you can even now converse with the vast majority of them, realize what they love (and despise), and hear how they portray your product.

Your most punctual clients may be companions, business associations, and colleagues. Or on the other hand, If you need increasingly fair input, you can utilize an apparatus like Product Search Ship that permits you to make custom greeting pages and fabricate a crowd of people of Productcentered early clients.

Any way you do it, get early clients to test, approve, and jab openings in all that you're doing. Along these lines, when the opportunity arrives to demonstrate your product to the world, you realize individuals will adore it.

2. Request Product and Marketing Feedback

Criticism is the most significant thing you're searching for pre-launch. Be that as it may, I'm not merely discussing Product criticism like bugs or UX issues. While these are significant for cleaning your product, there is a lot more you can gain from conversing with your clients, for example,

- What language do they use to communicate their encounters?
- Where do they get genuine incentives from your product?
- What unusual use cases or needs do they have?

This kind of criticism is essential for promoting groups as it gives you an immediate line into your optimal client's head. You get the chance to hear how they contemplate your product and can refine your worth prop around that.

As you plan for your launch, begin to pepper this language into your product and showcase pages. Test various forms of your greeting page to perceive what resounds the most. Give your showcasing group a similar open door as your Product group to tune in to clients, absorb that data, repeat, and test.

3. Be forceful about refuting you're. Not right.

The most significant misstep you can make as an author is placing your sense of self before your business.

When picking your test clients, it's anything but difficult to fall into the snare of just choosing individuals you realize will adore your product. Propelling another Product can be a defenseless procedure. Yet, you have to open yourself to the rawest, generally legit, and brutal criticism.

As you test your product and showcasing, pose a couple of critical inquiries:

Did you test with a beta gathering that was too disposed of even to consider liking the product? If you carefully select organizations or clients that aren't eager to state "no" to you, you will get a bogus footing. They'll attempt. Also, they'll give input. Be that as it may, they won't accept.

Did you predisposition your clients through your pitch? The authors are an enthusiastic gathering. In any case, your product needs to remain all alone without you in the room. In case you're affecting individuals a lot without giving them genuine worth, you're simply making a reality-bending field.

Are you making the correct inquiries? When you converse with clients, don't simply ask, "do you like it?" Ask them, "Are you utilizing it consistently? Are you discovering an incentive in it? What amount would you pay for that worth you're getting?" It's insufficient to satisfy your clients. You have to make them useful. Burrow profound and let them be straightforward.

Before you launch, you should be certain beyond a shadow of a doubt you're making esteem. So at whatever point conceivable, search for something contrary to what you expect. If you can demonstrate your Product sucks, it isn't prepared to launch.

4. Keep your coaches, guides, and different supporters on top of it

Your initial clients won't be the main ones utilizing your Product pre-launch. In case you're conversing with coaches or approaching individuals for appeal, you should be similarly as cautious about keeping up those connections.

Propelling a product is inconceivably tedious. In any case, these individuals need to support you. You can't merely request some help and afterward, drop off the substance of the planet. Instead, put it in your schedule to catch up week after week or month to month with a snappy update on what you did since you last talked, why, what you're anticipating straightaway and something you need assistance.

5. Don't forget the rule: do less when you are not certain

This criticism can have an unintended outcome: investigation loss of motion. With conclusions and remarks originating from all bearings, it can feel like you're suffocating in choices. Be that as it may, if all else fails, adhere to the brilliant principle of Product launches: Do less.

You may think you need ten highlights to launch with, however, believe it or not, you most likely simply need one. Here's a model: When we previously assembled Close, it was as an inward device for our redistributed deals organization, ElasticSales. It functioned admirably for us since we knew the entirety of its highlights and eccentricities. Be that as it may, when we chose to launch it to general society, we would not like to overpower or befuddle new clients. So we stripped it directly back to merely the center highlights.

At whatever point you're settling on Product choices pre-launch, think from the viewpoint of your clients. Launch with merely the fundamentals and let your clients mention to you what to work straightaway.

6. Pick your launch day and stick to it

Probably the most significant inquiry I get about how to launch a product is when to start. The ideal launch date is whatever works for you. You would prefer not to attempt to launch your product simultaneously as a vast Apple occasion, yet other than that, you should simply mark the calendar, check with your group, and afterward put it all on the line.

When you have a date picked, stick to it. You'll work in reverse from it with the remainder of your Product launch promoting plan.

7. Pick your top launch platform and play the game on it

By and large, you're going to need to pick a solitary platform to concentrate your Product launch on. This is the place you'll send clients, accumulate input, and measure your prosperity. What's more, whatever platform you pick, you have to play the game on it a long time before propelling.

Once upon a time, this implied fabricating a relationship with a TechCrunch correspondent. Be that as it may, today, there are such vast numbers of channels where you don't need to depend on a guard. You can launch on Product Search, Facebook, Reddit, LinkedIn, and so on… Anyplace your optimal clients are a decent spot to launch.

For me (and most other startup originators), be that as it may, the best alternative is Product Search. In case you're new, Product Search is a site devoted to revealing and discussing the most recent Products. Yet, more than that, it's a functioning network of product engaged individuals who will attempt what you've made and give you quick input.

Anybody can present their Product on Product Search. Yet, to capitalize on it, you have to make altruism and worth it previously. Be a piece of the network and lock-in. Don't simply upvote and like Products, however, set aside the effort to leave insightful remarks and guidance. It takes work, however, even a week or month of exertion will assist you with building a name and following for yourself.

8. Don't strive for perfection

Launch days will unavoidably be a scramble. Furthermore, I firmly prescribe preparing all that you have to go ahead of time. This implies structures and showcasing illustrations (enhanced for the platforms you're utilizing), duplicate, onboarding streams, messages, and so forth…

Make a product launch plan list of all that you need half a month out from launch day and add it to your Product launch plan.

9. Set objectives, not desires

Launch days are unusual. And keeping in mind that it sucks to state it, a ton of your prosperity will come down to karma. You have to disregard the things you can't 100% control (press, information exchanges, downloads) and instead set progressively reasonable objectives.

It's critical to make a stride back and consider the comprehensive view here. Regardless of what you're propelling, your ultimate objective is to create exceptionally held clients. That implies you ought to be attempting to assemble mindfulness, get input, and interface with individuals who will assist you with pushing ahead and emphasize after launch day.

Ask yourself what you need to find out about your product. Your initial clients will give you theory, and your launch day objective ought to be to demonstrate (or negate) it.

Disregard top-of-pipe vanity measurements like snaps, likes, and offers (that don't generally mean anything), and spotlight on criticism, remarks, surveys, and significant commitment with clients and influencers. Far better—center around new clients that evaluate your product use it, and continue utilizing it!

10. Utilize your own story to construct promotional buzz and expectation

New businesses (and SaaS organizations mainly) are awful at building publicity around their Product launches. Such a large number of authors become involved with what they know and overlook they're propelling to individuals who've never observed or utilized their product.

The scene is simply too dangerous not to have a story associated with your product. Your clients need to know what your identity is. They have to resound with your excursion. Your central goal.Your energy. They have to understand what your character is, and why they should confide in you to take care of this issue for them.

Start early, characterize your story, and spread it any place you can before launch day—blog on your webpage or Medium. Do meets and web recordings—guest post on destinations or in networks. Be the place your clients and network are and mention to them what you're doing.

11. Set yourself up to get the most ROI from launch day

Your launch day is only the start of your excursion, not the end. And keeping in mind that it's beautiful to take a couple of seconds to praise your difficult work; you have to ensure you're benefiting from it.

Before you hit "launch" you have to realize your group is prepared to work. This implies reacting to remarks, supporting new clients, helping individuals join or get arrangements, giving deals, and promoting all the devices and assets they need, having a procedure for gathering criticism and following element demands.

Be prepared to answer messages or turn on live visits on your presentation page If you have it. This is your opportunity to get before many individuals at the same time. Try not to squander it. Take part in whatever number of significant discussions with qualified possibilities as could be expected under the circumstances.

Product Launch day

As you can most likely tell at this point, I don't think launch day itself is close to as significant as the work you do paving the way to it. Yet, that doesn't mean you get the chance to kick back and put things on autopilot. If you need your launch day to go smoothly, you have to unite your whole group and lead them into fights.

1. Why you need to launch on Product Search (and how to do it)

If you followed my pre-launch exhortation and are propelling on Product Search, there are a couple of explicit systems you ought to follow to amplify your odds of progress. These are only the essentials as there are full aides committed to propelling on Product Search (even one from the group themselves).

To start with, compose your declaration remark in advance. When you put your Product Search posting live, you'll need to drop the main comment as a "producer." This is the place you clarify the product, talk about use cases, and offer the excursion of why you fabricated it and what you need to realize. End the remark by requesting input from your crowd.

Next, screen your page for the day and answer remarks rapidly. Product search isn't a launch and-leave network. They anticipate that you should be near and answer inquiries for the day. Ensure one of the product's "creators" is accessible.

At long last, monitor recruits and catch up with them. The Product Search people group will bolster you long after your launch day if you keep them refreshed. Not long after your launch day, send everybody an email with a recap of what occurred, what you realized, and afterward request proceeded with assistance managing your Product guide.

2. Utilize internet-based life to show the right instances of your product

When your Product Search posting is live, it's an excellent opportunity to begin directing people to it. In any case, if your concept of driving traffic is hurling a couple of irregular tweets and Facebook posts, you will be damn disillusioned.

Instead, you need to show individuals the worth your product makes. Not merely let them know. Here's an extraordinary model from my companion and sequential product propelled, Hiten Shah:

3. Influence your systems and contacts to carry social verification to your launch

Online life encourages you to show your product. Yet, when you're educating individuals regarding it, it's substantially more remarkable for that story to originate from another person.

Social verification is one of the most useful assets advertisers, and Product creators have. Furthermore, the more individuals you can get discussing your launch, the better. Contact those tutors, companions, and associations you've been refreshing about your advance and request that they share and lock-in.

Each platform and system you share your launch on is a potential spot to get input. Monitor all that you're doing and check-in for the day to draw in with new clients and catch up with questions and remarks.

Product Post-launch

You've endured the day and popped a container. Also, kick your feet up. Be that as it may, do you believe you've finished? No way. Realizing how to launch a product likewise implies comprehending what to do after launch day.

1. Converse with people that disliked your product

In case you're similar to the vast majority, the main thing at the forefront of your thoughts after the residue settles from launch day is: What would it be a good idea for us to work straight away? In any case, why squander this criticism and extraordinary associations by going straightforwardly once again into assembling mode?

For the following 1-2 months after launch day, you ought to talk and gaining from whatever number individuals as could be expected under the circumstances. Here's the reason:

All you know is the thing that you heard before launch and on the day. Not what they know now in the wake of being clients for half a month.

You'll have an alternate blend of individuals coming into your product when you launch. This gathering is far progressively illustrative of who your client base will be than simply the early adopters.

To start with, discover individuals who haven't proceeded with the product and ask them for what reason. You can gain as much from individuals who quit utilizing your product as the individuals who changed over. Connect with them and state, "you're one of the primary individuals to utilize the Product, and I need to get notification from you." Let them be fiercely legit because that is the best criticism you will get.

Next, connect with individuals who kept on working and get an incentive from the product. For the individuals who stayed, you'll need to accomplish more than a primary email. Attempt to get a meeting with these individuals and hear how they talk about the product. This is a goldmine of input that will assist you with improving both the product and your showcasing.

2. **Tidy up the house (for example fix all the things you broke to get the chance to launch day)**

Regardless of how much pre-launch work you put in, launch day is quite often a scramble. Furthermore, to arrive, your group presumably cut a couple of corners and made more than a couple of wrecks that should be tidied up before you can push ahead.

Here is a couple of you should search for:

Deals: If you had a business group set up before your launch, they most likely were extemporizing and working without a business procedure. In any case, that won't work for long. This is the ideal opportunity to take what you realized during the launch and build up a repeatable framework.

Showcasing: Launches are a smidgen of everything, except effective promoting is focused on and intentional. Make a stride back and truly delve into your top showcasing channels. This is likewise a decent time to dive deep into SEO and ensure you're beginning to get some natural traffic.

Product and designing: In the race to get the product out the entryway, your group most likely made all around specialized obligation—wasteful code that should be fixed before you can scale. You most likely additionally need to set up all the more testing to check whether your product can endure the clients you'll ideally be getting.

It's continually energizing to complete launch and surge onto the following thing. Nevertheless, in case you're expanding on a messed up establishment, your product is bound to come up short.

3. Keep your group persuaded and genuinely within proper limits

Ultimately, remember the individuals who got you where you are present. Is your group prepared to push ahead, or would they say they are exhausted? Do they approach all the criticism from launch day? It is safe to say that they are prepared and ready to move from every day, intending to setting quarterly achievements?

There's likewise the enthusiastic side of exciting points. Launch day can be an exciting and energizing, passionate rollercoaster. Be that as it may, the days after can feel like an accident. You've relinquished such pressure and feeling, and in the days to come, you will be either smashed on your prosperity or discouraged from your disappointment. As a pioneer, you have to do a few things to check this:

Envision those reactions and oversee them: Understand that post-launch won't merely be nothing new. You should be hyper-mindful of your group's psychological state and ability. You can keep things moving without wearing out.

Ensure feelings aren't hindering acceptable dynamic: In the dimness of a post-launch crash, it's anything but difficult to let the opinions of the day cloud your choices. As a pioneer, you have to help ensure individuals aren't getting excessively made up for the lost time and that you're settling on brilliant business choices.

Remember that without your group, you have nothing. Individuals cause your product to occur.

4. Imagine a scenario where you propelled, and nobody purchased.

Regardless of whether you followed every one of these means, there's consistently the opportunity your Product launch floundered. Each author I know has wound up in this situation at a certain point (myself included!), But because your business isn't the place you need it to be, it doesn't mean it won't be there in the long run. Each disappointment is a chance to learn, adjust, and develop.

To start with, let yourself an alarm. Indeed, this seems like horrendous counsel; however, getting annoyed with your bombed launch is characteristic. Furthermore, I'd state it's even useful. Freezing doesn't mean going around and shouting. It implies understanding this is significant, and you have to discover an answer now.

An excessive number of authors get tied up with their reasons ("Oh, we simply need this new component" or "However four clients revealed to us they cherished it!") as opposed to paying attention to this second.

Next, ask yourself: "Is the circumstance actually that desperate?" Step back and evaluate the harm. What's your financing circumstance? Do you have a year of runway to returned from this launch, or would you say you were wagering everything on a touchy beginning? Take one moment to audit your desires. Indeed, even the best Product launches just get around a 10% change, yet most authors anticipate that closer should 50-60%

Ensure you have enough information to settle on a brilliant choice. Don't simply take the central arrangement and surge out. Search for gaps where you need more data. Were your clients the correct ones? Did you launch on the right platform? Did you play the game? Revisit the pre-launch list and check whether you missed any significant focuses.

At last, converse with everybody and plan your turn. You assembled something, it didn't work, you took in a bundle from launch, and now it's an excellent opportunity to take a gander at that data, talk as a group, and settle on a choice of where to take it. This is a pivotal turning point. Also, there are a couple of steps you have to follow instead of becoming overly energetic:

Converse with your group: Come up with a harsh course of action and unite everybody to get their input. Each emergency needs a pioneer. Be straightforward, yet additionally, have a type of elevated level arrangement mapped out to keep individuals positive.

Converse with the clients you do have: Was the issue in informing, valuing, or even client advancement? Discover what individuals cherished and loathed and how you can improve it for them.

Converse with your sounding board: Asking for help is troublesome. Be that as it may, it's perhaps the best thing you can do. Before you settle on an official conclusion, connect with somebody who comprehends your circumstance yet isn't put resources into your business. This could be your folks, companions, or significantly another originator. Talk them through your response and inquire as to whether they think it bodes well.

Only one out of every odd launch will succeed. Yet, everyone is an opportunity to learn, emphasize, and develop.

You continuously learn how to launch a product. Crowds change. Platforms change. The market changes. Also, every time you put something new out into the world, it's an opportunity to try, learn, emphasize, and develop.

So disregard launch day presenting to you a million new clients (and If it does, awesome!) And instead, use it as an opportunity to get the input you have to keep assembling your business, bringing your client's worth, and beating the opposition. Since I've said it previously, and I'll state it once more: In the end, whoever knows their client the best, wins.

Amazon A9 Algorithm

Starting in 2019, more than 2.5 million dealers are now working together on the Amazon commercial center over the world. Given the straightforwardness with which individuals can launch another Product business on Amazon, thousands have just rushed to the site, with the numbers expanding continuously.

If you are hoping to get one of them, you have to understand that the opposition will be furious, independent of the specialty you pick. Gone are the days when you could without much of a stretch make six-figure incomes in the blink of an eye on Amazon.

Regardless of whether you have a product under a private mark, your image, or simply exchanging it, odds are there is another person previously doing likewise with great deals. Henceforth, during a solemn scene, it is imperative for you as a merchant to recognize your product in any capacity you can.

This makes your activity of propelling another Product even more troublesome. The inquiry emerges – how would you launch another Product such that draws the consideration of the clients and prompts not too bad deals?

The Vicious Cycle of Ranking on Amazon

In addition to other things, Amazon is additionally famously known for making it somewhat precarious for new dealers to move their business.

For another Product to sell, it should be noticeable at the highest point of the query Products since, how about we face, odds of somebody heading off to the profundities of the Amazon commercial center to discover a Product are negligible. Furthermore, for a product to be noticeable at the top, it needs to rank very high, which, sit tight for it, is driven by its business history.

Do you see the problem? You need a decent position to drive deals and deals to get a proper place. As it were, you have to produce sales and lift your location simultaneously!

Cracking the Amazon A9 Code

At first, it might appear to be a dubious code to split, and it is. Anything beneficial requires a great deal of exertion, hard and intelligent work, and steadiness. The key here is to comprehend Amazon's A9 calculation and utilize that information adroitly in your business.

You have to understand that while there are a ton of components that Amazon considers to rank product, there are three primary measurements that assume a significant job. They are interconnected, and If you get them right, a large portion of the fight is won.

The velocity of Sales: It is only the rate at which you are selling your product. The quicker you sell, the more your product is popular on the commercial center, and like this, Amazon will push it up in the rankings for additional individuals to see.

CTR (Click Through Rate): CTR is the level of clients who see your postings in the query Products and snap on it to visit your fundamental Product page. A high CTR infers that the assignment applies to the inquiry being referred to. Starting here on, the client will make his/her choice to purchase the product, depending on the data gave on the posting page.

Conversion Rate: This is the level of individuals who purchase the product.

To get each of the three rights, you need to concentrate on a couple of things, and you must do it from the second you launch your product on Amazon. How about we investigate.

How to beat Amazon's A9 Algorithm

Before doing anything identified with a product launch or deals, the primary thing you have to do is guarantee that your Product posting page is enhanced for changes.

A client visiting your Product page is now three-fourths of the path there – you currently need to persuade him/her to buy the product. You can do this with the assistance of a convincing, productive duplicate that unmistakably clarifies the highlights, advantages, and employments of the product.

You have to offer some benefits to your clients by tending to all the inquiries they may have identified with the product. Utilize top-notch pictures, relevant keywords that reflect real client search questions, compact visual cues, and, if conceivable, Enhanced Brand Content.

To guarantee that your posting is on target, get it dissected by our Listing Quality Index and distinguish the critical zones of your assignment that can profit by further improvement.

Phew! With that off the beaten path, we would now be able to delve into the procedures for a fruitful Product launch on Amazon.

Concentrate on Getting Reviews

Audits are an essential piece of any Amazon business – without them, it will be unimaginably hard to drive deals.

Individuals depend on legitimate client surveys to make a buy – as another vender, your most extreme need ought to be to get; however, many of them as could be expected under the circumstances. One approach is by joining the Amazon Early Reviewer Program. At whatever point somebody purchases your Product, Amazon will get in touch with them arbitrarily and request that they leave you a survey as an end-result of a gift voucher. Along these lines, as you approach advancing your Products on the web, you support your odds of getting the genuinely necessary criticism for your business.

Another excellent methodology to get surveys is by utilizing bundle embeds, mentioning clients to leave you an audit, give extraordinary client support, and work with elevated expectations. Also, send a mail your purchasers in the wake of conveying the product, taking their recommendations, and mentioning them to leave you an audit.

Master Tip: Do not be enticed to discover a route around Amazon's T&C concerning the equivalent and 'hack' the framework to help your deals. Amazon will find and take exacting activities. Continuously attempt to get surveys.

Utilize Promotions and Discounts

Make them an offer they can't cannot – individuals assembled organizations on this very way of thinking, and similar holds useful for Amazon as well. A perfect method to get your product off the ground is with advancements and limits – make worthwhile arrangements and offers that make individuals visit your posting and purchase your Products.

You can utilize various kinds of advancements on Amazon to improve the permeability of your image in the market.

Among the most famous is a giveaway, trailed by different variations like free delivery, rate of, web-based life promotion codes, among others. You can make it progressively select by setting your conditions.

With this methodology, you will accomplish three things:

- Create publicity about your Products in the market
- Make brand mindfulness
- Drive individuals to your postings that lead to surveys and ensuing deals

There are a couple of things you have to remember with regards to advancements. You have to choose the financial plan/hit you can bear to take on your Products. Since you are going to part with your Products for nothing or at a rebate, you have to guarantee that you accomplish your destinations without enduring a big cheese on your edges. As a beginner, it might be reasonable to work without a benefit for quite a while and put that cash in advancements to produce brand mindfulness.

With that, you likewise need to think about the sort of advancement, its length, Products to advance, in addition to other things.

Master Tip: If you have a product that is as of now performing admirably on Amazon, you can package it with the new product as a joined rebate bargain. That is, individuals get a rebate when they purchase those two Products together. On the other side, this arrangement is probably going to function as long as your new Product supplements the hit.

Advance Your Products on Social Media

Facebook, Twitter, and Instagram – the more significant part of the world is on these three platforms, and as a matter of course, they are your most fabulous crowd.

Without a doubt, this is the place you should showcase your Products, yet the secret to doing effectively is by giving something of significant worth to the individuals.

Limits and advancements have demonstrated to be among the ideal approaches to get individuals to purchase new Products. You will profit altogether more If you have an enormous gathering of companions/supporters via web-based networking media.

You can likewise tie-up with internet based life influencers to advance your Products. This will probably prompt better permeability, and brand mindfulness for your Products as influencers, by and large, have a ton of devotees. You might be forced to pay them a premium or work out an arrangement that may eat into your edges. This is the place you have to consider the sort of introduction you remain to get.

Exploit Amazon PPC Promotions

Amazon Sponsored Products, most ordinarily known as Amazon PPC, is the most remarkable advertising device you have as an Amazon merchant.

A lot of merchants have effectively propelled their new Products through Amazon PPC and acquired them to page one of the query Products.

Simultaneously, you have to recollect that even though PPC campaigns are staggeringly successful in boosting deals and permeability, an absence of principal comprehension of how they work will be inconvenient to your promotion spending plans.

You have to see how Amazon PPC campaigns work and the distinctive enhancement procedures to make the best of the battles.

For example, you can utilize the product focusing on the highlight and have your Product advertisements showed on the postings of those things that are doing outrageously well on Amazon. Thus, you can likewise concentrate on those Amazon Products showing up in Google Ads when individuals scan for them. There are numerous ways like this to utilize PPC to further your potential benefit. Visit this blog for further developed Amazon PPC procedures.

Keep in mind: Through our experience, we have seen that for PPC battles to be successful, the product needs to have a couple of audits. Clients are not that slanted to purchase a product that is showing up in the advertisements with zero surveys. In this way, before you investigate this way, ensure you have at any rate 3-5 audits on your postings.

Tap into Amazon FBA

Satisfaction by Amazon, all the more ordinarily known as Amazon FBA, is among the most favored method of working together on Amazon.

Your Products will gladly convey the smooth Amazon Prime identification, which will prompt improved permeability and more odds of getting changes.

More than that, Amazon will deal with the overwhelming legwork for you – it will utilize its satisfaction system to store your stock, transport, and convey the things to your clients. With that, it will likewise give client care and procedure discounts and returns.

Keep up a Full Inventory

Nothing drives a business down quicker than an unavailable product. If that occurs, you will lose your positioning in the indexed lists, and you should begin without any preparation to modify your situation in the market. Consequently, before you start, ensure that the Products are available so you can concentrate just on the business. You can likewise utilize propelled stock following programming to assist you with following your stock levels all the more successfully.

Conclusion

As should be obvious, propelling products on Amazon requires a great deal of work; however, If you do it right, there is no motivation behind why you can't be headed to earn substantial sums of money.

Chapter 7: AMS ADS (Advertising)

The advantage of utilizing AMS over different advertising methods is that it gives merchants an immediate chance to get their Products and brand before extra in-showcase customers on Amazon.com.

In particular, the capacity to target singular Product detail pages offers merchants a chance to present their Products straightforwardly close by contender Products when buyers are at the last platform before the transformation.

In the accompanying blog entry, we spread all that you have to think about Amazon Marketing Services, including:

What is Amazon Marketing Services (AMS)?

Amazon Marketing Services (AMS) propelled in 2012. From that point forward, Amazon publicizing contributions have experienced a whirlwind of changes, including the suspension of beginning Product Ads and Amazon Text Ads and renaming of eCommerce Ads to Product Display Ads.

They at last developed into three principles Amazon publicizing positions:

1. Amazon Headline Search Ads
2. Amazon Product Display Ads
3. Amazon Sponsored Products Ads

Amazon Marketing Services (AMS) are the administrations and apparatuses gave by Amazon, which permits merchants to run promotions all through the Amazon Marketplace. With three distinct sorts of advertisements to browsed, AMS empowers the seller to picked reasonable showcasing for product's needs; these are Headline Search promotions, Product Display promotions, and Sponsored Products. Each has their points of interest to improve your image's perceivability, drive the benefit for your image's Products, and, at last, improve deals. In case you're searching for a period compelling, carefully controlled technique for getting your Products saw on Amazon, then this could be the following platform for your business.

We should get familiar with a tad about the promotion alternatives accessible to you...

1. Amazon Headline Search Ads

When clicked, these promotions can take potential clients to an arrival where you may include your smash hit or explicitly picked Products. These promotions are arranged at the highest point of indexed lists pages as a flag, and show up when a client's inquiry matches with a focused on catchphrase in your battle. This sort of advertisement is regularly constrained to those with a Vendor Central record, yet Seller Central despite everything, must have alternatives accessible to you as a business.

2. Amazon Product Display Ads

This sort of promotion is perfect in case you're looking to straightforwardly target contender Products with attracting the client to your product. With Product Display advertisements, merchants can see execution measurements of their crusade, the dashboard indicating measurements, for example, clicks, impressions, spend, complete deals, and promoting cost of offer (ACoS). To catch the eye of buyers perusing the pages of contender Products, Product Display promotions show up on these Product detail pages, giving the customer the alternative to arrive on your Product page while weighing up the capacity or style of the contender.

3. Amazon Sponsored Products Ads

These advertisements can show up in an assortment of spots on the website page – top, center, base, or the right-hand side of output pages when a client's pursuit coordinates a watchword. Through tapping on this promotion, clients are legitimately taken to your product's detail page, wherein the wake of getting familiar with the product, they may wish to buy.

As a substantially more fundamental platform in contrast with Google Adwords, AMS could be the best choice for you, straightforward to utilize and exceptionally controlled.

10 ways to use AMS Advertising

1. Assemble so many top-notch keywords as you can — 300 least. (I incline toward creators and titles, because those have been the most solid wellspring of deals for me, yet I may simply smell at picking catchphrases.)
2. Utilize manual focusing on. Amazon, once in a while, has great recommendations, so take what's helpful. Utilize little financial plans, different campaigns, and unobtrusive offers to test your initial battles.
3. Increase your financial plan and offers when you realize your battle is mighty. I, for the most part, start at $10 every day. (Amazon is extremely, improbable to spend that sum.)
4. Attempt various varieties of your promotion duplicate to perceive what reverberates with your crowd.
5. Show restraint: it might take as long as about fourteen days for a deal to enlist on your AMS dashboard. Watch your KDP dashboard for approaching sales to give you an early thought of whether your campaigns are paying off.
6. If your book is in KU, know that KU downloads don't appear in the AMS dashboard by any means. Screen your downloads to check whether any builds may be owing to the advertisements.
7. If your crusade isn't getting any impressions, take a stab at reproducing the battle. Amazon can be unpredictable, and given two indistinguishable promotions, one may soar while the other doesn't get shown by any means.
8. If your campaigns are reliably not getting impressions, you may require more keywords or better catchphrases. Be sure they're pertinent to your book's type and subject.
9. If your campaign is getting impressions, however, hardly any snaps, that implies individuals aren't fascinated by your promotion. Investigate your spread to be sure it's

up to measures, reevaluate your focusing on (catchphrases), and attempt diverse promotion duplicate.

10. I've been taking a gander at AMS promotions to direct your likewise bought — however, If you additionally bought are spotless and reliable matches, they'd be the ideal possibility for keywords. The two function admirably together!

Note: AMS promotions are accessible to any individual who distributes through KDP; no selectiveness required.

Bonus Chapter: How to Setup AMS ADS UK

Getting to Amazon advertisements for the US store is simple. But, what if you need to publicize in the UK? Then, you must learn how to open an AMS ADS account in UK

If you have a US KDP account, you can get to the platform from your KDP dashboard without requiring a different promoting account. Be that as it may, there are a lot of writers (I'm one of them) who have at least one book that sells preferred in the UK over in the US. What's more, it helps If they can promote to that crowd.

Fortunately, it's conceivable to run adverts for your books in the UK. The awful news is that it's a little trickier than doing it in the US. It additionally implies setting up a unique UK Amazon promotions record and holding on to be endorsed. Be that as it may, when you've done that, you have all the advantages of the Amazon Advertising platform in the UK. It's less severe than the US (mostly because it's harder to access), and it's essential to creators who sell in the UK.

In this post, I'm going to tell you precisely the best way to set up an Amazon UK promotions account. You can follow these means whether or not you're situated in the UK, the US, or anyplace else.

Set Up a UK Amazon Advantage Account

To set up an Amazon UK promotions account, you'll need an Amazon Advantage to represent Amazon UK. Hypothetically this lets you sell Products you give through the Amazon UK store and boat yourself (which are unique with books distributed utilizing KDP, which are sold by Amazon, not by you). However, you won't use it for that, except if you build up a pleasant sideline selling the stock for your books (fortunate you).

1. To begin, go to https://advantage.amazon.co.uk
2. Snap-on the connection that says click here to apply for an Advantage account (or comparative: Amazon will change the wording from time to time).
3. Type in your name (this ought to be your name, not your business name) and email address. If you have a current Amazon UK account, it bodes well to utilize a similar email address.
   Presently you'll be considered a creation screen. In case you're making another record for the UK, round this out and click the make your Amazon account button. If you now have a UK record and you're upbeat utilizing that, click the sign in the interface at the base of the screen.
   In case you're making another record, you'll have to enter the check code that has been sent to your email address. It may approach you for this in case you're marking in with a current record contingent upon your settings.

4. Next, give your business name and snap the make account button. You'll be taken through the procedure to arrange a two-advance check, after which you'll be taken to the seller arrangement process.

    You don't have to round out as much data as a business that is utilizing the advantage to sell different Products (you're using KDP to do that). In any case, you should acknowledge the understanding.

    Try not to include your installment data as you'll add this in the subsequent platform when you utilize your Advantage record to get to Amazon Advertising (they don't make this simple, isn't that right?). You likewise don't have to round out the tax document (yahoo).

    So now you have an Advantage account. You'll never need to utilize it again, aside from as a method for getting to Amazon Advertising. This may sound incredibly nonsensical, yet I would say it's the most dependable method of getting to your UK Amazon promotions account.

Create an Amazon Advertising Account

To make your promotions, you don't utilize Amazon Advantage; instead, you use Amazon Advertising. Yet, you'll need your Advantage record to get to that.

Go to https://advertising.amazon.co.ukand click on the register button. You'll be inquired as to whether you have a current record. Snap-on, I have a bit of leeway focal history.

Presently sign in utilizing the record you made or used for your Advantage account.

You'll be provoked to enroll in a publicizing account. Type in your promoter name (regularly your engraving name) and check the container to state you acknowledge the understanding. At that point, click the make account button.

You'll be sent an email with affirmation subtleties. Snap the connection in that email to return to the arrangement procedure. Amazon will, at that point, audit your application for a publicizing record and email you when that procedure is finished.

When that is done, you'll approach adverts in the UK, through the Amazon Advertising dashboard.

You'll have the option to make three sorts of advertisement: Sponsored Product promotions, Sponsored Brands, and Product Display Ads.

Make an Ad page in Amazon

Supported Product promotions work in the very same manner as the supported Product advertisements you can make using the KDP dashboard.

Supported Brand promotions (recently called feature advertisements) probably won't be recognizable to you If you've just publicized employing the KDP dashboard previously. These promotions permit you to publicize up to three Products in a single advertisement at the highest point of the screen and can be valuable for books in an arrangement.

What's more, Product Display Ads will be natural to you if you publicized with KDP before the appearance of lock screen promotions. They work likewise for focusing on yet will be shown in a more significant number of spots than simply the Kindle lock screen.

Since you have set up an Amazon UK promotions account, you can explore different avenues regarding the three sorts of advertisements and see which ones work best for you and your books.

FAQs (Frequently Asked Questions)

Q. I just launched my Product on Amazon, yet it doesn't appear in the query Products. What would i be able to do?

It might require some investment for another Product to arrive at the highest point of the indexed lists if it is producing deals and has excellent client surveys.

In this situation, in any case, you would first be able to check whether your Product posting is recorded or not by entering the Product ASIN (10 digit number) and the principle Product watchword in the pursuit bar. If your product appears, it is listed.

To improve its position, you have to chip away at streamlining PPC promotions, and surveys as we referenced previously. You can likewise utilize the Keyword Tracker to screen your improvement endeavors and see where your Keywords are positioning in the list Products. If you have recently propelled your product, the positioning might be past page 10, and you have to invest some energy into improving its perceivability.

Q. What sort of Products would i be able to sell on Amazon?

You can necessarily sell anything on Amazon except for confined things. Be that as it may, it is an entire diverse inquiry whether you can make a flourishing business out of it. A dependable guideline is to sell a product that is in acceptable interest, has a low rivalry, and doesn't experience the ill effects of regularity. For more data on what sort of products to sell, look at this Amazon Product inquire about the guide.

Q. I just launched a Product, and Amazon evacuated my posting! What is the approach here?

Amazon may have expelled your posting since it was infringing upon its selling strategies. You probably got a notification concerning the equivalent. Experience it cautiously and comprehend the principles you disregarded – regardless of whether it is selling fakes, ill-advised posting, infringement of licensed innovation laws, and so forth. When you recognize the issue, fix it and request to Amazon to cancel its choice.

Social Media Marketing for Business #2020

Facebook, Instagram, YouTube, Twitter, Snapchat Secret Strategies to build up Your Personal Brand, become an Influencer in your niche & Monetize your Audience

By

Steven Sparrow

Introduction

Congratulations on downloading *Social Media Marketing for Business 2019* and thank you for doing so.

The following chapters will discuss the importance of social media marketing and its impact on the modern world of business. It will give you some helpful strategies and tips on how to implement social media into your own business.

Social media is a constant in our everyday lives now. It's used by nearly everyone.

If you're a business in today's world, and if you haven't already jumped into social media, now is the time. It is a valuable addition to any business, a brilliant way to reach customers. It is all 100% free.

Take this into account, no pun intended:

In the world, there are now 3-plus billion people using social media, a 13% jump from last year. Out of these over 3 billion people, all of them use social media at least once a month. The average American uses it for just over 2 hours a day.

With everyone on social media, your business should be too. 75% of marketers report that by increasing their social media efforts, their traffic has gone up. 50% say that their sales have improved. More than 1 third of people who use social media use social media to find out more information about a product.

Creating your own personal brand on social media is especially important. You need to make sure that you have a winning brand to really connect with your customers. This book will help you do that.

There are plenty of books on this subject on the market, so thanks again for choosing this one! Every effort was made to ensure it is full of as much useful information as possible. Please enjoy!

Chapter 1: Why Social Media is Getting a Primary Pole in Building Businesses Online

Let's keep this as simple as possible: your business needs an online presence, and a run of the mill website unfortunately just isn't good enough anymore.

What business you have doesn't matter all that much. Your business could be a tiny local store with only 200 customers a day or a huge international, multi-million-dollar chain of coffee shops, you need to be on some form of social media. You could be a freelancer with 3 clients or a model who regularly books thousands of dollars in jobs, everybody who has a business and is looking to make more money needs a social media page.

It is an essential part of any business strategy, and if it's not yet a part of yours, now is the time. While there are a lot of people out there who don't use social media, that number gets smaller and smaller every single day, as more and more people sign up for an account.

In the past decade, the landscape of the internet has changed drastically, and most of this change is thanks to social media. As a result, it has become a tool for brands and businesses, opening doors to changing your relationship with the public, engage with your base, and increase sales.

Do keep this in mind: businesses can do well without social media. They can make a profit, and break even. But if you want to continue growing, if you want to constantly be improving sales and making more money, if you want to improve your relationship with your customers and engage with them while at the same time not spending too much money, social media is a great way to do this.

Also, don't forget, as more and more of the world gets in social media, more and more people will expect to be able to find their favorite businesses and brands online. They want to communicate with you, to know about their product, and they want to know that you care. Making your customers feel connected to you will help your profits go up because they will feel connected to the product they are buying.

Getting into social media marketing can be tough, and overwhelming. It can feel like a huge, giant project, and often business owners, because of this feeling, decide that it's not worth it.

But it is. It is 100% worth it.

And here's why.

It builds awareness.

It's a part of life now: people talk about what they're doing on social media. Everything, from where we work, what we're eating, where we're vacationing, what we're wearing, who we're dating, where we like to go, what we like, where we live, it's all put up online. When someone puts something up on social media, all 500 of their closest friends get to see it. If 10 of these friends share whatever they have posted, all 500 of their closest friends see it. That adds up to 5,500 people seeing whatever the original post, and it doesn't stop there. People keep sharing your post, and more and more people see it and learn about your company.

The average consumer talks about brands with their family, friends, and co-works about 90 times a week. Even better, 50% of people looking to make a purchase have actually made a purchase all thanks to a recommendation made on social media. Think about it: half of the entire population on social media have made a purchase thanks to social media. By actively participating in social media, you are bringing more people to your page, to your company, to your products, and to more profits.

It's not just local viewings either. Social media gives you the opportunity to spread awareness all over the world, taking it internationally if you so choose. Say you run a quilting business; well, through a simple Instagram post you could get a commission from halfway around the world! If you're a cafe shop who make a specialty drink or pastry, tweeting out about it could get somebody coming to your cafe just for the sole reason of trying it.

You control your image.

By putting your own name out there, you control a good amount of what the public sees and hears about you. Think of it this way: what do you get when you google the word "McDonalds"? You'll get a list of them nearby, their website, and most importantly, their social media pages, specifically their twitter and Facebook. If McDonald's had no presence online, what would show up?

Well, you'd probably get some articles criticizing their food, some disgruntled social media posts and comments, and maybe one or two positive reviews. Of course, when you do type "McDonalds" into Google, you don't get this, because McDonald's has a website and social media pages, they control that first google search. They control the first things you see about the company.

You can do it too. If you have a Facebook page, most likely when you google your business name, that will be the first thing that will come up. As a result, this will be the first thing your potential customer will click on, meaning that you control absolutely everything they see about you.

Shows authenticity.

People want to see what's behind the screen. They want to know who you are, what you do, and they want to feel like they know who you are. Social media gives you the ability to really humanize your brand, and make it feel like there are real people in it. We've all seen these ads from various companies showing their employees actually working, and this is because it gives the company a flavor of realism. Suddenly, you are no longer a corporation just looking to make more sales: you are a business that employs people, who care about their community and puts effort into making sure every product is amazing. You are authentic, and people want to buy from you.

Encourages engagement.

Engagement is the act of communicating with someone on social media, through comments, likes, and shares. On social media, this is essential for communication with your followers.

One company that engages with their customer base really, really well is a beauty company called Lush. If you have never heard of them, they make all-natural skin and hair products, and their social media team is brilliant. Type the hashtag "Lush" into any search bar on nearly any social media page, and you'll get hundreds of thousands of videos of people dropping bath bombs into water, showing pictures of them wearing mud masks, and long posts describing the effects they've had on their skin or hair. That's because Lush often poses questions to their followers, and encourages them to post photos and use hashtags that they recommend on their pages.

This makes their audience feel actively involved in the company and the creation of Lush products. By giving your followers a real close up look into your company, and giving them things to do, you're encouraging them to get involved with who you are. You're opening the door into your world for them, and they feel like they're a part of who you are.

Provides support.

Anyone who has gone through the horror that is calling customer service can understand how frustrating and exhausting it can be. This is especially irritating when your problem is something you could easily solve if you only had the information provided to you in a quick and easy fashion. While this problem could be resolved by a simple Q & A section on your Facebook page or website, you can also reply to your client's questions directly in the comments section, or even direct messaging them. It has all the benefits of calling with none of the frustration. Just make sure that when this happens, you respond quickly.

You get to know your target audience.

The only people who are really going to be following you online are people who are genuinely interested in you as a company and your products. They're going to be the ones who believe in your message, and actively are either using or wanting to use your products. This proves advantageous: you actually get to know exactly who you're selling to, and you really can know exactly what your followers want from you. Many social media websites, including Twitter and Instagram, provide the option of actually polling your followers, which is brilliant. You could offer up two different services or products, and get to know exactly what your customers want.

You're on their mind.

In social media, you can post 10 times a day or 100 times a day. There isn't a limit, although keep in mind that posting 100 times a day might be overkill, and there is a specified amount of times you should post every day to bring positive engagement to your company. By consistently posting and engaging with your followers, you're staying on the forefront of their mind.

If you sell clothing, and one of your followers is looking to buy clothing, if they log onto their Facebook page and see that you have a new shipment in, where do you think they're going to go? By never missing a chance to remind them who you are and what you do, they'll automatically start to associate you with whatever product you're selling. Just think about it: how many times have you seen an advertisement for a kind of coffee, or any other kind of product, before being at the grocery, needing coffee, and going for it because it's what on your mind?

It's not a huge investment.

Economics is at the very center of every single issue in today's world and every single conflict and every single business. The number one question on everybody's mind at the end of the day is: can we pay for it? This is especially true in business, where breaking even is the most important thing at the end of the day, and how your business will survive.

Marketing campaigns in businesses are pretty common; big companies always have at least one person in charge of advertisements. But they can also be very expensive, and the bills can add up very fast. Small businesses often can't afford them. This is why social media is so valuable to small businesses. It's cheap, and even better, doesn't take up too much valuable time. After all, time is money.

If you learn how to use social media in a way that's valuable and effective, you can make the same as you would with a huge, thousand-dollar marketing campaign for a fraction of the cost.

It's not difficult to learn how to use it.

Yes, social media may feel incredibly overwhelming, especially if you're someone who's older and didn't grow up with it. Thankfully, it's not too hard to get involved in it. No, really, it may seem like a complicated thing, and there is definitely a feeling of "I need to prepare for weeks or months," but it's actually quite simple. With a bit of time and some patience, along with help from this book, you can become a master at it.

Nowadays, people in the majority use social media on their phones, so you can do it too. You can literally update your feed as you're going on with your day right from your phone. There are apps for every single form of social media talked about in this book. Some are just apps and you have no way of using them from a desktop!

The most important thing to remember about social media marketing is that it's not going anywhere. Social media is here to stay, so the best time to be getting into it is now. No, seriously, right now. The sooner your business comes out with a well thought out social media strategy that represents your brand in a way that's positive and memorable, the better.

First, of course, you need to figure out which social media site works best for you.

Of course, your first thought is to get onto the most popular social media site, followed quickly by as many as possible. No. This is a bad idea. If you're just starting out, biting off more than you can chew is a huge mistake. All it does is head you straight into feeling inadequate and overwhelmed. It can also be bad for your business.

While, yes, it does make sense to get on the most popular social media websites and use as many of them as possible, but every single social media website is aimed at a different demographic. You might not find your ideal customer base if you're on the wrong one.

It's also not a good idea to jump right into every social media platform when you're just starting out. Would you start playing Beethoven the first time you sit beside a piano? No, you'd start with a simple song like "twinkle twinkle little star."

There's no shame in taking a small step, especially when you're trying something new. A good, easy first step into social media marketing is figuring out exactly what you want from social media, and as a result, figuring out your perfect match.

Use the information below to help you. This is an entire list of available social media networks, ordered by their user numbers, with a small idea of how they work and why they might be the best choice for your business.

Facebook: Facebook is the king of the kings when it comes to social media, often considered the father of all social media (MySpace would be the grandfather). Facebook came out at the time just as social media was about to hit its stride, meaning that it very quickly became hugely popular, a fact that still stands today. Facebook currently has 2.2 billion active users, almost a third of the world's population! It's also the website you really can't ignore as a marketer. It's easy to learn formula and the fact that it's always adapting to its users' needs make it invaluable.

In terms of what kind of businesses should be using it, really everybody has a place on Facebook. There are over 65 million business pages on Facebook right now, and this is mostly because it's easy to use, as well as having a lot of valuable features. Pretty much every content format you can think of works on Facebook, including text, photos, live video, and stories. You can even use their messenger service as advertising! Facebook is great for any kind of business, but if you're trying to aim more at teens, their interest has cooled the past few years, with only about half of them using the service regularly. But 80% of millennials are still on the platform.

YouTube: A video sharing platform where you can spend hours upon hours looking at cat videos, YouTube has almost 2 billion active users and that number keeps rising. It also happens to be one of the biggest search engines online, second only to its owner Google. All it takes to start a channel is to make a short video, upload it, and boom, your subscribers can like, comment, and share the video.

YouTube is great for influencers who want to review products and talk about their experiences with different people and companies. They're also great for How-To videos and Behind-The-Scenes shots. If you make cookware, you could post tutorials on how to use your pots and pans properly. If you sell vegetables, you could show the entire process of how you grow them, and hold interviews with your employees. Video media is especially effective in social media, but remember, it can take the extra mile of effort. Is it worth it? That's really up to you.

Instagram: A popular photo-sharing app, Instagram boasts of over 400 million active users. It is often used to post information about food, fashion, travel, art, and lifestyle. It has several different features, all of which are relatively easy to use, including stories and live videos. It has also recently launched IGTV, which is similar to YouTube, for longer videos.

While it still remains to be seen what IGTV will do for the app, Instagram as a photo sharing platform is great. If your brand is very visual, like an artist or a model, Instagram is a great way to showcase your work. It's also great for travel, fashion, and food blogs, but remember, it is an app. You unfortunately can't use it from a regular computer.

Twitter: As a social media feed with 330 million active users, Twitter is focused on "real time". As in what's happening right at this very moment in news, sports, politics, and entertainment. You're also allowed only 280 characters per post, which can be a deal breaker for some, but actually works to the advantage of your business. People respond well to short posts, and they're more likely to be shared.

Twitter is what actually started the idea of customer service through social media. Celebrities and companies started using Twitter as a way to directly communicate with their fans more, and as a result, more fans went to Twitter to talk to them. Nowadays, more than 80% of social customer service requests take place on Twitter. Some people will of course not like the idea of being limited to 280 characters, and the fact that you have to post constantly throughout the day can be a little tiring, but it's a venture that can be very worth it.

Snapchat: The originator of the "story" format, a short, quick video that disappears after a certain amount of time, Snapchat boasts of 250 million active users. The concept is to send out images and videos, usually with doodles, writing and silly filters on them, adding them to your "story" so your friends can see them. While there are some reports that Snapchat users have gone down, it is still very popular with teenagers and young adults.

People aged 18 to 24 make up 45% of the platform and 76% of American teenagers use Snapchat. If your product is specifically targeted towards a younger generation, it's probably a good idea to at least consider using Snapchat. The decline of Snapchat is mostly thanks to the fact that other major social media platforms, including Instagram, Facebook, and even YouTube, have started to include it in their formula, which people have started using.

Pinterest: Pinterest is the place to get inspired, to find ideas, and most importantly, save that inspiration and these ideas for you to find later. Even better, you can organize them in folders, and have dozens of folders dedicated to projects you're definitely going to get around to one day. It boasts of 200 million monthly users, which seems significantly lower than others on this list, but don't brush it off. Get this: Pinterest is the social media site with the second most influence over people's purchases, second to Facebook.

Pinterest is specifically a place to look for ideas, meaning that people want to see new brands to try on their feed, with 93% of pinners, almost all of them, using it to specifically look for new products to try. If you sell many different products (or multiple versions of the same product) Pinterest is a great place to sort out everything you have. And, if you have a run of the mill blog or website, it's a great way to get more traffic to your website, no matter what kind of articles you're using.

Chapter 2: Becoming an Influencer

Here's the good thing about getting into social media at the current time: there is somebody out there, somewhere, who has made the mistakes that you don't have to. You can learn, not just from your own mistakes, but from theirs as well. By checking out other business and influencers pages, you can see what works and what doesn't work.

Influencers have particularly got this idea down to a science. They're becoming more and more popular in recent years, and are a valuable consideration to add to your business plan.

Do keep in mind that you can use the information provided above to act like an Influencer of your company. A lot of this information can be applied to business pages as well, on any social media platform.

What are Influencers, and why are they so popular with businesses all of a sudden?

Influencers are people selected by businesses with large social media followings and a lot of "influence" over these followers. They are paid to make posts on social media, usually in the form of a positive review of a product or experience, to their large following. As a result, the following often flocks to the product thanks to this recommendation, and buys it.

Some of these people can make thousands of dollars over a simple Instagram photo or 100-character tweet.

Influencers are a valuable addition to consider because consumers are actually losing trust in the businesses and brands they shop at, with less than 10% of the population putting their trust in them. Not only that but ad campaign click-through rates are dwindling.

This is where influencers come in. By telling their thousands or millions of followers to buy the product, a lot of them probably will because they see the influencer using it. Influencers have become masters at making their followers feel like their friends, and can actually increase revenue by a simple recommendation and coupon code. People trust people they like, and who follows somebody they don't like?

Most influencers won't charge you a thousand dollars per post, their price will depend on their follower count and the amount of engagement they get for each post. They are often a considerably cheaper option of paying for large-scale advertising, so they can be a valuable investment if you so choose.

To use influencers to their full potential, you first need to understand exactly how they work, and how they do what they do. You can also learn a lot from them in terms of how to run your business page: taking ideas from accounts you admire is never a bad idea.

The Secrets to Being an Influencer

For started, influencers are very careful to choose products that they believe in and what they are passionate about.

While there are a few out there who will partner with anyone who throws cash their way, most don't do this. They will often request samples of the product, so they can make sure they're recommending something that they know is great. They don't want their followers to think they've recommended a bad product. They will also pick a niche their passionate about, and you should definitely make sure it aligns with yours. (There is more information about that in chapter 3.)

Everything about their profile is about the hook. The bio, their posts, their profile picture, everything about their profile is showing the best of the best. They're also very careful to make sure that it is relatable. That the person on the other side of the screen can picture them in that situation.

Think of it almost like a fashion magazine: in a fashion magazine, you're constantly showing gorgeous people with unattainable beauty standards, often wearing clothing in a way that's completely impractical for everyday use. What influencers online do is take these clothes and show just how a normal person would wear them. Take any product, and apply it to the same idea, and you'll get the same result.

They make a very high point of engaging their followers. They answer their questions, like their comments, and often run polls on their profiles. They tell their fans to use certain hashtags and give them special bonuses if they do. For a good influencer, their number one goal is not only being relatable but to show that these things are possible. They want to feel real, not a made-up facade, but an actual person behind the screen that is doing all the things that the follower has ever dreamed of.

A good way influencers do this is being genuine. They share stories, tidbits of their lives, always making sure that their followers have an in-depth look into who they are and what they stand for. They often talk about things such as insecurities, and their struggles. If they can somehow work a product or a coupon code into that, even better. Think that fashion model again, only this time she is talking about her insecurities.

They're also careful to not be too personal. Anything that influencers do post that does happen to be personal is carefully cultivated and always matches their brand. Being an influencer is all about the image, the careful, made up facade of being perfect but not too perfect. They do understand that at the end of the day, their followers don't really care all that much. People are following them for the ideas, the inspiration, not for their actual real life.

If an influencer is a food blog, and posts about their dog passing away, when the dog has had nothing to do with the blog in any way, can lead to some unfollows. Now, if the dog had been mentioned on the social media page and had been a constant presence, that's entirely different. At the end of the day, just remember what your page is for: promoting your business.

They know exactly what they are and what their message is. This is a mistake a lot of businesses, and influencers, make. They don't know exactly what their message is and what they're trying to do with their pages. Influencers usually pick a topic or theme that resonates with them, something they enjoy talking about and doesn't mind it being their entire life. You should already be passionate about your business and brand to really resonate with your followers. If you don't care about your brand, your followers won't either.

They make plans. Influencers often plan their posts days or weeks in advance and carefully choose the best time of day to post along with hashtags and filters for whatever photos they're using. They make a point to go through each post, make sure that it adds to the theme of their social media page, and are dedicated to making sure they only post things their followers want to see.

Influencers go out of their way to make sure that they know their own social media platform inside and out. A good influencer is constantly looking for new ideas on what to do in terms of hashtags, filters, and fresh ways to reach out to new followers, get their current followers engaged, and find more people to make them aware of their brand. Your business should be doing this too.

Influencers often follow people they admire and look at their ideas. This is actually the way a lot of them get started in influencing, by watching other people online doing the same thing. Business should follow this model, and remember, that there is somebody out there who has already tried what you want to try. They already know if it's a mistake and what's not a mistake.

If there is an influencer whose brand is similar to your brand, take time to look at their profile. You could also choose businesses that are almost the same and look to them for ideas. Take note of the how often they post, the kind of posts they make, the hashtags they use. Think of it almost like market research: actually, no, that's exactly what it is.

The Importance of Staying on Brand

Consistency is valuable on every single layer of business. Consistent with the value of the product, consistent with how the product is, and in terms of advertising, consistent with what your brand is. Social media is no different.

While posting often, and on schedule, is very valuable, your brand, and sticking with it, is irreplaceable. It allows your brand to build up from its original platform while changing your brand over and over again means you start over with the foundation every single time.

It can translate to your followers not really knowing what you stand for, telling them that even you don't know. If they don't know what you stand for, they can't take a real passionate, invested interest in what you do. This is why it's important to find the perfect balance between being consistent and surprising your followers, keeping them a vested interest in your page.

There is a great quote by a man named Alexis Nasard, who also happens to be the former CMO of Heineken, a Dutch brewing company: "at the end of the day, the secret is to be consistent but not predictable."

Basically, this means that, yes, surprising your followers and keeping them entertained is important, it's equally important to make sure that it makes what you already have even richer.

If you don't even know what your brand is yet, this is definitely important. There's a section about this in chapter 3 on how to figure out exactly what your brand, your niche, and your audience are.

But if you already know, or have an idea, then here are some easy tips on how to stay consistent, but also put forward the idea of "new and improved."

Create clear guidelines. Make a long list of all that you can't do, but for everything on that list, add something to the "can do" list. If you have a brainstorming team, make sure to give them some freedom. Just make sure they definitely know what message they should be putting across.

Include your brand assets, every single time, and early on. If you have a slogan or a specific image relative to your brand, use it! Have you ever seen a McDonald's advertisement without the big yellow M or the "I'm lovin' it"?

Think about what has worked before, and apply it to the new idea. How can you improve a chocolate cake recipe without ever trying it? If you've done advertising before, you should take from that experience and apply it to this one. If you haven't, check out other business pages and influencers and see what has and hasn't worked for them.

Influencer Mistakes to Definitely Avoid

Not having a precise set of goals in mind. Every single marketing campaign needs to have a precise goal in mind. Whether it's raising awareness, having a specific product to unload, or to get people talking. A lot of first-time marketers jump into it without knowing what this goal is.

To avoid this is simple: sit down with your team (if you have one), and really hash out exactly what you want. Define what you want to happen if the marketing is a huge success, and define what you would expect to happen if it's a failure. Even what will happen if it's neutral in the success zone, where you don't get quite the turnout you want but you still get a good start. When you begin with a clear goal, you're able to build your marketing around that, and you can set yourself up for success in terms of whatever goals you have.

Not knowing your audience. This is a big one. You have to know exactly who this marketing scheme is aimed towards. Are you aiming towards little kids? Parents of little kids? Teenagers? Young adults just starting to make their way into the world and finding themselves? Older generations who are just looking to relax?

If you want to know your audience, you have to know your product. Think of whom you were thinking of when you designed the product. Who do you imagine purchasing it, finding good use out of it, and enjoying it? What really resonates with them? How do you communicate with them in a way that is effective? By knowing your audience, you'll know exactly what to say and how to talk to them.

Not knowing what platform works best for you. Every platform is different and has its negatives and positives. Each one is designed for a very specific use, and depending on what your business is, one of them will be the right one for you.

To avoid, do thorough research on any platform that you're interested in. There is a chapter devoted to six of the most popular platforms online in this book, along with information about what kind of businesses use them best, how to get followers, how to build your profile in a pleasing way, and how to use them to the best of their ability.

Not making any plans (or planning poorly). Planning is a staple of any business plan. It can really cripple a campaign if you don't have a realistic, set plan to put in motion. You could end up not knowing what to do next and running into a brick wall.

Constantly coming up with ideas, sometimes weeks, months, or even years ahead, is a good idea. You should always be thinking of new ideas, writing them down, and making sure that you are prepared if something goes wrong. If you're really struggling with this, there are great social media planning apps to help you. One of the most well-known, of course, is Hootsuite, but there's a ton of other options.

Working with the wrong influencers: While most influencers will carefully examine and test out a product before even considering it, there are some which will literally take any job that's offered to them. Or maybe there's an influencer that already loves your product and wants to work with you. If you don't carefully screen the influencer, you could end up with one who doesn't reflect any of the messaging you're trying to get across.

Just like an influencer screens what products they plan on using and talking about, you should be screening what influencers approaches are. Your brand and business will reflect what influencers you work with, just as whatever brand an influencer might work with is screened. You need to make sure that they fit in with what you want your company to represent. Also, do keep in mind that your influencer's page should have something in common with your product.

Overestimating an influencer's influence. Just because an influencer has a large following, that doesn't mean that it will have a large impact. This might be good for raising awareness, yes, but if you have other goals in mind you might want to look at other factors. Another thing to consider is that you never know if an influencer has bought their followers. This means that a majority of their followers, who aren't real people, won't actually engage with the post, meaning that it won't get attention elsewhere.

Your first thought when choosing influencers to reach out to should be relevance, rather than how big they are. Find individuals who have influence and understand the industry. Then, if awareness is what you're going for, maybe someone with a large following is what you're looking for. But what you really want to look at is their engagement rate, because, believe it or not, the more followers you have, the less engagement they actually get. People of 1,000 or fewer followers' engagement rates is about 15%, while these with more than 100,000's engagement rate fell down to only 2%. In this case, less is more.

Not being personal enough. Most social media websites have rules that you have to let your followers know that it's an ad, in the process basically letting them know, yes, you're getting paid for this. One mistake a lot of influencers, and businesses make, is taking this too far, and practically just copying and pasting an ad right into their caption or post.

This is a mistake. Remember, the whole idea of influencers using social media to advertise is that it doesn't sound or look like an ad. People don't like looking at ads, and as ads become more and more of an annoyance in our everyday lives, people are getting better and better at ignoring them. You don't want to see an ad in your social media feed. Influencers manage to make their ads not be ads by balancing them with witty captions and letting their followers know just how much they love the product with a personal story or how they use it in their everyday life. They make it personal. It doesn't feel like an ad in that regard, so people don't mind looking at it.

Putting too much money into it. This is commonplace in a lot of businesses, unfortunately. People overestimate just how successful they will be in things, and when they're not, they wind up disappointed and struggling.

Don't just throw money at social media marketers and influencers. Do your research. Read this book. Talk to people you know who have also started a business through social media. Don't just put yourself in the hole with no thought as to how you're going to get it back.

Working with Influencers

With one of the biggest challenges of any business is getting your name out there. While traditional ad campaigns are definitely there to consider, they can often be extremely expensive. This is especially difficult if you're a new business who is just starting out, and can't spend millions of dollars on advertising.

This is the precise reason why it is really valuable to at least consider working with influencers. Influencers aren't just there to advertise your product, they're there to advocate for them. Influencers rarely ever take on a product they don't believe in because they understand that their relationship with their followers is crucial. If they lose that special trust with their followers, they lose their source of income.

Which is why it's important to make sure they are actually a genuine advocate of your product. You have to sell them on the product, and the product actually has to come through for them before they will even consider making a post about it.

Keep in mind, working with influencers is a mutually beneficial relationship. You should be promoting them as much as they promote you, especially if it helps drive traffic to you. Share their posts on your own social media pages! Mention them to your followers! The best relationships between brands and influencers are the ones that work together and help one another.

This means regularly communicating with them about what both of you want out of this business relationship. You both should know what success looks like to the other, and both have clear-cut goals in mind.

Good luck!

Chapter 3: Starting a Business on Social Media

Starting a business on social media, or putting your business on social media, can be a daunting experience. Especially for people who have never done it before, or have very little experience in it. Thankfully, there is a ton of things you can do before you get started to help yourself out.

Finding Your Niche (And Your Market)

Before you start any business, anywhere, you need to know exactly what you are as a business, and who you're selling to. A niche is the place that is appropriate for your business to flourish in, and it can be tricky to figure out exactly what it is. You can spend hours upon hours trying to find it, and you can still feel like you're going nowhere.

The first thing you can do is to list your passions. If you're starting your own business, your platform should be something that you are interested in and something you really care about. If your niche is something you're not invested in and want to succeed, your odds of quitting are much, much higher. This doesn't mean that you have to be passionate about every single part of the niche, you just need to be passionate about something in it. This will keep you going.

To find out what your passion is, ask yourself these questions.

- When you have free time, what do you enjoy doing?

- Are there club or organization you belong to? What kind is it, and what do you do in it?

- What topics do you enjoy learning about?

- What do you picture yourself doing all the time?

When you've done this, do research into whether or not there is a viable market for it. Really look into the kind of problems that your target customer is experience, and see if it's something you can resolve. Talk with people in the target market one-on-one by talking to people you know. Look at websites and forums. Search up keywords and see if whatever niche you've touched upon is ever talked about.

You should also look at your competition. See if they're offering the same product you are. See if you can make it better. Make note of what they're doing wrong and what they're doing right. Competition is seen as a bad thing in business, but it's really not. You can see whether or not there is a market for your product, and even better you can learn from their mistakes. If they're doing something that isn't so great, do it better.

Do some tests. It can take some to figure out exactly what your niche is, and this isn't a bad thing. It's just a thing. There isn't a perfect process for finding out what it is, and there is going to be some missteps along the way. Sometimes the best thing you can do for your business is just getting your name out there and getting started. Don't worry about the small stuff, and make sure you learn from your mistakes. Sometimes, it's just better to have your name out there and learning than to just be researching on how not to do this.

Finding and Keeping Your Customer Base

Who is your product aimed at?

This is the question every business which is just starting off asks themselves. Who are they hoping to sell to?

This can be determined by a number of things. Age, location, gender, race, career, relationship status, family status, the list of the different demographics goes on and on and on. If you already have customers, you should be looking at them closely and determining who they are, what they do, and why they're buying from you. Knowing your customer base can help you target more people like them, as you already know that people like them buy from you.

If you don't know what your target audience is yet, or you haven't started selling, this is the time to figure it out. If you already know your niche, the first thing you should do is check out your competition. Who is buying from them? Who are they marketing to?

Look closely at your own product. You should already know your product inside and out, and take the time to list out every single benefit of each feature of the product. When you have this, ask yourself what kind of person who ultimately benefit from the product and the benefits? Make a list, and target these demographics.

Demographics means a lot of different things. While things like age, gender, location, race, income level, education level, family status, marriage status, and occupation are all good places to start, there is an often-overlooked part of this. These are the actual personality characteristics and lifestyle your ideal customer leads. This includes things like attitude, values, interests, hobbies, behavior, and how they lead their everyday life.

Let's say you are selling a filter app for smartphone cameras. You likely are going to be aiming this kind of app at young people, mostly teenagers. But not every young person wants or needs an app like this, so really think of how a person who wants this kind of app would use it. How and when will they use the app? What features would be appealing to them? How will it fit into their everyday life? What kind of interests and hobbies do they have, and will the app make these more fun? These are questions you need to ask yourself.

Once you've figured all this out, really evaluate your decision. Consider if there are enough people who need this app, whether or not they will really benefit from it, and if they can afford it. Really try to get into their head and walk in their shoes.

Remember this: don't break down your target too far. You can have more than one group of people who want your product. You can aim your marketing at both of these groups.

Defining your target can be tricky on social media. But once you have figured this out, it gets easier to come up with posts, images, and videos that they're going to want to see. Now comes the fun part: making your account.

Starting Up Social Media

Once you've figured all this out, now is the time to get started with your account. Or accounts.

Starting up your business online is very similar to starting up your business in real life. A lot of the information you will find here will often show up online. The good news is that social media is a lot less complicated than people out there make it out to be. It's all about engagement and keeping your audience by giving them what they came for.

You should always start out with a plan. Every good business strategy starts and ends with a well thought out plan. This is a common denominator with social media. You need a plan so you know exactly what you're aiming for. A lot of businesses think that because it doesn't cost money and it's easy to do, that you should just dive in without any plan in mind.

You need a plan so you know exactly where you're heading and what you want from your social media efforts. Here's what you need to do to achieve this effectively:

- Figure out what you want. What are you looking to get out of social media? Are you hoping to attract new customers? Do you want to help your current customers by giving them easy to find information and a way to contact you directly? How much engagement do you expect for each post, and how do you get there?

- Consider an audit. If you've started social media and things aren't going the way you like, consider having your page audited. There are people online you can hire to do this for you, or you can look online to find a checklist of things your pages should have. You can evaluate what you are doing right, what you're doing wrong, and get new ideas on how to move forward.

- Take inspiration. From everywhere. Your competition. Other business accounts. Influencers. Businesses that aren't even on your radar, but have amazing pages and tons of engagement. Study them and learn from their mistakes.

- Understand just how important consistency is. Consistency in how often you post. Consistency in what you post. Consistency in how often you post. People are following you for a reason, and you need to stick to that reason. You have to continue posting because why else would people be following you?

- Look at each social media platform and figure out which one is right for you. Do some research on your demographic. Never make assumptions as to which social media platform they are using. You really don't know, but there are people out there who do. Look into it.

Once you are on social media, and your pages up and running, focus on building relationships.

Your followers should be more than just your followers. They need to be your friends, your partners, and people you want to talk to and engage with. People can argue all day about whether or not follower count matters, but at the end of it, 100 followers who actually comment, like, and want to see your posts are infinitely better than 100,000 followers who just ignore you.

Build relationships by engaging with people. Answer questions, follow back, reply to comments, give the people what they want and ask them what they want. Focus on helping your followers and customers, rather than selling to them. Yes, you're a business, but you don't want to come off as if you don't care whether or not this product adds value to their life. The more you make your customer feel like a friend, the more likely they are to buy from you.

Plan your posts. Just like advertisers plan their ads week or months in advance, you should be planning your posts in the same way. When it's getting into October, you should already have at least 10-20 posts worth of Halloween material (this number depends on your business and what kind of social media page you have). Planning a good while ahead means you'll never run out of things to post. You'll always have something to share with your followers.

Cross-promote. Most businesses have more than one social media account, and they often have a website. Always make sure to mention your other accounts regularly. Thankfully, a lot of social media accounts work very well together. You can often share new posts on one account with the other. For example, Instagram has a feature where you can automatically share your post with Facebook and Twitter.

Stay active. An inactive social media page is the death of that social media page. Why would somebody follow you for the posts if you're not posting? The amount of posts per day or week depends on the platform, but you should be at least posting once a day. People who follow you want to hear from you. Remember that.

Be human. This is so, so important in the world of social media brands. Look at a lot of company's pages on various platforms, and you'll find brands communicating with their followers like they would their friends. They crack jokes, answer their questions, thank them for their comments, and really humanize the company. Remember: people want to buy from companies who feel like they really care about them and their needs, not just companies looking out to make money.

Your Profile

On any social media page, your profile is essential. It's the first thing a prospective follower or buyer will see. In terms of photos and videos, it's especially important because they need to be of the same theme and color layout. Your entire profile acts as the selling point. Think of it almost like walking past a jean store and seeing all the jeans in the window.

Actually, let's take that metaphor a little further: if you have only ever liked one pair of jeans from the store out of hundreds of pairs, would you continue to go back there on the sole chance that you will like another pair of jeans? No, you already know that you only ever liked one of their products, why would you go back?

Your profile should look good, and every single post should look good against each other and be of high quality.

Understanding Keywords

A keyword can be defined as what a person types into the search bar to find something. Every business has keywords on their websites, they just might not be using them to their fullest potential, or just not putting the right ones in.

People use keywords in searching all the time. Just ask yourself: how many times do you use Google or Bing every day? Probably at least 10 times a day, asking it things like basic yes or no to complicated social problems. Crazy, right? "To Google" is even considered a verb now.

You should be using keywords all over your social media site. To get started, make a list of as many words as you can think of that have to do with your website. Then use them as much as you can in your posts. Example: if you have a card making business, and you're posting a new design. Use words like "card," "design," and "new."

The Importance of Consistency and Tone

Consistency is essential in any sort of business. Consistency of product, consistency of advertising, and consistency of quality. The same rules apply for social media marketing and your page.

Consistency is a lot more than about your brand and how often you post. It's also about your tone and personality. Think of your friends. How would you feel if they changed their personality and interests every few days? You probably wouldn't be friends anymore, because you would never know what you were going to get. You would never know if you would like the person every time you saw them.

Tone on social media is generally the same thing. If your brand is more playful and silly, your posts should reflect that. If your brand is more direct and to the point, your posts should say that. This allows people to recognize who you are and what your company and products are about. It's definitely a tightrope act: finding a way to communicate with your audience in a way that's real and resonates with them while staying true to who you are as a company.

For audiences to recognize what your niche/brand is, they need to see what kind of things you are posting. If you're constantly posting about something different, they don't know what you're really about. If you're only posting once every six weeks, they won't even bother following you because it makes it out to seem like you don't care about staying in touch. Every time you post, it is an opportunity to connect with your audience and make them want to reach out to you.

Your consistency should echo throughout every part of your social media page. In every post, the tone should be spot on. Every time you share something from someone else's page, it should resonate with your brand on some level or another. It's also important to consider the source and the information. It never hurts to double check or fact check information you find online.

And, last but not least, always remember that each post you make should add to each other, visually. Your entire profile should be appealing in appearance. Humans are very visual creatures. Everything, from the header image to your video posts should match up together and looks nice against each other. Variety in the type of formats you decide to use can really help with this. Variety is always essential in keeping your audience interested.

In this book, there is an individual chapter on each social media network you might consider using. You'll find information in each on how to build your profile, the best kind of posts, and how to engage your followers. This is just the beginning.

Chapter 4: Monetize Your Audience

None of the information in this book means absolutely anything to you if you can't make money off of it. The real question for any business is this: How can I make money off of this?

Generating more revenue is really the biggest reason why businesses turned to social media. They wanted a new way to reach new customers, in the process selling more products, and earning more cash. The bottom line is always the end goal.

But once you've gotten them to buy a product, or follow you, how do you actually make money? How do you keep them interested? How do you get your customers who have already bought something to buy more?

Thankfully, half the battle is already done. If someone is following your business online, congratulations! They're already invested and interested in you and your product, and if they haven't bought it already, it won't be hard to sway them to buy it. They probably already agree with your message and want to live by it.

Half the climb is already done, and now you just need to get them over that hill.

1) **Direct sales.** If somebody slides into you direct messages looking for more information, give it to them! Just because it's through social media doesn't mean you can't communicate directly with your customers and tell them exactly where to go. You can give them a direct sales pitch about the product, the benefits, the history of it, and how it fits into their life, all from your computer or phone. This way you actually establish a personal connection with your potential customer, the same way you would if you were in a store, standing two feet away from each other.

2) **Post the positive reviews.** You know how when you buy a book, sometimes they've copied and pasted the reviews on the cover? Do the same thing for your product. If it gets a positive review, toss it up online. Quote the article in a caption of a photo. Bring attention to the fact that other people want it. You could even post satisfied customers (with their permission). People tend to want what other people have.

3) **Keep them up to date on new products and offers.** Your business should constantly be coming up with new ideas anyway, and always letting your customers know. There's a reason why McDonald's still run ads: because they're still coming up with new meals to share with people. If there is something new in your business, let your followers know. Again, they are already interested in what you sell, remember that. They might just need a push, and that push could be a product that suddenly aligns with what they want. In every post doing this, make it a point to say exactly where it's going to be and at what time, and how long you will have it.

4) **Offer discounts and offers to your followers**. Do this occasionally, and make a huge deal over it. You could even make it clear that it's only the first 10\100\1000 that get the offer. This is how a lot of businesses get their company off the ground: they offer a big discount to a certain number of people and these people flock. Your follower base is just another form of loyal customers, so they should be the ones getting the discount. Are you a store that is just opening? Post that the first 10 shirts will get 20% off!! Maybe you're running a course. Then the first 100 people to sign up can access it for half of what you'd normally pay. These are just some examples. You want to keep your customers coming back for more, and at the same time just continuing to let them know how much you appreciate them.

5) **Give them a taste.** We've all been to the grocery store and had someone wearing a hairnet and an apron offer us a free sample? It's usually a product you would never think of getting, but sometimes you end up really liking it and buying it. You would have never even considered buying that product twice unless there were free samples of it. It's the same with online business. Sometimes you really need to give your followers a taste of something to sell them on it. If you're selling a course, give them a watered-down version of it. If you're selling an eBook, give them the first two chapters. Everybody loves free samples.

6) **Do tutorials.** This works really well if you're coming out with a product for people to use in their everyday life but might not know exactly how to use it. Think cookware, handyman tools, electronics, etcetera. If you're selling a food product, show people how to use it in recipes. All you really need for this is a good camera and a person willing to show your fans how.

7) **Create shareable content**. The biggest mistake of a lot of businesses online is that their content is just not appealing. Their content is dry, boring, or worse, and nobody wants to share it with their friends and put it up on their feed. Do your best to create appealing content that people actually want to see or read. The more people share your stuff, the more you're likely to get more sales.

8) **Post articles**. If you're looking to make more ad revenue on your blog, posting your articles to other social media sites is a great way to get more people to click. Just make sure that the cover image and title are appealing, and it's a subject people want to talk about.

Chapter 5: Facebook Marketing

Facebook is the King of social media. While you could say that MySpace is the father, Facebook is definitely the King. It currently has over 2 billion active users, 1.4 of them tuning in daily, and is the most popular social media network online.

Facebook was launched in 2004 by the now infamous Mark Zuckerberg. Originally only open to Harvard college students, it eventually expanded to include schools all across the USA, Canada, and the UK, before opening itself to the public in 2006. Facebook figured out the formula early on: they constantly had to adapt to suit the wants of their users.

This is precisely why Facebook is going to remain the top social media network for a very long time. It is constantly adapting, changing, and reworking itself to fit the needs of its users, in contrast to MySpace, which crashed and burned thanks to its inability to change.

Facebook is the one social media network that marketers really can't ignore. Not only because of its massive user base, but also because of this ability to adapt. They are always adding new features, often using ideas from other social media sites, and pushing the boundaries. Every content variation you can think of, Facebook likely has it.

Facebook may be cooling with the younger generation, who prefer apps like Snapchat or Instagram, but it is still very much a powerhouse. More than half of Americans in every age group say they are on Facebook. YouTube is the only other social media network with more range across their users. The younger generation is even using it: 76% of kids aged 12 to 17 admit to having an account and using the platform.

Facebook is the most important social media network to get onto for all of the reasons above. It's here to stay. You might as well embrace it.

Your Facebook Page

Facebook is very good to its businesses. You get a lot of features and bonuses once you create a Facebook business page. One of the best qualities is Facebook insight.

Facebook Insights is a way to see all your engagements in one place, and even better, it is easy to understand even for someone who has never used that kind of data before. You can see just how many likes, comments, reactions, and any other kind of engagement you get with Facebook Insight.

You can really get into it and see how certain posts are doing. You can see which posts are getting a lot of engagement and which ones aren't, and compare the two. You can even decide you only want to see one kind of post, and sort by type.

There are other benefits besides Facebook Insights of course. You can add the following things to your business profile, all of which can help you market your business in a well thought out and thought-provoking way:

- Hours of operation

- Address

- Phone number

- Reviews

In terms of actually building your Facebook profile, it's easy to learn. The name of your profile should be the same as your business. Use your logo as your profile picture, and a picture that accurately represents the business as your cover photo.

Describe your business. You only have 155 characters, which isn't a lot. Make every sentence count. There is another place on your profile to provide a longer description, but don't worry about it. The most important one is the one that your potential customers will see as soon as they see your page.

Make sure everything on this page has no spelling errors and that it all accurately reflects the brand. If you have other social media networks, you can put the links in the other about me section, along with a longer description of the business. The longer about me is located under "edit story" on the right side of the page.

Posting

Facebook has many different kinds of posts, and they are always adding more to the roster. They will likely have at least one more on this list before the year is out.

Text Post

The original kind of Facebook post, and the most basic. A text post sparks engagement and gets your followers talking. Ask your followers questions about what they want from you and what you can do to make their lives easier, and this will get you some great engagement.

Image Post

Image posts have a lot to offer. Studies have shown that posts with photos actually get more engagement than those without. It doesn't necessarily have to be one of your own photos. There are plenty of free stock photo websites out there that you can use. Just make sure that it has something to do with the message you're trying to send out.

Video Post

Video in marketing is particularly powerful, especially when selling a product. Especially a video that shows you exactly how the product works. Video clips start automatically playing in the Facebook newsfeed, meaning that you really only need a moment to catch someone's attention.

While a short video is always a good option, longer videos have almost made Facebook a replacement for YouTube. There are companies posting blogs, reviews, and tutorials, all without leaving Facebook, with people watching over a combined 100 million hours of video every day.

Live Video

Live video is exactly what it sounds like: a video that is live. It can be a great way to connect with your followers and give them behind the scene looks at your company, your product, or even the personality behind the brand. Just remember, anything can happen during a live broadcast, so be sure to prepare yourself well for any problems that could take place.

Linked Content

Linking content on Facebook is a very popular and very easy way to get more engagement to your own website, or other content online. Be careful to only share content to your page that is relevant to you, and that you think your followers will want to share as well. Sharing is caring, everybody!

Pinned Post

Having a pinned post is when you pin a post at the top of the page. This is great for you if you have something that you feel like needs attention, and should be the first post that your potential customers see as they click on your page. (ex. You're trying to sell tickets to a show. Your pinned post should be a review or a picture of the production.)

Gaining More Likes

The biggest goal of any social media marketing strategy is to get as much engagement as possible, and Facebook is no different. Thankfully, using Facebook in a way to create more business for yourself and bringing awareness to your brand is a lot simpler than it seems.

The most important thing you can do is create shareable content. Your content should be things that other people want to post about on their profile and share with their friends. This is what will get you a good amount of exposure. Make sure to always use good photos, that everything is in good quality, and it's done professionally.

Be consistent. Post at least 5 times a week, but don't post more than 2 times a day. On Facebook, spamming can lead to some thumb downs. You should also post at the best time for your business: what that is will depend on your brand. But it seems the afternoon is the best place for Facebook posting.

Short and sweet. Studies show that posts with less than 150 characters get 17% higher engagement. The quicker it is to read; the more likely people will actually read it.

Be relevant. Every single post on your page should somehow lead back to exactly who you are as a business. If you're a real estate agent, you really shouldn't be posting about dogs.

Consider tailoring your post to the seasons. If you're a baking company, post a lot of Christmas cookies around the holidays. If you're a travel blogger, in the autumn you should be posting a lot of pictures of the leaves.

Include a call to action. If you're hosting a live event, add something like: "we're streaming in 20 minutes! I can't wait to see you there!!"

Creating a Facebook Group

Facebook groups are exactly what they sound like, a group on Facebook of people with a shared interest, but they're more than that. They are a group of people, getting together online to share ideas, information, and debates, such as like-minded people. Once you've started to really build up your following, a Facebook group is something to seriously consider.

An easy and effective way to gather up all your fans into one place and encourage them to interact with each other, you can use this to your advantage. Your followers will likely share their own ideas about the company and you won't have to do a thing to encourage it. It's a great way to so communicate with followers and get to know what they really want. You can generate conversation, but it's not necessary.

Sometimes people create their own groups with a brand in mine. They often share a common interest and want to talk about it. If you are looking for ideas on things to post, you could see if you find any that are similar to your brand. They might have some ideas and, even better, you could probably attract some of the fanbase to you.

Facebook Shop

Well, nowadays, Facebook isn't just a place for marketing your product anymore. Now you can actually sell the product *right on Facebook*. Yes, you read that. Facebook now lets you have the ability to create a Facebook shop page and directly sell items to your followers.

This is another feature that is very, very new, and not very many people are taking advantage of it.

Your first thought might be "no way" but stop and think about it. Facebook is the most popular website in the world, and average users spend about 20 minutes per day on the platform. That adds up to over two hours every week. That's a lot of time.

It's also not that hard to believe, considering our own experiences with social media. We've all fallen down the rabbit hole, haven't we? Where we spend at least an hour scrolling through our feed, tapping links, and liking posts?

There's no harm in taking advantage of Facebook as a social media platform, so there's certainly no harm in using it as a selling platform. It's not a fully evolved one, with all the bells and whistles, like Etsy or eBay, but it does its job.

To do this, you're first going to need a Facebook business page. On your page, Locate the shop tab to the left and click on it. You're going to have to give Facebook information such as your tax number and your address. For payment, you can link your bank account.

After this is all done, you're ready to go! You can add a product to your shop/s.

People may see Facebook as an odd place to sell things, at least directly, but think of it's this way: you're making the time they have to wait to pay shorter, meaning they have a small window to change their mind.

Messenger

Messenger is the Facebook messaging app. It's used by almost everyone with a smartphone, mostly because in 2014, Facebook removed the messaging feature from their regular app, forcing people to download messenger.

Messenger is a powerful tool for businesses because it's direct and much more personal. Unlike a post which a person can just scroll past, a direct message is right there in your messenger box and is often tailored to you specifically.

Customers want to use direct messages to communicate with businesses. 63% of customers said that their own messaging with businesses has increased the last two years, and 56% would rather message than call a business for customer service.

You can also use Messenger as a marketing tool. Here's why and how:

1) You directly deliver the content. This most common way of delivering content is to use email, but Messenger is much more direct and much faster. It also gets much higher engagement rates that email does.

2) You help your followers find the content they want. If a follower wants to specify the kind of content they want to read, you can set up a Messenger chatbot to help them. This is a non-intrusive way to introduce new content to your followers.

3) You remind your followers of important events. You can set up a chatbot to send your followers reminders of events coming ups.

4) You re-engage customers that haven't been in touch for a while. Occasionally nudging your followers isn't a bad thing, as long as it's done in a gentle and non-evasive.

5) You talk to your audience one on one. Facebook is full of ads. It's just a fact. So, imagine a way to get away from all that noise and really engage with your customer one on one. You can pitch them, the way you would in a store, on messenger.

6) You provide fast and easy customer service. The best thing about messaging is that a customer doesn't have to hog up their phone line and take hours to wait to get through to a customer service agent. It can take less than a minute to get an answer to a question they want to be answered.

Chat Bots

Now, if you're interested in learning about Chatbots, and don't have the time to spend answering every single message that is sent to your Facebook page, it can be a bit overwhelming. People assume it takes a lot of complicated coding to make a chatbot. Most don't even try.

There's a way to make this all so much easier. There are platforms out there that will actually help you create one, and run it on the platform for you. One of them is called Chatfuel, another is called Botsify.

These websites will often walk you through the entire Chatbot process, and really help you figure it all out. Don't worry, you've

got this.

Facebook, at the end of the day, is here to stay. It's not going anywhere. So, you might as well get used to it.

Chapter 6: Facebook Ads

Facebook's user base is the biggest user base online, with over 2 billion monthly users. This is the exact reason why it's such a valuable ad space. Also, bonus, it's really simple and flexible, which makes it perfect for someone who is just dipping their toes into the water of social media ads. Facebook ads also have the benefit of showing up on Instagram as well.

Facebook ads are proven to be highly effective. 65 million businesses are using Facebook ads. 96% of marketers admit to considering using the platform as an option when they start to think about ads. Facebook ads are also very easy to set up, use, and understand. Managing your Facebook ads is a significantly easier process than if you used Google AdWords, which is known to be difficult for new users to master.

You can get started without too much of a large effort, and see results pretty fast. The most important thing is that you do it right, and you can do this without spending a lot of money or putting days or weeks of work into it.

You will always reach your target audience. In Facebook Ads, the target audiences are highly customizable. You can specify exactly who you want to reach based on their location, their interests, the engagements on their Facebook pages, and more.

Facebook Ads also offers a host of different kind of ads (see the list below) that you can choose from. They include video ads, article ads, and photo ads, and are constantly adding more to choose from. You'll definitely find the right one for your business. Facebook's biggest strength is that they're always looking to expand and improve on what they already got: they're dedicated to always adapting to suit their user's needs. Their ad system is no different.

Finding Your Objective

Your marketing objective is the strategy set by a business when promoting its products and participating in advertising. It's the strategy set forth to achieve its goals.

Facebook has arranged 11 different marketing objectives to choose from, so there's plenty of options to choose from.

These are the following:

- Brand awareness: increasing the number of people who are aware of your brand

- Reach: reaching as many people as possible in a certain amount of time

- App installs: encouraging people to download your app

- Conversation: get people talking about your brand and wanting to know more

- Video views: putting a video ad out there, before getting them to look at more of your videos

- Engagement: driving up the number of likes, comments, reactions, and shares you get in your Facebook feed.

- Lead generations: getting new prospects into your sales

- Track performance

- Traffic: driving up the number of clicks and engagement you get to a specific webpage (or even just your Facebook page)

- Messages: increase in the number of people subscribing to hearing from you regularly through Facebook messenger

How do you know which one is right for you?

Choosing the right objective is crucial. It will affect your whole campaign, and what you get out of it. To make it simple, pick the objective that most aligns with what you want to get out of it.

Awareness: do you want to generate interest? Do you want more people to know about your brand?

Consideration: do you want people to think of you when they're considering looking into your brand of service or product? Do you want them to ask questions and want more information?

Conversion: are you trying to encourage sales? Is your aim to find more people to use your service?

Keep in mind that as you use Facebook ads more and more, your objectives might get more specific (*think I want more people to like my page, I want more people to sign up for the course*). But when you're just starting out, using the above examples is a great place to start.

Types of Ads

Just like how Facebook is always going to be coming up with new marketing objectives and new features, it will always be coming up with more ideas for ads. It is an ever-changing beast, and that can only mean good things for you. The more variety Facebook provides, the more likely you are to find an ad format that fits every need you're looking for.

The ads below are separated on what they bring to the table.

Sales for Your Service or Product

If you're a company who's running a store, whether a local business or e-commerce, Facebook is great for showing a wide range of products. Believe it or not, a lot of these ads don't even need to leave the Facebook website or app for them to work: people can fill them out and learn more right on the site.

Multi Products: think of a long line of images that you scroll through. You can show up to 10 images and is extremely useful if you're looking to promote multiple products from your business, or you have one product but it comes in a bunch of different colors. You could also use it to promote different posts and offers to see what customers are clicking on.

Dynamic Product Ads: These ads target you based on your past actions on Facebook's website or app. All you have to do is upload your product catalog to Facebook, and make sure that your Facebook Pixel is installed correctly on your site's pages. And you're there.

Lead Ads: It's all in the title: lead ads are for getting leads. The ad lets people get your content and sign up for your offer without actually having to leave the website.

Traffic for Your Website

Driving traffic to your website is no doubt very important. Ads leading to your website should showcase the absolute best of your website, and be a great preview of what's to come.

Link Click Ads: These are the ads you think of when you think of Facebook ads. They perform very well and are known to generate likes for your page.

Video ads: Video ads are one of the most popular forms of advertising online, and with good reason. You can put a lot out there about yourself with just a 15-second video. Video ads on Facebook really are just another form of link click ads.

Page Boost Posts: These are the posts that look exactly like a regular post, only they have the "sponsored" note at the top. Every time a business makes a post, they have the option to "boost it."

Likes and Engagement

Getting as many likes and engagements as possible is very important in Facebook. The more engagement you get, the more attention will come to your business. This is why ads that encourage exactly that are so popular.

Page Ads: just a simple ad of your page, probably with a little description as to who you are

Page Photo Post Ads: a post showing a chosen photo post that you've posted, along with a like button beside it to like the page

Page Video Post Ad: the same thing as the ad above, only with a video

Page Post Ad: the same thing as the top two, but only with a regular text post. Keep in mind that this one has the lowest engagement rates, so you might want to look the other way.

Creating a Great Ad

Ads have to do a lot of things. They have to sell you on the product, portray both the product and the company in a great life, and make it relatable to the consumer's life. Finding the recipe for success can take some time and effort. There will probably be a few missteps along the way.

Ask yourself these questions.

- What makes you stand out from the crowd?

- What is it that makes your brand unique?

- What makes you stand out?

- How is your product or service different from the rest?

- What can you offer that they can't or won't?

- What would attract you to this product or service?

- What do you have that your competition does not?

Keep the headline interesting, but short and snappy. In social media, you need to grab someone's attention quickly. They can just scroll past it if you don't, or skip it. Your headline needs to be short, but also very effective. A headline can make or break your ad. Remember: there are more people who will read your headline than those who actually read it.

Give them a bargain. People have a hard time resisting the concept of saving money, even if it's something they don't really need. How many times have you bought something because it was a buy one, get one free deal? Make them an offer they can't refuse.

Call to action. You should never just tell your customers that this great product exists. You should always tell them to actually do something. Click on the link, like the page, buy the product, pay for the service. Remind them that this product or service could absolutely be in their life if they do something.

Make it urgent. People often see ads and make a mental note to look into it more closely later. Unfortunately, people are busy, and usually just move on with their lives. Make it out to seem that this deal is going to disappear, and they will never get this opportunity to do so again. Every single ad should be done with the intent that the buyer will only ever see it once.

Using What You Have on Multiple Platform

Facebook is the best platform for social media ads, especially if you're just beginning. It's easy, they walk you all the way through it, and there's no reason to really explore other options. It's also the most effective of all social media advertising. It also uses advanced targeting than any other platform, using user's history to determine what they want to see.

But if you do, it is not too hard to transfer what you have to other platforms. YouTube is the second biggest advertising module on the internet, but Google Ads can be very complicated and difficult to understand for someone who has never used it before. Twitter also has its own advertising.

If you plan on using multiple advertising across multiple different social media platforms, do your best to use an advertising format that works for all of them. Video advertising is your best bet.

Why Video Ads, and Why They're Powerful

Video ads are often considered the most effective form of advertising, both inside and outside social media. Video content is the most popular content on the internet. People love content that engages them, and video ads do this. On Facebook, video content is what gets the most engagement, with videos reaching 135% more organic reach on Facebook when compared with photos. It is estimated that in 2020, 75% of mobile traffic will be video streaming.

On Facebook, 100 million hours of video a day are being watched on average. This means that, with a lot of people making videos, it won't be too expensive. A lot of marketers see video ads as being a giant hassle. This is true: they can be a hassle and take up considerably more effort than a plain old picture ad. But if you're not convinced that they're worth it after seeing these numbers, well, I'm sure nobody can convince you.

Chapter 7: Instagram Marketing

If there is any social media platform that adequately sums up the phrase "a picture is worth a thousand words" it would be Instagram. The platform launched in 2010 and has been owned by Facebook since 2012. As of 2018, it has 400 million active users. It started off as solely a photo-sharing platform but has since evolved into videos, stories, and IGTV, a platform similar to YouTube.

Visual content is the most popular form of content online. It's the kind of that gets shared the most, and gets the most engagement, which is why it's probably not a bad idea to look into Instagram, especially if your business depends on visuals.

One of the biggest differences between Instagram and other social networks, at least at first, that Instagram was solely an app at first. Now, it does have a website, but you can only post photos and videos from the app.

Instagram is extremely popular with people under 30, them making up 59% of the platform, and people under 25 use Instagram for an average of 32 minutes a day. In terms of teenagers, 72% of them use Instagram use Instagram every day, second only to Snapchat, and since Instagram has put in a story option similar to Snapchat's formula, that number is getting higher. This is an extremely valuable tool if your product is more aimed towards that generation.

If you want your business to be picked up internationally, 80% of Instagram users are outside the US. This is especially valuable if your product is something that can be ordered or used online, like a course or a blog. If you're located in a tourist town, this is also a thing to consider.

Instagram is all about visuals, and because of this, it is one of the best apps out there for businesses that really depend on these visuals. It's also very easy to share Instagram photos and videos to places like Facebook and Twitter.

For example, if you're a blog about cooking, Instagram is a great way to promote new articles you're going to be posting. You can post images of the food you're going to teach them how to use, cookbooks you enjoy, and fresh produce. You can really pull in somebody to a website or more information thanks to a simple picture.

And here's how.

How to Use Instagram

Making your Profile

The most valuable real estate of your profile is your bio. On Instagram, you get about 200 characters, which can run out pretty quick, meaning that you really need to spend time crafting the perfect one. Every word counts, and your bio should reflect exactly who you are as a company.

In your bio, you should try to include the following information:

- Who you are

- What services you should provide

- Why should you follow them

- A link to your website for more information.

Tips for a Great Bio

- If your business has a slogan, this is a great place to put it: the whole point of a slogan is to really put forward the message of your business and that's exactly what a bio is

- You should include emojis: emojis are a fun way to add personality into your bio and to set the tone: you don't even have to include fun ones, just ones that reflect what you do (ex: if you're a photographer, use a camera emoji!!)

- Use hashtags. A lot of big companies use hashtags specifically marketed for their campaigns, and it shows on Instagram. Nike's #justdoit campaign has, as of December 2018, been tagged 16 million times on Instagram. But don't use too many: just one is fine. If your followers do tag you, you want it all to be in one place, and too many hashtags can clog up your bio and turn followers away.

- Put what you do in your header title. No, not your username, but your header title. (Ex: Samantha Samerson, Seashells. This means when somebody puts "seashells" into the search bar, their name will show up.)

- Give your followers a "bonus." Think, a coupon code, a link to a free eBook that they will get if they subscribe to your email list. Just a little taste of what you provide and what they'll get if they buy from you.

- Anything you can't fit into the bio, you can put into your story.

In terms of your profile picture, it should definitely be a clear indicator of exactly who you are and what you do. A lot of businesses use their logo, but there are other options. Really, just think a well photographed, focused image that is everything you are.

Following and Followers

Who you follow can actually affect who follows you, so be careful. The accounts and hashtags that you choose to follow should be ones that you want to mimic. A good place to start is with brands that you admire.

Following brands whose accounts you enjoy looking at can be a good experience because it teaches you what works and what doesn't. You can look at their engagement rates, which photos get the most likes and comments. This is a great way to determine their value and why customers follow your competition.

Liking and commenting can also bring attention to your own page. If you're a travel page and constantly are liking travel pictures and commenting on them, other people will see that you comment and like a lot of these photos, and check out your page.

Posting Photos

The whole point of Instagram is to post pictures. It is the most important part.

The best method as to what photos to post is not just thinking of things that reflect who you are and your brand, you should also be thinking of a magazine.

In a magazine, editors take careful consideration into what photos look best beside each other, the overall theme of the magazine, and think of the entire magazine as the selling point. Your photos should look great up against each other, almost like a collage in a magazine.

If this is something you really struggle with, there are apps out there that can present to you exactly how your profile will look. A great app is one called Preview, available in both the Apple app store and Google Play. It is free, or you can take out a subscription.

You should also consider investing in a photo editing app. Some businesses actually use the same photo editing formula for every photo, so they look similar. Instagram does have editing features, but they're not the best that you could be using. Good apps to use are Snapseed and the very popular VSCO. VSCO has a subscription service for about $20 a year.

The best times to post on Instagram are from 12 PM to 1 PM Monday to Friday. Take advantage of this, because Instagram's algorithm is not based on chronological order, but how much engagement the post has, and how much the user is likely to want to see it. Tip: if you can, keep a bunch of posts in your drafts. It's an easy way to post at exactly the time you should, but without any hassle of planning a post on the spot.

Hashtags

Hashtags are the signposts of Instagram. When people are looking for accounts to follow, more often than not they head into hashtags. If they like looking at pictures of food, they will look up food. If they want to see sunset pictures, they will head into the sunset hashtag. You get the idea. This has only become truer since they introduced the concept of being able to follow just the hashtags, meaning that the best posts from the hashtag end up in your feed. This could lead to more follows for you if you use hashtags correctly.

The kind of hashtags you use really depends on the kind of account you are, and the kind of followers you want to be gaining. If your goal is to gain as much engagement as possible, you should go for the most popular hashtags in the space your business operates in. But, if you want more long-term followers and loyal customers, you should really aim for more specific hashtags (ex: if you're a local business that is only accessible in that area, hashtag your city). Every Instagram post has a limit of 30 hashtags, and stories have a limit of 10. Use all of them, but always make sure they actually make sense with the post.

Some Hashtag Tips

- To make it easier for yourself, create a memo in a memo app on your phone so you can just copy and paste it into your post

- If your business has a hashtag that you want your followers to use, use it. If you want maximum impact, use it in your caption.

- Do you want to put in all 30 hashtags, and want to share it on other platforms but don't want the hashtags making the post look too hashtaggy? Instead, comment the hashtags, it has the same effect.

Just in case you're running a bit of a blank, here are some hashtags divided into categories you can use. Not every one of these posts can be used for every post in this category, to be noted. Every time you use hashtags, it should fit the individual post, so be careful with which you use. Avoid just copying and pasting from a website.

Food: #foodie, #foodporn, #food, #foodgasm, #yummy, #yum, #goodeats, #eatingfortheinsta, #chefmode, #hungry, #cleaneating, #instagood, #delicious, #eating, #sweet, #breakfast, #lunch, #dinner, #delish, #tasty, #nomnom, #eatingright, #ilovefood, #iloveeating, #foodgrammers, #foodgram

Travel: #travelgram, #travel, #traveltheworld, #instatravel, #travelgram, #theworld, #traveltheglobe, #instagramtravelers, #worldtravelers, #travelingtheworld, #ilovetravel, #traveling, #globetrotter, #beach, #cities, #skyline, #view, #backpackerlife, #backpacker

Fitness: #fitness, #instafit, #getmoving, #heath, #healthyeating, #fitnessmodel, #motivation, #healthyfood, #fit, #instahealth, #healthychoices, #workout, #bodybuilding, #cardio, #gym, #active, #strong, #lifestyle

Stories

Stories are a relatively new addition to Instagram in the past few years. Instagram Stories were viewed as an obvious plagiarism of Snapchat, which popularized the idea. But people used it anyway, and now every day, over 300 million stories are posted, with one in five getting a direct message. This is huge.

Even better, because they disappear after 24 hours, they are a great place to promote one-day offers or bring attention to new content in the same style that twitter does without it taking over your feed.

Stories are also a great place to really add personality to your brand. In stories, you can really showcase what your brand is really about. You can add hashtags, stickers, and links. One brilliant feature that has been added very recently is polls.

In it, you can actually ask your followers questions, and get answers. This is a direct way to ask your followers exactly what they want from you, and even better, get a lot of engagement.

Ideas for Stories

- Behind the scenes. Is something happening at your company that you're super excited about? Is there some behind the scenes shenanigans that you think your followers should see? Take your followers through your day and add some real authenticity to your company. Show the realness.

- Promotion. You have a one-day sale, and need to talk about it. Your new post is up. Stories is a great place for promotion because of its disappearing formula.

- Takeovers. If you have an influencer that regularly works with you, get them to takeover your story for a few hours. This is a great idea for both you and the influencer: it brings attention to both you and them.

- Q & A. This is another Instagram feature where you can tell your followers to ask you questions, about you, the company, what kind of products, and you can answer them in your story.

Highlights

Highlights is a feature where you can organize the best moments of your story into easily accessible highlight reels. Highlights are a great place to put anything you can't put in your bio.

Ideas for Highlights

- Q & A highlight. Have a question that is always asked by your followers? An FAQ highlight provides a place where you can put all their questions in an easy to find space.

- Behind the scenes. If you have some great shots that really add to the realness and authenticity of your company, such as showing off your employees or the way a product is made, put it in there.

- About us. Anything that you can't put in the bio that you feel is important, like the company's history, your employees, all the products you have, amazing customers, that should be in a highlight reel as well.

Instagram is best used when a company is especially visual. It's all about the visuals, remember that. Happy Gramming!

Chapter 8: Twitter Marketing

Twitter is really where the idea for brands being on social media started. It was the first social media network in which people could communicate directly with their favorite brands, and became very popular. Twitter was launched in 2006 and has amassed about 330 million active users.

It really started the whole communicate with the brands through celebrities. Celebrities like Lindsay Lohan, Paris Hilton, and even politicians like Barack Obama realized they could communicate directly with their fans on Twitter. On Twitter, the ground is even; a fan can tweet their favorite celebrity and get a response. Brands realized that this was a good business model, and followed their example.

Nowadays, Twitter is often considered one of the best platforms for engagement. Why?

Well, it goes back to the common ground point. On a lot of brands twitters like Denny's, LinkedIn, and JetBlue Airlines, you'll find them constantly communicating with customers, whether they're tweeting back at them, retweeting success stories, and asking their followers questions about their day to day lives. On Twitter, you don't go through hours of customer service: you just send a tweet directly to the source. A lot of social media sites like Facebook have implemented this into their business page (on Facebook you can post on a business's wall, for example), but Twitter is the place to go.

Their user base is incredibly diverse. Unlike with most social media where the ratio of men to women usually has a large gap, Twitter's is literally 50/50. It's especially popular with millennials. 36% of Americans aged 18 to 29 years old use Twitter, and Twitter itself claims that 80% of its user base are millennials. 28% of people with college degrees use Twitter. It's also very global: 79% of their user base is not in the USA.

Twitter thrives on things that specifically support and encourage engagement. Things like photos, hashtags, and numerals (tweets containing stats or sports scores). They also have a feature where you can poll your followers. Brands have even been known to communicate and tease each other, bringing attention to both brands and starting engagement among followers.

And the most important reason why: it's real time, and it's fast. Twitter was built specifically on the idea of "what's happening in my life and in the world right now?" On it, you can share quick updates on projects, talk about what's going on in your day, and ask your followers questions in a quick and easy formula. It's 260-character limit actually works to their advantage: the shorter a tweet is, the more engagement it's likely to get.

Is Twitter right for you? Yes, yes it is. Twitter can work for almost any business, whether you're a local brand or a multimillion-dollar chain of brands. The only issue is whether or not your clients/customers are on Twitter, and well, they probably are.

How to Use Your Twitter

Building Your Profile

Building your Twitter profile is a simple task, and it's a good place to get used to shaving everything down. The hardest part of any bio on Twitter is the bio. You only have 160 characters, and you have to fit everything you want to say in it. It can be difficult. Your bio has to be memorable, entice followers, and really express everything you are. Don't worry about writing the perfect bio: you rarely will get it right on the first try.

Use keywords. Make sure to be specific on exactly what you do in your bio. It doesn't have to be a long sentence, it can even just be the title or what you do. You could even reference the year since you've been doing it. Think: "selling potatoes since 2003". This means people will search "potatoes."

Put your slogan into your bio. This is a no-brainer. If you have a slogan, make sure you put it in your bio. You will almost always be the exact message that your business is built on.

Be personal. Personality is everything. You have to come off as authentic and transparent. But most importantly, you have to make your followers feel likethey follow you, they're part of a community. For example, if you sell makeup and other beauty products, something "Beauty Gurus unite!" brings a smile to a prospective follower's face, and makes them feel like you're talking directly to them.

Use humor. A lot of businesses will use humor in their bio to entice people to look more closely at their profile. This isn't necessary, but it's shown to raise followers. Tip: if you have an inside joke that only people who have known about you for a long time and that is easy to get into, use it.

One or two hashtags don't hurt. Hashtags are Twitter's way of sorting out users and tweets based on categories. Using a hashtag not only puts you in that category, but it also encourages engagement. Just don't make your entire bio hashtags. Just the keywords of what category you want to fall into.

Sending Tweets

The general rule of tweets on Twitter is this: the more you tweet, the more followers you will get. Twitter's feed is constantly moving and changing because it's so much about being in the now. While they do have a "highlight" feature where when you log into Twitter, the most engaged tweets on your feed show, it quickly returns to that "in the now," constantly moving feed.

This means that even if all of your followers log in every day, they might not actually see your tweet. To make the most of this, you should probably tweet 5 to 20 times a day, and do it throughout the day. Twitter is incredibly global, so what's 6 AM for you might be 5 PM for one of your followers. Some of these tweets can be retweets, so don't be too concerned or feel overwhelmed.

Actually engage with your followers. Sometimes you see brands where all they do is post advertisements and links. This is not how you should be using Twitter. Ask your followers questions, reply to their questions, and retweet often.

Tweet about what's happening in the now. Twitter has a great system where you can see what trending on Twitter. These things can be jokes, current events, or stories. Tweet about it, using the appropriate hashtags!

Something to keep in mind—and is actually quite important—is that Twitter, despite a lot of users asking for it, has yet to add an edit feature. So, make sure you always carefully proofread your tweets to avoid having to delete something, or worse, that your fans check it out and point it out. But if this does happen (you're not perfect), roll with it. It humanizes your brand.

Retweeting

Retweeting is basically just sharing like Facebook but on Twitter. You can retweet your followers, companies you admire, or things that resonate with you and your brand. You have the option of adding something to the tweet or not. You can even retweet yourself, updating your followers on something that happened earlier or bringing attention to a special offer that's happening.

Following

On Twitter, people can see who you follow. They might look at your list of people you follow to look for more people to follow or even just to get an idea of what kind of people you want to see on your feed. Follow people you'd actually want to talk to in real life.

Before you first start following accounts on Twitter, you should try to tweet a few times before you do. That means if you follow someone, and they check out your account, they'll have an idea of what your brand is just by your tweets. Not just an empty black hole because you haven't gotten started yet. You should always have something to show right out of the gate.

Twitter Lists

Twitter lists are one of the least utilized tools on Twitter, and it's a shame considering how useful they actually are. To explain them in the simplest terms possible, they're basically just lists of accounts by you, organized by category. You can create lists, and follow lists that you like. They have a limit of 5,000 people.

You can separate your lists into many categories, the sky's the limit, and here are just a few ideas:

Geography: if you're a business that is only available in one place, like a store or a cafe, you could arrange lists based on other businesses in your area. You can use them to keep track of what's happening locally.

People you admire: if they have a following you identify with, if you think their profile is really great, if you like the ideas they put out there, put them all together. This way you can actively take a part in the conversation, and get some ideas on how you can start the conversation.

Your Industry: You should always be keeping up with people who are also a part of your industry or have a business similar to yours. You can stay in the loop as to what's going on, get ideas for your own business, and make connections in your industry.

Pinned Tweets

Pinned tweets are tweets that are pinned to the top of your profile. They can be changed every few weeks or every few years. It should really be the most important thing you can say about yourself in that very moment. You can tweet about an event or a sale you're having, and then pin it at the top of your profile. That means when someone visits your profile, it will be the first thing they see. If you find value in that, use it.

Hashtags

Hashtags, which is a staple on almost every single social media site in today's world, started on Twitter. It was conceived as a way to keep Twitter users and their tweets in categories. Twitter, as of yet, has not implemented a way to follow hashtags, but it's probably coming. Especially since Instagram has put it into use.

Because you only have 240 characters, you can't use a lot of hashtags, as opposed to Instagram where you can put 30, and still write a caption in. Only use one or two, and build the tweet around them, or add it at the end. One trick a lot of brands do to stay in the moment and be relevant is to check out what hashtags are trending and use these.

Overall, Twitter is a powerful platform, and easy to use. It's a social media site that is used best along with one or two others and is a great place to directly engage with your customers. You can follow trends and see what you should be talking about, right now. Happy tweeting!

Chapter 9: YouTube Marketing

YouTube is the ultimate video sharing platform. It was launched in 2005, and quickly became one of the staples of the internet. It was thanks to this extremely quick growth that it was bought by Google in 2006. It still is one of the most popular websites in the world. YouTube is second only to Facebook in terms of monthly users, with 1.8 billion users every month. This doesn't even count people who don't have accounts, as it's not needed if you just want to watch videos rather than comment, subscribe, and like.

Videos are the most engaged format of post online. They're more likely to be liked, commented on, and shared. Videos take very little effort to pay attention to and can grab your attention in a second.

YouTube is the one social media network that doesn't really count as a social media network, despite constantly being referred to as such. YouTube is more a search engine, the second most used in the world, after Google.

While in social media, posts will usually disappear and be forgotten after they no longer become relevant, YouTube is different because anyone could type the key phrase into the Google search bar or the YouTube search bar, and it would still show up.

Say someone posts a video about drawing human figures. If somebody types into the search bar "how to draw human figures" their video will show up, no matter how old it is. The only thing that really affects the order of the videos is according to how much engagement the video has gotten as well as based on the user's previous searches.

Unlike a social media post, most of which will disappear into the bottom of your page after a certain amount of time, YouTube doesn't have this algorithm. Your feed suggestion is based on what you have watched in the past, no matter how long it's been on the site. This means that if you do decide to start using it as a place for marketing, you don't have to repeat yourself nearly as much as you would on another social media page. What you can do is just constantly keep posting the video links to your other pages.

YouTube can take some serious dedication, especially if you plan on only using YouTube (not recommended). Not only because of the fact that if you plan to do it all the time rather than occasional video, but you also won't be getting subscribers. It's because there is a lot more effort involved in making streamlined, well-edited, well-written videos. Good content matters especially on YouTube, because every minute, 400 hours of video are uploaded on the site. Your content has to be well put together to stand out, so some practice with an editing system probably wouldn't be a bad idea.

Despite all this hard work, YouTube is a great addition to any marketing campaign. It flows well with the majority of other social networks out there, and because it's a search engine, you don't have to constantly be making up new content (if getting a lot of subscribers is not your goal). The important thing to do is to just be bringing attention to it on your other pages.

YouTube is aimed at literally everybody. At its core, it's a video platform. There is something on it for everybody: who doesn't love videos? It doesn't really matter what you are interested in watching or building a business around, you'll likely find it. And if you don't, that's just better for you, isn't it? No competition. It's because of this diversity in its users and content is why it's so valuable to marketers, and why you should at least consider adding it to your strategy.

In terms of economics, YouTube videos should not cost all that much to make. If your phone has a good camera, use that or borrow one from a friend. It doesn't take industry standard equipment to make them. As long as you focus on it looking good, it doesn't matter how it's made. As long as you're making quality, watchable, shareable content, nobody cares how much it cost to make it.

The most valuable place to use YouTube is along with other social media sites like Twitter and Facebook. Just using YouTube by itself can lead you straight into a brick wall, and leave you feeling frustrated. If you already have a page, or pages, on other social media sites, make sure to promote your YouTube videos on them.

Putting Together Your Channel

Putting together a YouTube channel is pretty simple to do. The website does a great job of walking you through it, and with a little exploring, you'll be a master.

About Section

The About section is often overlooked and not given nearly as much attention as it should on YouTube. This is mostly because when you look at somebody's profile, it's hidden in another tab, rather than right at the front, in contrast to the majority of other social media networks where it's right at the front.

While your character limit is not nearly as cramped as others, it should still be short, sweet, and simple. Treat it like you only have 100 characters, and only put the most important things there. Say what you do, your message, and your goals. You don't have to use hashtags.

At the end of your description, don't forget to add in all the links to your other social media pages, and if you have a website too. YouTube allows up to 5 links, which should be plenty. You can even customize hyperlinks up to 30 characters. You should also consider putting your business email, in case there are people who want to collaborate with you.

Your Cover and Profile Image

Keep both your profile image and your cover image simple. Your logo can act as your profile picture, and for your cover image, consider a large image with your slogan, or a small description of who you are. Keeping it simple, at least at first, is a good bet. Just make sure it's visually pleasing.

Your YouTube Trailer

YouTube actually allows you to choose a video to put right front and center on your page. One idea is to put together a trailer, clips, and things all put together to really show what your channel is about. For just starting out, just keep putting your best work up there. The absolute best video you've got, the one that best represents your company and your channel should be the first video your potential customers see.

Making your Videos

Make sure that each video is unique, but fit into the same theme as your brand. Keep a list of video ideas, and filter out the best ones. Watch other videos, of good quality who are in the same niche as you. And when you do plan to pick up a camera and start filming, a plan is never a bad thing.

It is not expensive to make a good quality YouTube video. Really, the only things you need is a camera, a tripod, and an editor. A script is also a good idea, writing down exactly what you say and what you want to cover in the video. Go into the video knowing exactly what you want to say. Also, don't forget lighting. If you can, stand in front of a window where natural daylight comes through, and film using that. If you can't, there are some great tutorials out there on how to make DIY lighting.

End the video with a call to action. Don't just end the video with a simple 'goodbye.' Make sure you tell them to subscribe, tell them where they can find the products you use in the video, and that they should comment below, telling you what they think, and like the video. Encourage constructive criticism, and ask them what they want next. This will encourage engagement.

Titles, Descriptions, and Keywords

Titles are important in YouTube. Just like how when you google a question, and websites show up with that exact question as a title, YouTube will do the same thing. The subject of your video 110% needs to be in your title.

Descriptions are also another great place to put keywords, but the best keywords should no doubt go into your titles. Descriptions should not be too long, same as your about me section. Try to stick to well-written ones, and avoid spelling and grammar errors. That's the easiest way for people to not take you professionally.

Probably the most overlooked factor in most beginners on YouTube is the thumbnail, the title page of your YouTube videos. First impressions matter! People like to say "Don't judge a book by its cover," but that is not a factor in terms of any form of social media. Make sure your thumbnail is polished, has the title in the image, and is well lit and focused. Your video thumbnail needs to stand out, and looking nice and polished is a good way to do that.

Promotion

Like stated above, you should be promoting your channel across all social media. If YouTube is going to become a staple in your marketing campaign, this is essential. Take full advantage of that share button, and make sure to let your followers know when you're posting a new video. YouTube doesn't really work as a stand-alone, as something that you use all by itself. It works much better as a companion to something else.

But, as more and more platforms work to add video streaming and content into their platforms, like Instagram with IGTV and Facebook with their video content, it might be used less and less in this way. Just something to keep in mind.

Some Basic Tips

If you really plan on using YouTube to grow, it's going to take some dedication and hard work. YouTube is entirely video content, which can take a considerable amount of more time than other platforms. Remember this before you decide that it's the best fit.

1) The best time to post content is between 12 PM and 4 PM on weekdays, and 9 AM - 11 AM. You can schedule videos to become public at these times if you don't want to think about that.

2) Constantly promote your videos on other platforms. Tweet about them. Talk about them in your Instagram story, or put a small clip in it as a taste. Make a post on Facebook describing them. Really chat it up.

3) Post at least 5 to 10 videos before you do this. This will make it out to be like you really know what you're doing, and show dedication.

4) Be consistent with content. You should always have certain times you post, like every Wednesday at 2 PM for example. If you really want your channel to grow, posting good quality content on a regular schedule has a lot more possibilities than occasionally posting a video on a random schedule and every eight months.

5) Choose content you can make on the regular. If you're making videos that take 2 months to make, you're not going to get much growth. Create a formula where you can easily put together at least one video a week.

6) Promote at the end of your video. Talk up your channel, ask them to subscribe and engage with the video by liking or commenting. Put some thought into where the person watching would want to go after watching this video, and recommend one of your own.

Types of Videos

Tutorials: Have a product? Show them how to use it, or set it up. If your service is offering a service, show them how it can effect their lives!

Q & A: If you have questions that are always asked, answer them in a video. Make this your featured video if it just answers the basics.

Listicles: Basically, just think "Top Tens." Like "Top 10 ways to Use Your Product" or "5 Reasons Why You Need This."

Behind the Scenes: this is a great way to humanize your brand and prove that you're more than just a product. You are all human, you all work hard, and you all enjoy what you do. Show this to your fans, and you will seem more real.

Vlogs: Show them what a day working for at your business looks like. Talk to the camera, and carry it around with you all day, just going about a normal day. If you yourself don't want to do this, do it with one of your employees (if you have them).

YouTube Analytics

Once you create a high-quality video and work out all your keywords, it's time to learn about YouTube Analytics. YouTube provides you with all the information to see what kind of videos are getting the most views and engagement, what kind of videos make users subscribe to, and more. You can learn a lot about your channel and what works in it.

On YouTube Analytics, you can see everything about your viewers, from how long they stay on your videos, to their demographics. It breaks down where people are watching your videos, where they're finding them, and what device they're watching them on.

Using this information, you can figure out exactly what is working, and what isn't. It's a valuable tool that should not go unnoticed. Make good use of this, and your YouTube channel will thrive.

Chapter 10: SnapChat

If you want to aim at young people, SnapChat is the way to go.

Snapchat is an app, for both Apple and Android, that is used for photo/texting/video, and the idea is remarkably simple: it sends the photo, text message or video, and then, after a certain amount of time, it disappears. This app is most popular with people aged 18 to 34. Teenagers are especially drawn to the app, with 47% thinking it's better than Facebook.

While on paper, this idea seems almost silly, it was actually laughed out of the classroom the first time it was pitched in 2011. Snapchat is most famous for this disappearing feature. This feature is the thing that makes or breaks the app for the majority of its potential users. But ironically, that is not where Snapchat has experienced the most success, and that is not the feature that is "borrowed" by other social media networks such as Instagram and Facebook.

Of course, this is the story feature.

The whole idea of the story filter is to tell a story about your day, and it disappears after 24 hours. This is especially good for businesses who hold a lot of contests and special offers. For example, you can post a coupon code into your story, but if it disappears after 24 hours, your customers are much more likely to make an impulse buy.

Snapchat is an app predominantly used by young people, so if you have a product whose base is largely teenagers or young adults, Snapchat is a good option. Snapchat's brand is all about what's happening in the now, spontaneity, and creativity, and has a playful and outgoing energy to it. If your brand falls into any of these categories, Snapchat is definitely for you.

Come off As Unfiltered

Snapchat is all about the moment, in time, between friends. It's a platform for fun. Your stories and postings should recognize this. They should be filled with fun, spontaneous, and funny moments, things people go on Snapchat for. While a lot of other social media networks have a serious side to them, Snapchat is all about the fun. By showing that you're fun too, you can strike a deeper connection with your followers, and inspiring loyalty by showing yourself off as authentic.

Personal experiences also have a giant mark with Snapchat users. Pitching for a faceless brand isn't going to be as successful as it would on a social media network like Pinterest. Snapchat is all about being connected and making moments count with your friends. Your brand needs to adapt to that idea

When you do take photos, be silly with them. Add emojis, draw on them, use filters. Snapchat is meant to be fun, and your Snapchat story should reflect that. Remember the majority of people who use Snapchat are teenagers. You're appealing to them and should bring yourself to their level.

Posting

Snapchat comes with a ton of goofy filters and silly stickers to add to your pictures. You can also write messages, show the time, and use location mode. They can be fun to add to your pictures. Be creative!

If you're a little lost as to what you should exactly be posting in your story, take some of these suggestions into consideration. They might help you come up with your own, unique ideas!

1) Reveal the backstage moments. By backstage moments, I mean the fun, silly ones. The ones that hurt your gut laughing. Get someone to tour the place where the business is based and have them narrate their way through, introducing your followers to everyone the company works for. Show the people who are working hard every day to make this business as amazing as it is.

2) Consider account takeover. Account takeovers are fun, and they're mutually beneficial. What you do is you pick an influencer that reflects your brand, and they take over your Snapchat feed for a certain amount of time, whether hours or days (this can also be done with Instagram). This is a partnership that really goes both ways: it brings attention to your brand from the influencer's followers, and it brings attention to the influencer from your followers. Win-win!

3) Promo codes. The nature of Snapchat makes it ideal for advertisement of limited time offers or events. It's going to disappear in 24 hours, and after it disappears, it will no longer be valid. If you're having a sale or an offer, that's a great place to put it as only the people who viewed that story can actually take advantage of it.

4) Put information only on your story that they can't get anywhere else. Exclusive news. Facts about upcoming projects. Sharing information like this is not only a great way to make your followers feel like they're in the loop and they're the first ones to know, it will also encourage others to seek you out and follow you to make themselves feel like they're a part of that group. Your followers are the best people in the world, they deserve that exclusive content!

5) Relevance is your friend. Talk about current issues. Things that are happening right now. That can be anything from a silly meme that has become popular recently or something that is big in the news right now. Talking about relevant issues shows that you're really in touch with the world. Just make sure that it somehow relates back to your brand, and that your followers would actually expect you to talk about it.

6) Event promo. If there is an event coming up, throw it up on Snapchat. When you're at the event, hand over the app to several different people so they can get the event from all different angles onto the story.

Things to Consider

If something is related to your brand in some way, snap it. Seriously. See a quote? Meet someone the company works with? Have a photoshoot. Snap it. Your followers should be there for every single step of the way.

Don't worry too much about being perfect. Snapchat is different from Instagram in that it's not about the perfection factor. Snapchat, because it's all about what's happening in the moment. No one is perfect in every single moment. It's just not possible. It's about these humane moments where all your cracks are exposed and you're just having a good time. Your brand will be more relatable if you post your funny and embarrassing failings just as much as you post your successes.

Keep them short. Your snaps should be short clips of your life, not a reality TV show. You're not a Kardashian. You should be giving your followers a slice, not the whole pie. If you're going to stream an event, just post snippets of what happened. If you really want to post an entire video, post in Snapchat that there will be a video posted on YouTube later, and just post a small piece of it to your story. That way, your fans will go check out your YouTube page, generating more views for you.

Make sure you share your Snapchat to your other pages. Make a post about your Snapchat occasionally on your pages, and watch as people look to it. Sometimes, a little nudge towards where you want them to go is exactly what potential followers need.

People may say that SnapChat is from the past, but it's just not true. It's still a huge platform, used by young people, and not taking advantage of that is silly. Happy Snapping!!!!

Chapter 11: Pinterest Marketing

Pinterest in the social marketing game is often overlooked, which is unfortunate. It's an underrated and incredible platform for businesses, especially if you have a lot of different products to sell. Launched in 2010, it has gained 200 million active users. In comparison to Facebook, that number seems small, but get this: 93% of Pinterest users have admitted to using Pinterest to plan purchases, and 50% of them have made a purchase through a promoted pin. These numbers should catch the attention of any marketer, and get them on the site.

The best way to describe Pinterest is a virtual pinboard. You collect pictures, videos, articles, and most forms of media online into folders, or "pinboards." Other members are able to see your pins, collect them into their own pinboards, like and comment. They can also follow you, or just an individual pinboard. It's a great place to gain inspiration and ideas for your life.

Pinterest is often mistaken for a visual scrapbook which people put together for wishful thinking. But it's more than that. It's a To-Do List. It allows people to visualize what they want their life to be. It allows people to find ideas on ways to do this. It gets their goals together in an organized fashion.

It is exactly the wishful thinking that makes Pinterest such a powerful marketing tool. Pinterest users are looking for things to add to their lives, and ways to make it better. It provides a visual representation of these things. Basically, Pinterest is one giant department store, and people can go around registering for what they want. Their users buy more off the website than users of any other social media network, including giants like Facebook and Twitter.

Pinterest also generates a huge amount of website traffic, because every pin leads back to its original source. If someone pins a recipe of yours, everyone that follows them, or the pinboard, and sees the pin, goes back to your website. Pinterest creates more referred website traffic than YouTube, LinkedIn, and Tumblr combined.

Not only that, but pinners actually want to see your content on their pinboard. 78% of them say it's useful seeing content from brands on their pinboards, with the top categories being art supplies and hobbies. They want to see your products. They want to buy from you.

If your business is related to crafts and DIY projects, or even if you're selling a physical product, Pinterest is definitely a great place for you. But it's also great for travel blogs as well, with 49% of travellers on Pinterest saying that they use it to plan trips.

In conclusion, Pinterest may be underrated when it comes to how much impact it has on the internet, but its users are more likely to actually buy from you. That is never a bad thing in the world of business.

Using Pinterest

Your Profile

Business Account

This is important to remember if you're creating a Pinterest account specifically for business use, then you absolutely must get a business account. You can switch in your settings. The reason why is that using a personal account to promote your products on the site actually violates their terms of service.

In the future, Pinterest is likely to add more features to its business pages, as right now they're not all that different from personal accounts. As more and more businesses flock to Pinterest, Pinterest will get more incentive to do so.

Your Bio and Profile Picture

In your bio, really sell the benefits of your company, and use keywords. Keywords are especially important on Pinterest because people are using it to search for new ideas, much like they use Google. Make sure you link your main business webpage or other social media platforms. If you have a mailing list, link that too.

Consider using your logo for your profile picture. But, if you don't want to use that, your profile picture should revolve around one subject having to do with your brand, being good quality, and brightly colored.

Creating Boards

Boards are the sections in which your pins are organized into, and they are your biggest marketing tool. They usually are created with a theme in mind. You should also sort them by kind of product or service you offer. Let's say you're a Christmas ornaments business, and you make 3 different kinds of ornaments in various colors. These should be separated into different boards.

When naming your boards, do your best to keep them short and snappy, but always include at least one of your keyboards. Example: if your board is all about baby showers, Baby Shower should be your title.

Pinners can choose to follow just your board, rather than your actual profile, so they can be a valuable tool. This is why it's important to repin as well. If you're a cupcake company, you shouldn't just be pinning images of your own cupcakes. Make sure you pin cupcakes from other companies or designs you want to try.

Types of Boards to Consider

- Customer feedback

- Employees

- Behind the Scenes

- Customer spotlights

- Read all about it (a whole bunch of articles relating to your business that are interesting and informative)

- Success stories

- Graphics

- Quotes

Pinning

Pinning is the act of actually putting your pins into these boards. When you pin, about 50% of your pinning should be repinning other people's content. This keeps your pins varied, and shows that you're always looking for more ideas. This also could lead to some repinning from other businesses of your pins in return.

There isn't really a bad time to pin, but the afternoon, between 1 PM and 5 PM seems to work best. When you pin, don't forget to fill out the description, and use keywords. Include a call to action as well, asking your followers to either repin or asking them what they think.

You should also be pinning from websites. Most blogging websites have a pinning option (just click the Pinterest logo somewhere on the site). When you do this, make sure to pick an image rather than just the text as the cover of your pin. This is a mistake that a lot of beginner pinners make; Pinterest is about the visual, remember.

Some Tips to Remember

- Stay within your brand. Know your niche and stick with it. Don't pin things that aren't in some shape or form directly having to do something with your business.

- Think lifestyle. Pinterest is about organizing your life and making plans as to what you want it to be. Your brand should emit a certain lifestyle.

- Try not to pin too many things with human faces. Research shows that abstract images do better.

Unfortunately, because Pinterest has not really been explored as an option for businesses to use, the business side of Pinterest's potential is not obvious to a lot of people. It's a crying shame. No doubt, based on all the information you've just consumed, Pinterest is valuable to any business's marketing plan.

Chapter 12: Things to Remember

There is a lot of information in this book. You're probably feeling a bit overwhelmed. So, this chapter will leave you with what are the most important things you can take with you and a quick run over of exactly how this all works.

What are the most important things to remember?

Consistency. Anything you post on your profile should relate directly to your brand, in some shape or form. Consistency should be in the quality of your photos, how often you post, the number of times you post, and everywhere in between.

Transparency. You should be sharing behind-the-scenes information and photos, and really showing the feel and culture of the workplace. Is it one of your employee's birthday? Do you have traditions that you always partake in the morning? Share them: it humanizes your brand.

Authenticity. Always be yourself. Never try to be another business. Your business and brand are what you are. If you think another page is better than yours, that's fine. Learn from them. Don't just blindly copy them.

Variety. Always be on the lookout to engage your customers in new and exciting ways. Don't stick to the same old formula all the time; keep track of several different ways of doing things, and switch them out whenever things get stale.

Current events. Pay attention to what's happening in the world. See if you can somehow swing the latest trending hashtag into something that works to promote yourself. Be actively involved in the community your brand is a part of, and keep it there in a positive way.

Visualization. Everything should be seen on your profile. Everything should be in high quality and fit into a theme of colors. No exceptions. First impressions truly matter.

Have a plan. Plan. Plan. Plan. You should always have a plan.

Know your brand. If you don't know your brand, you will start over from scratch from every single post.

Engage, engage, engage, engage, engage. You will never hear how important that is enough. Talk to your customers. They're giving you money.

Learn from your mistakes. This leads us right into the next section.

Social Media Mistakes to Avoid

You probably won't be able to avoid at least mistakes in social media, but you can read a list of ones that have already been made.

To not have at least an idea of what you're getting into. Know your brand. Know your product. Know your goals. Know who you are as a company. If you don't, you will hit a wall at some point.

To not understand your goals. You might know your goals, but if you don't know exactly how you're going to get there, you're going to hit a wall. To do this, create a step by step plan, and do some research on having achievable goals. Make a step by step plan on how you will get there.

Having high expectations. No, your first post is not going to go viral, and you won't have a million followers overnight. Social media marketing is a marathon, not a sprint.

Not humanizing your customers. Your customers are more than just people to squeeze money out of. They're human beings with families, goals, and a want to make their life better. You have to appeal to that side of them and prove to them that you can make their life better. To do this well, you have to listen to their feedback and actually use it.

Not thinking before you post. Proofread. Double check your sources. Making sure everything is high quality. Be smart before you post.

Being tone deaf. Think of it this way. If someone's house was burning down, and you were a carpenter, would you walk up to them and hand them your business card? If you're going to post about something that is trending, make sure to look into it first, to make sure that your post reflects the tone of the event.

Sharing too much. This is called TMI: Too Much Information. Some things are just better left unsaid and private. If something really negative happened at your company today, your audience doesn't need to know this. Only directly address it if you feel it's absolutely needed.

Sharing an opinion that has nothing to do with your business. Especially controversial ones (think political or controversial). If you want to come off as professional, don't isolate part of your audience by stating something that they might disagree with in a strong way. Of course, if you feel that your beliefs actually reflect the company well, go for it. Just be cautious, and remember you might lose some potential customers.

When you do make a mistake, don't worry. There aren't a lot of mistakes in social media that aren't fixable. Most of them are very fixable, and very easy to fix, whether it's just deleting the post, or even sometimes apologizing if there is a backlash.

The most important thing is that you learn from these mistakes, and take careful steps into making sure that they don't happen again.

Social media can be fun. Remember that. It can be so much fun to communicate on a daily basis with your customers, finding out what they want from you, and learning about your base. You add more richness to your company and improve the most important relationship for any business: your customers. They're the most important part, after all.

Conclusion

Thanks for making it through to the end of *Social Media Marketing for Business 2019*. Let's hope it was informative and able to provide you with all of the tools you need to achieve your goals whatever they may be.

The next step is to take all that you have learned in this book and take it to your various social media profiles. Put all these tips and tricks to really good use and make your profile shine. Remember experimentation is key: it will probably not be perfect the first few times you do, and that's totally and completely OK. The best advice you can get is to just keep trying, and keep note of what is working and what isn't working. Always make sure you learn from your mistakes. As long as you keep trying and keep putting quality content out there, you are golden.

Follow the information provided in this guide as close as you can, but there is no shame in experimentation, and trying things that aren't written in this book. Remember to trust your gut, and that you know what is best for your company, not me or anyone else. You do.

In this guide, I have explained strategies and given you information to help you grow your business through social media marketing. I have given you tips, explained to you the importance of social media, and given you ideas for your future posts.

Made in the USA
Middletown, DE
20 July 2021